IN THE LAND OF
GOD AND MAN

CONFRONTING OUR
SEXUAL CULTURE

IN THE LAND OF GOD AND MAN

CONFRONTING OUR SEXUAL CULTURE

Silvana
Paternostro

A DUTTON BOOK

AUTHOR'S NOTE
The author wishes to note that certain names and details in this book have been changed to protect the privacy of individuals who generously shared their stories.

DUTTON
Published by the Penguin Group
Penguin Putnam Inc., 375 Hudson Street,
New York, New York 10014, U.S.A.
Penguin Books, Ltd, 27 Wrights Lane,
London W8 5TZ, England
Penguin Books Australia Ltd, Ringwood,
Victoria, Australia
Penguin Books Canada Ltd, 10 Alcorn Avenue,
Toronto, Ontario, Canada M4V 3B2
Penguin Books (N.Z.) Ltd, 182–190 Wairau Road,
Auckland 10, New Zealand

Penguin Books Ltd, Registered Offices:
Harmondsworth, Middlesex, England

First published by Dutton,
a member of Penguin Putnam Inc.

First Printing, November, 1998
10 9 8 7 6 5 4 3 2 1

REGISTERED TRADEMARK—MARCA REGISTRADA

LIBRARY OF CONGRESS CATALOGING-IN-PUBLICATION DATA:

Paternostro, Silvana.
    In the land of God and man : confronting sexual culture in Latin
America / Silvana Paternostro.
        p.   cm.
    Includes index.
    ISBN 0-525-94422-2 (alk. paper)
    1. Sex customs—Latin America. 2. Men—Latin America—Sexual
behavior. I. Title.
HQ18.L29P38   1998
306.7'098—dc21   98-29084
                                                          CIP

Printed in the United States of America
Set in Simoncini Garamond
Designed by Leonard Telesca

This book is printed on acid-free paper. ∞

For my family for understanding
and
in memory of François
and Dr. Jonathan Mann

Contents

I. The Invitation 1

II. Makers of Angels 48

III. The Man of My Dreams 108

IV. A Love Story 196

V. Northern Ladies 270

    Epilogue 308

    Acknowledgments 313

    Bibliography 315

    Index 320

I have no knowledge of these things,
except that I came to this place,
so that, if true that I am female,
none substantiate that state.
   I know, too, that *uxor*, woman,
designed, in the Latin,
only those who wed;
and either gender may be virgin,
as I will never be a woman
who as wife may serve a man.
I know only that my body,
not to either state inclined,
is neuter, abstract, guardian
of only what my soul consigns.

                   —Sor Juana Inés de la Cruz

I.
The Invitation

I like you when you're silent:
It's as if you are not there.

Me gustas cuando callas
porque estas como ausente
   —Pablo Neruda, Poema xv

A man rang the doorbell at my parents' house in Bogotá and handed me an envelope addressed to them in fancy calligraphy. I thanked the messenger and opened the unsealed envelope—an engraved invitation to a reception honoring high-level cabinet members of the Colombian government.

The names on the cream-colored cardboard took me back to my childhood in Barranquilla. Ana María and her husband would be hosting the party. She and I had been close growing up; our families took trips together and we slept over at each other's houses. Alvaro, who was in tenth grade when I was in seventh and was friends with the unapproachable boy I had a crush on, was the country's new vice-minister of energy. And the vice-minister of agriculture, much to my amusement, was Arturo, who had insistently kissed me when I turned fifteen. Our mothers would have liked it if we had kissed more, because we would probably be married today. In 1976 girls in Barranquilla married the first boy they kissed, mostly, because kissing seemed to go hand in hand with getting pregnant. If I had stayed there, I would be the wife and the mother of the children of a vice-minister with a bright future, a role I was brought up to perform. But I am not wife or mother, a reality that neither I nor anyone who knew me then would have predicted.

The invitation was tempting. Without hesitation I decided not to go back home to New York that week as planned, but to stay for Ana María's party.

I felt excitement at the thought of talking to Arturo again, more than fifteen years later. He was a university student in Bogotá when we first met, at a funeral, and I was a ninth grader at the American school in Barranquilla, but whenever he was home for holidays he would hurry over to see me. I have fond memories of his visits. Because I had a boyfriend then, his visits were a little illicit, but the truth was that I enjoyed spending time with Arturo more than with José Luis, my *novio oficial*. I would sit for hours in Arturo's car, parked out in the driveway, and listen to him talk about his life in big, metropolitan Bogotá where he shared an apartment with friends, about the classes he took at the university and the books he read. But what interested me most was when he talked to me about *la política*.

José Luis didn't really talk to me about much, other than telling me a million times every day that he loved me forever and that I was his girlfriend and that I would one day be his wife. When we went out he discussed soccer, cars, and the top forty hits on Miami's Y-100 radio station while I sat next to him in silence and he held my hand. José Luis liked telling me what clothes to wear and when to be home. If he called and I was not there, he became impossibly possessive—"Where were you? Who were you there with? Who did you talk to?" One evening he drove away without me because he disapproved of what I was wearing and I refused to change. When I showed up at the party without him, I was told by his friends that I was being disrespectful and that I had better return home immediately. My girlfriends agreed I should not stay at the party. If he had wanted me to change, they added, why was I making such a big deal? It only meant that he was serious about me, that he was really in love with me. I had felt humiliated and angered by José Luis's request. They thought it was romantic.

José Luis and I made up after that fight, but he continued to ask me to change. My skirts were getting shorter and my tops skimpier. I had learned early that it was through being beautiful and seductive that I would be noticed. Every father's dream was that his daughter would grow up to be a Miss Colombia. I was not tall enough to be told that I would be Señorita Colombia, and my face did not have the delicate features of a statuette of the Virgen María. But plenty had shown interest in the forming curves of *mi cuerpo* and the roundness of *mis tetas* as I went from child to señorita and I was allowed to wear high heels and stay till midnight at the parties at El Country Club. I went all out. At fifteen I looked like a brown-skinned Lolita with glossy, pouting lips, tight jeans, and six-inch heels. I transformed my mother's scarves into strapless bandeaux which I tied across my chest, and I wore bathing suits that were tinier than the ones most of my friends wore. For a costume party, Mercedes, Claudia and I wore Playboy-bunny outfits.

To José Luis's complaints I soon had to add my mother's, my sister's, my grandmother's. My mother yelled at me because my shorts were too short. To make a point of how small my green and purple bathing suit was, my sister tried it on her doll. I am a little over five two, but my body was definitely more formed than the doll's. I knew that in my swimsuits my breasts looked like Farrah Fawcett's in the poster all the boys liked, and I liked the way my buttocks sneaked out of my cutoffs like slivers of crescent moons. But it was confusing to be reprimanded for the one thing that I had been hearing a girl should most want to be.

The way I looked reflected little about the way I acted. My mother told me I looked like a *putica*, a little slut, every time I wore those cutoffs. But I knew *putas* were the girls who slept around, and I had barely been kissed. I had, sort of, kissed José Luis and Arturo, but I really had not encouraged it. The first time José Luis kissed me, I gagged. It felt like such an intrusion. But he pressed me so much that I would let him, just to get it over with. I assumed I had to—he was my boyfriend. When he did, I closed my eyes tight, opened my lips, and waited as he slid his tongue inside my mouth. It felt just like when the doctor checked my throat with a wooden stick, telling me to open wide and say aaaahhhh.

I preferred kissing Arturo. Somehow it felt less forced. Plus, Arturo was the first person who had shown any interest in what I had to say. One day he tried to kiss me and I did not want to. He did not press for my kiss, as my boyfriend did, but he got angry, and although I didn't mean to make him angry, it was not clear to me why it was necessary to kiss when talking felt better—more satisfying and somehow more intimate.

I never discussed how it felt to kiss Arturo or José Luis with anybody, not even with my best friend, although I knew Eugenia and Carlos also kissed. Carlos was one of José Luis's close friends and sometimes on Friday nights the four of us would drive around the thirty blocks of upscale Barranquilla that circumscribed our small world, listening to Barry White and Julio Iglesias. José Luis drove and I sat next to him changing the tapes. Eugenia and Carlos kissed in the backseat. After a while, Carlos drove while we sat in the back and kissed. Eugenia tells me now that she loved to kiss Carlos but Carlos, unlike José Luis, was not her *novio* and she was heartbroken when, at the end of that year, he had to get married. Vicky, his real *novia*, was pregnant.

Three, sometimes four times a night the four of us would drive past El Gusano, Barranquilla's hottest discotheque. It was on the Boulevard del Prado, the city's main drag where prostitutes and men with fully developed breasts, coiffed hair, and heels strolled up and down the avenue or leaned against the dry palm trees. We all knew about the prostitutes, but I did not know that the transvestites wore so much gold lamé to attract customers—other men who paid to have sex with them.

Every time we drove by the nightclub, which was owned by José Luis's friend, whoever was at the wheel would honk at the club's doorman. Sometimes José Luis and Carlos parked the car and walked inside—to buy cigarettes, they said—while Eugenia and I stayed in the car. José Luis would always bring back lemonade and Chiclets for me. Shortly before midnight he drove by for the last time, signaling to the doorman that they would be back. Eugenia and I would be driven home and dropped off in time for our midnight curfews. They would head back to The Worm. Whenever I asked to be taken there José Luis insisted it was not a place where I—a good girl—could go.

Being with Arturo was different. When he called, I felt that instead of policing my days he actually wanted to talk with me.

When he was with me, I don't think he noticed much what I wore. I am pretty sure he too went to The Worm, but when he was with me he was never in a hurry to meet up with his friends. In fact, sometimes he stood them up and stayed with me longer. We would talk and kiss until very late, way past my curfew. I liked the fact that Arturo did not respect my father's rules. José Luis by contrast felt like the executioner, one of many reasons that made him the perfect boyfriend in my parents' eyes. My friends also found him pretty enviable. He visited and phoned daily and showered me with gifts—delicate gold bracelets, tiny heart-shaped diamonds, and tons of Toblerone.

Arturo gave me a book. From Bogotá he brought me Machiavelli's *The Prince*. "I'm happy," he announced, "I found it with a prologue by Napoleon." When he handed it to me, he called me *muñeca* and said, "Here, start learning something about the world." I never really read it then, but I loved opening it to the page where he had written with his gold Cross pen: "This, undoubtedly a major classic about Politics, leads us inevitably to think that *la Vida y la Política* are a long Machiavellian comedy of desires, aspirations, successes, and failures where the human soul will find enough elements to develop its feelings." Arturo's words, like the allegory of the fox and the state, made little sense to me then, but I liked the feeling owning that book gave me. I liked his handwriting, which seemed so grown-up to me. The way he signed his name, pressing hard on the paper, reminded me of my father's formal script. They were signatures that emanated self-confidence, authority, and importance. They belonged to men, about whom I was consumed with curiosity. What they did, how they talked seemed much more alive than what the women did.

I felt I owned knowledge and shared some of that self-assurance every time I held the thin paperback edition I kept, for years, inside the drawer of my pink night table. Unlike José Luis's tokens of love, which to me felt like things that I should want but actually didn't, Arturo's book made me feel special, like he was talking with me, not making me. At night, after my sister had gone to sleep, I opened it, turned pages without reading them, read sentences without understanding them, wondering, after turning out the lights, what he meant every time he talked about the importance of politics. Later on, however, I would understand that the politics Arturo talked about—like Machiavelli, my boyfriend, my father, and for that matter any man I came into contact with—was a world that I could not enter for one simple reason. I was not a man.

I have always lived among men who were born to talk *política*, to do *política*, even to rule. Because I was curious, I was allowed an occasional taste of their exclusive world. I was allowed to dance around them, to ask a few questions, to dabble with a few opinions, but if I probed further I was sent rapidly back to my place. I was to be next to them as a daughter, eventually as a potential wife, but not on a par with them, not as an equal. I was born into a class where the men rise to be leaders, and I was shown early on that I was not to become one. My place as a woman was as a follower, and how presumptuous of me to think otherwise. Both men and women knew that this inequality was sanctioned and enforced by rule, customary law, culture, religion, tradition, and history. Machismo, or whatever one calls it, is a rigid system that both men and women promulgate. "It is not attractive to be so opinionated," a boyfriend's mother once told me as a piece of complicit feminine advice.

Men and women today roll their eyes at me, subtly edge away, or change the topic of conversation whenever mention is made of this book. Many like to argue that things are different and that I do not know it because I am out of touch with my culture. Friends will remind me that I haven't really lived in Latin America, that I left twenty years ago. Things have changed, they say. In some ways, I know, they have. Women now do not need their husbands' permission to work outside the home or open a bank account. Today, women make up half of the labor force. I am also aware that in Colombia, for example, half the university graduates are women. I even recognize there has been some room in politics. Latin women have served as attorney general, prime minister, vice president, even as president. In 1997, twenty-three women served as ministers, two as presidents of Congress. Ecuador and Costa Rica have women as vice presidents. Women are aspiring to the presidencies of Colombia, Venezuela, and Honduras. Nonetheless, I am not satisfied. Women have entered the work force as secretaries, bank tellers, even officers and a few high-ranking executives, but the reality is that less than one percent are decision makers and most women work as domestic servants or *maquila* operators receiving exploitative wages and no health benefits. Regardless of the hype about the number of women in government, they only occupy about twelve percent of the legislative seats. It is men who are still making the rules.

Spaces open up for women if they enter public life ready to follow men's rules. When, in 1996, Ecuadoreans elected a woman as vice president, Rosalía Arteaga was able to name three women to the cabinet. Guadalupe León, known as a social researcher working on gender issues, was named minister of labor, the first woman to hold the post. A few days before she was sworn in, she attended a dinner given by the president to introduce his new cabinet. She had heard through a friend, male, also a member of the new government, that some members were nervous about her nomination. He called early the next morning to congratulate her. Everyone—he reiterated, everyone—was commenting on how impressed they had all been with her, how professional she had seemed.

She was startled. "But," she told her friend, "I didn't utter a word all night."

"That's exactly right."

Few women challenge the more-than-five-hundred-year-old system that makes men the executors of our lives: as our fathers, as our husbands, as our spiritual and secular leaders, as our governors. In Barranquilla, I grew up guided by big and small signals that would prompt me to follow this rule unquestioningly. I was educated to follow God and men, programmed to think of myself as an obedient daughter until the day I was handed to a husband, someone *con buen apellido*, a member of El Country, a photocopy of my father. My future was predetermined by everyone around me. I was to be the wife of a man like José Luis or Arturo.

But a few months after I turned fifteen, my parents decided to send me away to school, and I left behind the path that had been traced for me the day I was carried home from the hospital with my tiny earlobes pierced, wearing pink. I finished high school in the United States, where I stayed on for college. Ever since, I have been a rootless contradiction: too impetuous, emotional, and erratic for New York; too independent for Barranquilla where *una mujer que vive sola* really means she is loose.

When the counselor at the Academy of the Sacred Heart called me into her office to talk to me about college plans, I had none. I had never thought that, like Arturo, I could go to college. Unlike my classmates who had been practicing for their SATs for years, all I had heard about my future was about *el día que te cases*. It was marriage, not college, that would hand me a life. Then suddenly, at that formative age, the heavy rules I had known, and had always had a hard time following, were breached. I was able to see, hear, experience differently—so much so that today, almost twenty years later, it is still hard for me to go back to Colombia and feel comfortable being the woman I have become.

I looked at the invitation again. My friend Ana María's name had changed. Joined by the seemingly insignificant but so meaningful two-letter word *de*, "of," she had added her husband's surname after hers. Though I had been surrounded by women whose names included this possessive preposition—my mother, my grandmothers, their mothers, my teachers, my aunts all use it—I was always struck on seeing it added to any woman's name. But I was especially jarred when I saw it next to the names of my childhood friends—surprised that none of them minded becoming in such a public and formal way a man's belonging.

It would be easier to understand if the *de* were something I saw only among those girlfriends who never left Barranquilla to study abroad, who never lived on their own, who went from their twin beds to their marital beds. Julieta, who married a distant relative of mine when she was, at the most, seventeen, was among the brightest in her class, but she stopped studying the day she got married—pregnant, of course. She moved in with her husband's parents while he finished medical school and she became a wife and mother who stayed home. During my confusing first week as a freshman at the University of Michigan, I received a letter from Julieta which didn't help clarify my thoughts. I still remember feeling a tinge of envy when I saw the return address on the tiny envelope filled with teddy bears and balloons in which she announced the birth of her son. While I was struggling with sharing a small room with Jodi, my strange roommate who liked to be called Jazz and whose eyes were as open as Marty Feldman's, Julieta shared her bed with a man who had given her a name— Julieta S. de Gutiérrez—the passport to enter a real life. At her age, she could not vote, yet she belonged to a man and that made her into a grown-up. As I reread her letter, today, I realize it is the note of a child:

¡Hola Silvana!
How are you? *q'tal el cole* . . . The baby is born, he is pretty, blond, chubby and blue-eyed. Everyone is crazy about him. My dad is all excited because he looks like him.
Can you imagine—me, a mom. I myself can hardly believe it.
Write to me, kisses
Juli

But Ana María, like me, had been exposed to more: boarding school in New York City, college on the East Coast, frequent trips to Europe. After graduating from college in Virginia, she returned to Bogotá and started working for her father, the president of one of Colombia's largest engineering firms. Ana María became her father's right hand, a position that put her in touch with the country's lines of power. She was soon working around the clock, hopping on a helicopter to visit a bridge in construction or negotiating a contract for a new road for the government. At a meeting at the Ministry of Public Works she met the undersecretary who less than a year later became her husband.

Ana María married with all the pomp that was expected. The cheeses were imported from Curaçao. The carrots were flown in from Miami. She was the first one of my friends who did not have to marry in a hurry—she was not pregnant. She also continued to work and waited more than a year to have her first child. To my mother, she is admirable. She is an *ejecutiva*, my mother tells me, trumpeting her success loud enough for me to feel uncomfortable, especially when she gets to the part about how she is also a wonderful wife, a great hostess, and a devoted mother. But whenever I hear the praises, I cannot stop myself from thinking that she, too, signs her name as a possession. I tell myself that maybe Ana María doesn't see it that way. But how can calling yourself and signing your name Señora de—Mrs. of—not give you a sense of being owned? What is her need for doing so? I've always wondered.

When Julieta and Ana María married—Julieta in 1978 and Ana María in 1982—they had, by law, to sign their names thus, to be identified as the possession of a man. In Ecuador, the civil code still requires the "de," and in Venezuela, not using it was considered by the law a "grave insult" and was grounds for divorce. Until recently, men had patriarchal authority, *patria potestad,* over all decisions involving a couple and their children. Under Latin American law, which is based on the Napoleonic code, men are the sole heads of the marital unit because women, like children and the retarded, are seen by the state as creatures incapable of full development and therefore in need of protection, protection provided by men—fathers, brothers, husbands. The management of the family is in the husband's hands. Without his consent, the wife could not accept or relinquish an inheritance, act as a guardian, or exercise a profession. By taking on the names of their husbands, my friends had acquiesced in such imprisonment.

Latin America's constitutions have been rewritten since then. There is legal recognition of the individuality and equality of women. As of 1988, Colombian women do not have to use the infamous two-letter word. But customs, which are followed more strictly than law, have yet to catch up. Most women in Latin America still use the *de* attached to their names. I am surprised not only to see my friends using it but to see it attached to the names of women who are working on women's issues. A woman who considered herself a feminist was asked why she used it. She was quick to point out that she was married to a very good man. Does that then make it okay?

And still there are laws that perpetuate inequality. In Bolivia, a married woman cannot buy property without the consent of her husband, and, as in Guatemala, he can prohibit her from taking certain jobs. Children born out of wedlock are automatically in the custody of the "supposed" father. In Peru, women are not allowed to work the night shift, or to work in mining, in construction, or in anything that will jeopardize their health or their "good manners." Young boys swarm the streets of Lima shining shoes, selling newspapers, flowers, candy, or lottery tickets. Girls cannot. In Panama, if a married woman wants to open her own business, she needs to present an authorizing letter from her husband to the ministry of commerce in order to get an operating license. In Ecuador, a divorced woman who wants to remarry needs a certificate that states that she is not pregnant. In Chile, there is no divorce.

I had been in Colombia only a few days when the invitation to Ana María's reception arrived. Being back was always tense. I feel my life stops when I'm in Colombia and I'm thrown into the whirlwind of the mundane and now foreign concerns of others. My family's and my friends' lives—their meals, their laundry, their ringing phones, their cocktail parties, even the way they express themselves—do not belong to me. A friend tells me she could not visit her brother in Miami because her husband "didn't let me go" and a friend of my sister's, a working woman, says that she cannot go away on a work trip because her husband "does not allow me to spend a night out of the house." Words like this leave me feeling as if I've landed, not in my childhood home, but on Mars. This regimented world where every day, after lunch, the men go to work and the women stay behind—sitting at the table, smoking a cigarette—has always felt uncomfortable. I have sat through many meals, I have smoked many cigarettes, yet I've been unable to play the part of "woman" the way they play it. If I were married to Arturo, as I dreamt of all those years ago when he gave me *The Prince*, how would I feel asking for his permission to write this book or to go on a trip?

When I told Arturo I was leaving for the United States, he told me that if he were my father, he would never send his daughter to the States. Girls are different there, he said. If I went, I would get a bad reputation. My mother's friends told her the same. She tried to explain I was going to an all-girl Catholic school, the prestigious Sacred Heart where all the Kennedy girls go, but it was impossible to get them to change their image of the United States where girls are *libertinas*, a disparaging word freely used to describe girls who have sex with their boyfriends. My mother talked to me before I left. Don't feel any pressure to be like them, she kept telling me as my departure grew closer. Do not forget, she said, the principles you have learned in your home. Completely sincere in my promise, I reassured her that I wouldn't.

As she had warned me, my new classmates seemed to fit the bill of libertines. In 1978 the sexual revolution had even reached the halls of the Academy of the Sacred Heart. My American friends not only had sex with their boyfriends but they actually planned for it. Laura had her boyfriend Tim stay for the weekend whenever her parents went away.

Situations like this shocked me at first and, when alone, I would hold tight to Arturo's words and my mother's advice. Barranquilla's mores were so deeply ingrained, so hard to root out, that it was only during my junior year in college that I was finally ready to allow a boyfriend into my bed. When Laura found out that my boyfriend was spending the night, she made sure she talked to me about birth control—and, oh boy, was I not open to her concern. Three years after my arrival in the United States, I was living on my own, yet I had never spoken to anyone about sex. Laura's questioning offended me—did she think I was one of them? How could I tell her we weren't really doing "it," that we just kissed and slept, that if she walked with me past the lions guarding the steps of the graduate library, she could hear them roar. College lore had it that the imposing statues knew when a virgin passed by—but no one had heard their call since 1868.

What would have happened to me if I had not left when I did? Those that stayed—Eugenia, Julieta, many others—were pregnant before finishing high school and, most probably, before ever having a discussion about sex, let alone one about birth control. While girls in Barranquilla kissed and got pregnant, girls in the U.S. talked about sleeping with their boyfriends and were likely to be on the pill or to know how to use a diaphragm. And I, at the time, only thought of my new classmates as being a bad influence on me, not as contributing to my becoming responsible about my sexuality.

Because I left, I did not have to marry the first boy I kissed. My friends did, and today they have children in their teens. When

I go back, my outspoken aunts and my friends ask with amusement and with shock, And so who are you with now? I have become the *gringa libertina* they predicted. If someone asked my parents today for advice on whether to send their daughters to study abroad, they, I think, would agree with Arturo. I'm sure glad they sent me, though.

I heard my mother's voice through the kitchen entrance. She was telling the cook what to prepare for dinner as I walked in with Ana María's invitation.

"I think I'll stay for this," I said, handing her the envelope.

"It's a great idea," she said. "You'll get to see all your old friends."

"That's what I thought."

When my father was my age, he had a wife and three kids, sat on a different board of directors every day of the week, presided over Barranquilla's Chamber of Commerce, and worked closely with the Colombian president. Every Sunday we went to Mass, usually at six in the evening at the Inmaculada, where the lulling sound of the breeze against the coconut palms entered the open windows and rocked me into a doze. I would not really understand, or listen to, what the priest was saying; unlike the good feeling I got from Arturo's book, Mass was not something that interested or intrigued me. Sitting on a long pew, standing, and kneeling repeating over and over a litany of words that sounded as if something very important and very bad had been our fault seemed incomprehensible and unfair. What was it that was *por mi culpa, por mi culpa, por mi propia culpa?* My eyelids often felt very, very heavy as I pondered, as Padre Becerra spoke, what we had done that required repentance with such guilt and remorse. I couldn't think of anything I had done. Did calling my sister fat or locking myself in the bathroom to read Henry Miller qualify?

At eight I had my First Communion, which meant I would be a sinner if I didn't attend Mass with my parents every Sunday at dusk. By then, I also knew the prayers and every one of the priest's lines by heart and the only part I looked forward to was when the priest would lift his hands and bid us offer each other the sign of peace. People hugged their neighbors, kissed their families, waved and winked to their friends. In Barranquilla *darse la paz* took forever. But that was not enough to make me want to go back every Sunday. Trying to stay home to study for an invented test or complaining of a sudden stomachache never worked. I would hear how I should have done my homework before church and how going to church was as important as finishing schoolwork, especially after having had my First Communion. Faking a stomachache was scarier. The religion teacher had told us God knew everything, including, I assumed, if I had a real stomachache.

Communion, I was told, meant I was receiving the body of Christ. It was frightening and hard to imagine how it was possible that the same thin, long-haired, bearded man on the cross next to my grandmother's bed was going to be entering my body in the form of a thin and bland full moon, but when I asked I was told, sternly this time, that these were the mysteries of God and His Church. My front teeth were not yet fully out when, dressed like a child bride, I received the body of Christ for the first time. My long white dress came from Spain, where cloistered nuns had spent months embroidering it. I wore a veil with a train and I wanted to wear the ring with the yellow heart that I had received at a birthday party but my mother said no, the day was too special for a plastic ring. I woke up very early that morning, before my mother did, to comb my hair and practice saying amen in front of the mirror.

I never stopped being nervous whenever it was my turn for the priest to place the white wafer on my tongue. The religion teacher and my grandmother had told me to pray and think about Christ the moment we felt His body in our mouth. But all I could think of was how the tasteless wafer was sticking to the roof of my mouth and how I had been instructed not to chew but to suck. Sucking only made it stick more, and regardless of how hard I pressed my tongue to my palate, it stayed stuck. Mass would soon be over but the taste of the body of Christ remained.

As we walked out, my parents always ran into friends, married couples with children, families that looked like ours. The parents would exchange greetings, stop and chat under the almond tree in need of rain. The men—a senator, the city's governor, the mayor of the moment, the movers and shakers—gathered in a circle. The wives stood in silence or talked with each other outside the circle. They all looked well-dressed and poised but my mother was always the prettiest. While the other children ran back and forth from the parked cars to their parents' side, I would just stand by my father and listen to the men's conversation, which always started with the same line—"*Ajá y que hay de nuevo en la política.*"

My father, like Arturo, like all men I knew, talked incessantly about politics. At family gatherings, my grandfather and uncles and father sat around discussing the Conservative Party while the women sat in silence or made sure their husbands didn't need a new drink. During election time my father was always busy campaigning and fund-raising for his party. He was proud of the Christmas card he received every year from Alvaro Gómez Hurtado, the Party's leader, thanking him for all he had done.

The only time I saw my mother participate in politics was when, right before elections, the women, the wives of the *políticos*, would meet at one of their homes and help stuff envelopes with voting sheets. On election day they wore T-shirts stamped with their husband's faces and handed out envelopes at the voting stations. The servants in our homes were each handed one, and their *patrones* would tell them that they wanted them to vote for the Conservative or the Liberal candidates. It was hard to escape voting for the candidate of their choice, or to keep your vote private. Up until recently, the voter's index finger was submerged in blue ink if the vote was cast Conservative, in red if it had been Liberal. (This could have serious consequences. During the 1940s and 1950s, Conservatives and Liberals staged one of the most violent witchhunts in history—shooting, stabbing, burning each other's property, and leaving more than 250,000 Colombians dead.) Upper-class Colombians like to marry within their class and within their party, and the man of the house expects his sons, daughters, wives, and servants to vote with him.

This is not unusual. During Mexico's 1994 elections, women complained that their husbands were taking away their voting cards, preventing them from casting votes of their own. Machismo transcends country and class borders. Chicana workers in California, striking at a cannery in Watsonville, received little support from their *compañeros*, who preferred them to be at home cooking, not demanding better salaries. Many women were forbidden outright to stand on the picket line.

I was convinced Arturo was different. He was even supportive when I decided to go on to college. I am also sure that I chose to major in Political Science because it was what sounded the closest to what he talked to me about. I still carried around, unread, the little book he had given me. Freshman year, he wrote frequently. In his letters he sent strength and advice—"I hope that when I see you, you will have many things to teach me about that beautiful profession you chose." To keep me up to date with his successes, he sent all the newspaper stories that were being written about him. Right out of school, he was already some kind of public person. He had been named director for health services, and also selected as Ejecutivo del Año, as my father had been at his age. I was proud of Arturo's accomplishments, but what I really liked was that he shared them with me while calling me his *muñeca*. "When you return I will show you the books I read about politics. They are really excellent and they really deserve my hours of dedication. You will see."

In an effort to bring him together with what I was reading—Locke, Hobbes, Marx, Rousseau, an English edition of *The Prince*, flyers announcing demonstrations on campus, *U.S. hands off El Salvador, Disinvest in South Africa*—I kept his letters mixed with the mess on my desk. I anxiously anticipated our reunion in which I too would show him my books, in which I would kiss him fiercely before he would kiss me, in which I would no longer simply sit in admiration, listen, and ask questions but would also tell him what I had learned about his *política*.

Upon my return, I traveled to Monte Carmelo, my grandfather's *finca*, an incongrous name in this case, for the "farm" is bigger than some American national parks. Arturo's family's *finca* is nearby and I knew he was there that week. I called him and he promised to come over that evening. After a year of learning politics from lefty, ex-draft-dodging professors, the place where as a child I had milked its cows, swum its river, saddled its horses became a microcosm of income disparity and exploitation. When Arturo arrived I wanted him to be Che—he insisted on Machiavelli. As I walked him to the gate and he said good-bye, I knew that that would be the last time he would call me.

I would now see him at Ana María's party, I thought. We could reminisce about our talks, even laugh at our youthful intolerance. In Ann Arbor I had discovered liberation theology and leftist politics, theories about the culture of imperialism, CIA plots in Central America, sit-ins and demonstrations—the staples of a college campus at the end of the 1970s. My student days opened a Latin America that Arturo had maybe seen but had refused to recognize. We were adults now, he a minister, I a journalist. It would be fun, I thought as I passed my index finger over his name in haut-relief on the invitation.

Seeing Arturo's name next to an important title was not surprising to me. At an early age, young and privileged men like him are seduced by politics, by prestige, and by power. Being a vice-minister in your early thirties is, I think, an act of arrogance, but in a way this is an arrogance that is instilled in these men the day they are born. It is pretty much par for the course. Arturo is an upper-class man, in a world owned completely and absolutely by them. As far as the hierarchy goes, he is at the top. This is a world where some people—the rich, the white (or, more accurately, the less mixed), the *políticos*, the industrialists, landowners like Arturo's father, like my grandfather—have a lot, and where many more people have very little. But regardless of which side of the tracks you're born on, the rich or the poor, the men who own the land or the men who work it, it is a world where men have carte blanche in domination of their women. Just as my grandfather expected my grandmother to vote Conservative, our gardener expected his wife, our cook, to give him her salary. As recently as 1995, a Panamanian husband sought to divorce his wife because she did not cook him dinner or take his clothes to the dry cleaner. That she worked full-time was irrelevant in his view. Those chores, he argued, fall under her obligations.

More dramatically, and regardless of the fact that in the last two decades most constitutions have been rewritten, the judicial system throughout Latin America will rarely convict a man who kills his adulterous wife—men have a right to defend their honor. In Panama, until 1991, for a man to be adulterous, the relationship had to be scandalous and continuous. For a woman, it took one slip. A rape victim in Peru was told by the judge that, as she was not a virgin at the time, it did not really matter that she was raped. Her rapist would be relieved of prison if he offered to marry her. And as in thirteen other countries—Argentina, Brazil, Chile, Colombia, Costa Rica, the Dominican Republic, Ecuador, Guatemala, Honduras, Nicaragua, Panama, and Paraguay—a rapist may go free if he marries his victim with her consent. In Costa Rica, a rapist may go free even if he marries the raped woman *without* her consent.

In Argentina, last year, a cook accused of systematically raping his eleven-year-old stepdaughter every time the girl's mother—his wife—left for work was immediately released from prison when he announced he would marry the girl. Under Article 132 of the Penal Code, his ten-year sentence would be repealed if the marriage took place: "In the case of violation, rape, kidnap or dishonest abuse of a single woman, the delinquent who will marry the offended will be exempt of his sentence, if she consents after she is restituted to her parents' home or to another safe place."

The girl, who was pregnant, accepted the offer—with her mother's consent—to marry her mother's husband, her rapist, so that the newborn would have *un papá.*

The fascination I had felt listening to my father and to Arturo discuss politics mutated into real concern after college. I discovered that journalism would allow me to infiltrate their separate clusters. And I would be better equipped to crawl inside if I covered Latin America as the gringa they thought I was becoming. As one, I could comment on and question the *política* that once I had felt they kept me out of for the simple reason that I was not a man. While I lived in rented rooms in Managua and Mexico and squatted in friends' homes in Panama stringing for newspapers as a way to understand the politics that I had been surrounded by and at the same time shunned from, back home José Luis, Arturo and about a dozen more friends acted as patrician adults, walking the halls of power in Bogotá, leading the lives my father and their fathers led at their age. While I voted *en blanco* as a form of protest, my brother was ready to vote Conservative.

But following, in this case, was an act of preserving their self-interest. The State in Colombia has always guarded the economic interests of the country's patriarchal oligarchy—an elite that still depends for its survival on a class-divided society and on women being excluded from public life. When I become obnoxiously repetitive during family dinners about the fact that Bogotá's Jockey Club will not admit women as members, a friend, in jest, provides me with the clearest answer. "If we do," he says, "what will we have left?"

In Colombia—and, in Latin America from Mexico all the way down to Argentina—just as landowners are not eager to divide up their huge parcels of uncultivated land to the campesinos who live on it and work it, men are not ready to see women as free participants in the country's civil society. They are more than happy to continue to see women as wives, mothers, virgins, or whores, but not as engineers, journalists, lawyers, surgeons, or statesmen. We are still encouraged to want to be beauty queens and soap-opera heroines, beautiful and virginal. The ones who kiss with their mouths closed are always rewarded with the successful and handsome husbands.

I feel the eyes rolling again, of men and women who will accuse me of exaggerating. Look at how many women in Colombia are in *altos cargos*. Great! I say. Before Madeleine Albright was named secretary of state, Colombia named a woman minister of foreign affairs. True! And women all the way from Argentina to Mexico have been appointed to high governmental office. I know about those twenty-three ministerial posts, three vice presidencies, two presidents of Congress. But let me point something out. Men, knowing that it is politically necessary to name a few token women, do it with a certain discretion. They feel fine relinquishing the ministries of education, tourism, culture, not to mention family and women's affairs. As a matter of fact, of the twenty-three ministers, only three are in different ministries. In Colombia and Mexico, María Emma Mejía and Rosario Green are foreign ministers, and in Chile, Soledad Alvear heads the Justice Department.

But comments like the one I heard in Ecuador are more eloquent than the actual appointments about how men in power see the appointment of women. "It's really nice to have ladies in the meeting of Congress," the first secretary of government said, referring to the possible appointment of a woman to the Ministry of Tourism. "I would like it very much if Soledad Diab were made responsible for the Ministry of Tourism, not only because she is a beautiful woman but also because she knows about the field." Is it a coincidence that Irene Saez, the woman running for president of Venezuela is a former Miss Universe?

Venezuelan elections are scheduled for December 1998 and the thirty-six-year-old former Miss Universe appears to be a serious contender despite her limited political experience. She has served as mayor of Chacao, the richest part of Caracas, where she has started early morning tai-chi classes for the elderly, two orchestras, and a school of ballet. She has also outlawed "passionate" kissing in public. But as Agustín Blanco, a professor of history at the Catholic University of Venezuela, told the *New York Times*, "what people vote for is the image of a beautiful woman not a woman who is judged on her intelligence, her capacity and accomplishment."

Like my friends, like their friends, my parents married young. My father was twenty-two. My mother was eighteen. She went to a convent school, where she showered wearing a thin white robe over her body. She left before finishing to marry him, to be *de mi papá*, to go with him to New York while he finished a master's degree in economics. Three months after their marriage, she was pregnant with me.

I saw a picture taken in the midst of a Syracuse winter. She stands next to him, snow up to her ankles in a setting that for her must have felt like the moon. She had never felt cold or spoken English. Yet in her face I can sense that she feels protected by him on this new planet. Despite his young age, my father radiates power through the photograph. He looks like a bull ready to take on any matador, and she looks proud to be married to him, as if she needs nothing more in life.

My parents keep a picture of my brother on his graduation day from Culver Military Academy in a silver frame in the family study upstairs. Like my sister and me, and many of our friends, he too was educated abroad. We were all being prepared to take on the roles we were born to play in this Latin opera of feminine submission and masculine power. My sister and I attended an all-girl Catholic high school. Many of our girlfriends spent a year at finishing schools in Switzerland learning French, how to set a formal table and who painted the *Mona Lisa*. Instead, my brother attended a military academy where many privileged Latin boys his age—he had classmates from Colombia, Guatemala, El Salvador, Panama—learn discipline. "Very important that he learns discipline," says my father. What they learn, as far as I am concerned, is how to continue thinking the world is theirs. Flipping through my brother's yearbook, I ran across the quote next to the photograph of the graduate from Guatemala: "I want to be democratically elected as dictator of my country."

My brother was barely eighteen when he graduated with medals across his chest. But there is already a look to him in that photograph, regardless of his boyishness. He stares straight at the camera, conveying that he is capable of smashing it if something does not go his way. There is something similar about these two photographs—the way my father stands next to my mother, and the way my brother stands next to the school's gate, with their feet apart and their hands clasped in front—that sends the message that they are confident of their place in their world of power. A power that, in Latin America, is determined by their sex.

I walked into Ana María's grand apartment with my parents. I was nervous and excited, but the way I looked made it easier to stride into the world of white wine and whisky, where every man stood like my brother, stared like my father, and spoke like them both. My mother had spent the last few days maneuvering to make sure I wore something appropriate, so she was delighted. She really suffered every time I came back to visit and wore only blue jeans. The day I told her I would stay for the party, she went through my duffel bag and pulled out a crumpled black taffeta skirt.

"This needs a blouse," she said, lifting it up and heading to her bedroom to call Doña Berta, one of Bogotá's fanciest dressmakers. She pleaded with Doña Berta, who was saying it was impossible to have anything ready on such short notice. She was the busy couturiere of beauty queens and society ladies, and to make a quasi-glitzy blouse for me was not as interesting as the important wedding gowns and the long beaded evening dresses she was used to designing. But my mother, with her usual charm, convinced her. This was urgent.

As I scoured the room for Arturo, I was glad of my mother's insistence. I liked the feel of the black bodice that Berta had made for me. It was long-sleeved, with a round, low neckline, and it was sprinkled with little rhinestones. I looked around the apartment. It was hard for me to grasp that it belonged to someone I once shared teenage secrets with. The dark red damask on the decent replicas of French fauteuils, the perfectly framed scenes of English foxhunts hanging from the walls, and their three-year-old blond boy dressed in his best sailor suit all seemed too incongruous to have any relation to my life. I was a penniless cub reporter traveling like a gypsy from war-torn Nicaragua and polluted Mexico to sensual Rio de Janeiro and eerie Paraguay writing about military coups, drug trafficking, political corruption, and the transmission of AIDS in Latin America. This was the home of two people who were traditional, and comfortable with the way things were, who didn't question but followed, I thought. What had happened to me?

Nonetheless, there was a certain familiarity to the scene. Some time ago I learned how to act as a girl of privilege at a cocktail party and, like riding a bicycle, I have not forgotten it. My father held my forearm as he proudly steered me across the room where men stood in small circles holding their drinks.

"Remember my daughter Silvana?" he interrupted. "The one that's a journalist."

But since I am not as tall and striking as my sister, and they could not ask me about my husband or my children, they smiled politely and went back to their conversation about the price of coffee.

My mother called me over to the sofas where the women sat separated from the men. They welcomed me with careful kisses on the cheek, making sure not to smudge their red Chanel lips, and turned to my mother to tell her how happy she must be to have me home, if only for a few days.

"You don't think you'll come back to Colombia?" one of the ladies asked. "You like it there too much."

"She's too independent for here," another one replied.

A uniformed waiter holding a silver tray handed me a whisky. He was pouring water into my tall glass of Boheme crystal when I spotted Arturo across the room. He, like every other man there, was dressed in a gray suit. I walked over to where he was and stood straight in front of him with a big smile on my face. He stretched his right arm out, and offered me a handshake and an uninterested greeting.

I remained next to him waiting for more.

"So, how many kids do you have now?" he asked politely, in that intimate yet impersonal way people in politics practice so well.

"What?"

"*Tus niños,*" he repeated. "*¿No tienes niños?*"

My no was followed by my very own nervous laugh.

"Aren't you married?" he asked, surprised.

"Married. No. Me? No. To whom?" I thought he was joking, that this was his way of breaking the ice.

He insisted. "I don't know, but I thought by now, by now, you would be married. You must be, what, thirty. Right?"

"That's right. I am thirty."

"Well, I'm sure you do have a boyfriend." His voice had turned paternalistic. "Boyfriend, right?"

"Yes," I said, "boyfriend."

"Whenever I run into your cousin, the one who's married to Felipe, I always ask about you. I thought you had married. I do know you're living in New York, right?"

"Yeah, New York. Finishing my master's at Columbia, international affairs, and I've been reporting from Central America. As a matter of fact, oh, I was just in Mexico working, covering, covering . . . Mexico." I said it all in one breath, a ramble whose only purpose was to give some meaning to my life—a life and work I enjoy, a life that I am proud of and that Arturo with one question had just made all go up in smoke.

I was exculpating myself to Arturo for not being married, for not having children, for my unwillingness to play the game of a woman commanded by her need to be only mother and wife. I felt Arturo's reproach of who I had become and, for the first time, it hurt. Usually I disregard the comments of my mother and my female friends who today have teenage children, when they mention my unmarried status. But Arturo's implied criticism was different. I felt he was putting me down for having followed what he had once started.

I understood that what made me different was not that I was interested in having a career. My mother was right. Many of the women born into my privileged world had college degrees and careers. It was more a question of attitude, a question of how I saw myself vis-à-vis male authority. In this setting, my independence was not attractive, my brashness was unbecoming. I had not followed the advice Colombian women give other women: "A docile character assures happiness in marriage and will make a woman the ideal partner for a man until death."

I guess it's undecorous for vice-ministers to hug at cocktail parties given in their honor, but that's what I really would have liked. I wasn't there to congratulate him on his new job. I was interested in the person who had, for the first time and in many ways, opened my eyes to a different world from the one that was slated for me. In a way I was there to thank him, to show off a bit because I felt he could recognize his influence. I also wanted to ask him how it felt being so close to power. It must be titillating to feel you belong to the future of a country. At the same time I wanted to take him aside and warn him what happens in the game of politics played by those who follow the rules of the little book he had given me almost twenty years before. But Arturo turned his back and continued talking to the other men in gray suits. (Six months later, in one of the frequent cabinet shuffles, he was replaced.)

After my disappointing encounter, I turned to my mother and her friends. The ladies with the Hermès scarves around their necks and the big pearls clipped to their ears were always warm.

They always seemed to have a good time at cocktails sharing their juicy *chismes* while lighting each other's cigarettes with their 24K gold Dunhills. Instead of financial transactions, government contracts, and soccer scores, they chatted giddily, like girls at a sleepover, about recent divorces and upcoming shopping sprees in New York or Miami.

I arrived to hear a litany of praises for Ana María. The reception was so elegant, her husband was sooooo nice, her son so beautiful, she was so chic, nice, *conversadora, inteligente.* The lady with the longest nails said that she had heard that for Ernesto Mario—Ana María's father—she was indispensable in the office.

Like my mother, they dream of having a daughter like Ana María. She married into one of Colombia's more traditional families *con apellido importante.* She is charming and social as can be. They always sound surprised when they add that she has time to be a mother, a wife, an important businesswoman. She doesn't cease to amaze them: She cooks, goes on holidays, gives and attends dinner parties. She might need some help with her taste in clothes and antiques but, nonetheless, she is always *bien arreglada,* nicely turned out. My mother's praise for her strikes me as a hint that I should reexamine the way I live. Grow up, she tells me constantly. But what she really means is be a woman—like her, like her friends the charming Chanel ladies, like Ana María.

I gave up the life of a Latin princess when I decided to stay in New York. I traded a big house for four hundred square feet I call home. Instead of having breakfast served to me in bed on a tray I buy coffee at the corner Greek deli. I do not travel in a chauffeured car. My nails are short; my long hair is usually in need of a trim. I do not visit the beauty salon as often as they do. When I have friends over for dinner, I don't rely on several servants to make the soufflé rise and I don't look like I just stepped out of a Saks Fifth Avenue catalog. I do not have a husband who has power lunches, or wants me to use his last name—the one that appears on the gold American Express card that would allow me to go shopping in Miami.

Unlike the women who raised me and those who grew up with me, I've always lacked faith that those "things" that I so much should want would be able to protect me. I've never felt comfortable with taking the steps necessary to have the life I was raised to have. I've wondered many times if, in reality, this is what I truly want and I'm rejecting it because it is what I was told I would have and I don't have it. But it is impossible for me, today, to walk into the life I was born into and not feel the consequences of those shopping trips. I cannot enjoy a lunch with the ladies, *un almuerzo de señoras,* without thinking that while we are being served a sumptuous meal by servants in aproned uniforms, men, their husbands, are deciding the economic future of our country. While we eat at a table set with Christofle silverware on starched *manteles,* they are passing laws that will affect us directly. Unless more than 9.4 percent of the legislative seats of the Colombian Congress are filled by women, by women who will change the laws, rape will still be considered a crime against the state, not against an individual. Abortion will still be punished with prison while thousands of women will continue to die from them.

It became especially hard to sit still for these five-hour lunches after my visit to the Hispanic AIDS Forum in Jackson Heights, Queens, in 1991.

I was there to see its director, who would explain to me the pattern of transmission of AIDS in the Latino community in New York. Miguelina Maldonado swiveled her chair to grab a black plastic folder with the seal of the City of New York. She opened the report and, out loud, went down the list of categories marked as high risk: homosexuals, MSMs, IVDUs, and blood transfusions. I knew IVDU stood for intravenous drug user but I had to ask Maldonado what MSM meant.

"Oh, you know, *m'ija.* M-S-M," she said in a strong Puerto Rican accent, "stands for men who have sex with other men."

"Men who have sex with men?"

"Ahhmm."

"Wouldn't they be listed under homosexual transmission?"

She shook her head no and smirked, satisfied she was one up on me, another Latina.

"Bisexual?" I tried again.

"No. Simply men who happen to have sex with men. They are neither homosexual nor bisexual."

"Oh, of course," I said.

Of course.

Being a Latin American woman, as soon as I heard those words I knew what she was talking about. All the jokes and the comments came back: he is such a macho, he fucked another man; *marica es el que lo da,* faggot is the one who takes it. Stuff I had overheard in the background of boys' conversations all of a sudden became institutionalized, percentages in a study about AIDS. Miguelina and I had started speaking about AIDS and men having sex with other men in the sterilized language of a graduate student and the director of a state-funded social agency. After my second cup of coffee we shed the formalities. I was startled. We agreed that in Latin American culture, two men can have sex, and one of them—the active partner—would never think he has had homosexual sex. We talked for hours trying to come up with some kind of baroque explanation—a mixture of manhood, homophobia, and religious influence that could bring our men to the point of persuading themselves that two men can have sex without it being a homosexual act. But what was really disturbing for us was what this sexual behavior meant for women, partners of men who have sex with other men, with AIDS in the picture. "In this group," she said, "the use of condoms is lower than any other group."

Memories of my youth in Barranquilla sprang up—the car rides on Friday nights, the transvestites walking down the rich boulevard where I grew up, the conversations among men—even boys my age—who referred to men as either machos or *maricas,* sissies, faggots, *el que lo da.* Being called a girl was as much of an insult. I remembered my mother's suggestions about what it meant to be a girl, about saving myself for the day I got married, how she thought I shouldn't wear those shorts that made me look like a slut. I thought of Mrs. Gaspari, the religion teacher, who kept saying that God punishes those girls who look at their bodies naked and I was sure she had said it looking straight at me and I had thought oh my God, she knows, He told her. I also thought about Julieta, Ana María, Lali, Mercedes, Eugenia, my cousin

Rosanna—pretty girls who became mothers without ever being anything other than pampered daughters living by the codes of our strong fathers. We had strict curfews, we weren't allowed to go to El Gusano, and we were told only bad girls did. When we had boyfriends, they added their own authoritarian rules to those of our fathers: no talking to other boys, no short skirts or small swimsuits, and if there was kissing and touching it was never talked about. The boys respected our imposed curfews, dropping us off at midnight, eager to meet with their friends at El Gusano and, sometimes, at bordellos. It was right there sitting in Queens looking at the number of women being infected with AIDS by their husbands that I realized how dangerous the connection between our sexual culture and the Catholic Church and AIDS was, not only for my friends but for all Latin American women.

I left Maldonado's office with the statistics and with my heart pounding. If AIDS is seen as something only gays get, but men are having sex with other men without ever considering their act as a homosexual one but just as something that they occasionally do, where does that leave their women? Girlfriends who have been raised to think of their sexuality as sinful and unmentionable, and wives who have sex when they are ordered to?

I spent the following six months traveling around South America interviewing epidemiologists, sociologists, gay activists, transvestites, prostitutes, wives. My fear was confirmed when I read a study by the Colombian epidemiologist Dr. Juan Eduardo Céspedes. A housewife in Latin America, asserted Dr. Céspedes, is at higher risk of contracting AIDS than a prostitute.

"Why?"

"The hidden bisexuality of Latin men."

That same week I was told that eighty percent of the wives who had tested HIV-positive at Bogotá's Simón Bolívar Hospital had been infected because of the bisexual activity of their husbands. Most of these women had married as virgins. Their husbands were the only man they had made love to.

I faxed my story to Tom Schroder at the *Miami Herald*.

"Wow," he said. "This is pretty explosive. You are sure about what you are saying?"

"Yes," I said.

"Well, we are going to check it with our bureaus down there. We need to be very sure, you know. In Latin America when the *Miami Herald* says something, then it becomes a fact. People really read this paper carefully, and we are about to say that all these married men are having sex with other men and they don't think that's having sex with a man. I've never heard of such a thing."

"I'm sure, Tom," I said. "Listen, there are many references in literature. Vargas Llosa mentions it in *La ciudad y los perros*."

"That's literature. This is stating it. I need to be very careful. I need to get ready to answer a lot of angry calls and letters."

The *Miami Herald* received no phone calls and no letters, which to me meant it is better to leave the earth unturned when what is to be uncovered might prove impossible to deny.

When I decided to write this book, I knew a big part of my interest was selfish. I would be able to ponder the string of questions that, like clouds over my head, have accompanied me on my travels as I go from my small apartment in New York City to Ana María's floor-through in Bogotá to my grandparents' house in Barranquilla. My experience is not unique. It is that of a privileged white woman—*café con leche,* really—who grew up as the princess in a fairy tale and was given the chance of breathing a little of the air outside her provincial palace. Women like me have been accused of being influenced by the United States; we are told that our ideas are foreign and imperialist to our societies, that everyone is fine with the way things are, that machismo is a fact of life. "Relax. Lay back," everyone remarks when I try to explain. "You're becoming too American. Find a husband, *cásate.*" In other words, get married and shut up. They recognize that their husbands can be impossible, but come on, *los hombres, m'ija, son los hombres,* and with all your talking you are not going to change that. You are just going to scare them away. *Un poquito de astucia femenina, un poquito de resignación, y cada una con su cruz.*

I guess it is easier to justify if one lives in great comfort and with the status of a married woman. To them, my life might be as mysterious and as foreign as a French film but equally unappealing. They have no interest in living like me. New York is great—theatre, restaurants, stores—but, for a few days. Who could dream of life with no servants?

But as I talk to the women I do not know as well, the women who live in the favelas of Rio de Janeiro or São Paulo, the women who fought against the Somoza dictatorship in Nicaragua, the young women who support themselves by selling their bodies for sex in Bogotá or Recife, the street girls who sniff glue and beg for money in Montevideo, the housemaids with long black braids and Inca faces in the households of Quito, I realize that I cannot accept those answers and that the clouds of questions become larger, darker. A storm of resentment approaches those, even my friends, who do not see that they are victims of their own "perfect" condition.

My need to run out, to leave the lunches and explore why there are so many transvestites on the main avenues of Latin American cities, why millions of young boys and girls prefer to leave their homes, even if poor, for the streets where they are exposed to the inclemencies of weather, brutality, danger, and disease, is not because I want to satiate an isolated personal curiosity about untraditional sexual practices or because my heart weeps when an eight-year-old gamin with grimy, rosy cheeks asks me if I can give him a home. It is because I now recognize the chain of events that leads an eighteen-year-old to sell his body to pay for his ten-dollar room at night, even though he knows he is HIV-positive. Most women might think of transvestites as carnival creatures, and of street children as unfortunates but potential criminals whom they must keep at arm's length even when giving them a handout on the streets; I see them as a consequence of a set of practices and beliefs that are closer than these women ever thought to their bedroom lives.

"My clients?" says the eighteen-year-old boy sitting on the steps of the Terrazas Pasteur, the shopping center in downtown Bogotá where he starts soliciting work at three every afternoon. "I can't tell you exactly, because they are so different. My clients are soldiers, *viejos borrachos,* businessmen, married men, construction workers, even rich men who come with their Mercedes-Benz."

Transvestites have told me what they do for work, who their clients are, how many times they wear condoms. Street boys have spoken about why they ran away from home. Women in Cuba, in Nicaragua, and in Brazil who joined and worked closely with armed liberation movements have confirmed that the men who believed in Che Guevara also believe that a woman's place is in the mountains but doing the cooking. Priests who have challenged the orthodoxy of their Church and demanded social justice are not ready to challenge the Church on women's reproductive rights.

This is where this book stops being my own private cry, and I start seeing it as a call to all women from Mexico to Argentina—a call to ponder just for a second the world of behavior that results from having men decide for us and dictate our laws. Unless we stop this process, we can die from a dangerous self-induced abortion, we can find ourselves being HIV-positive having slept with just one man, or we can be forced to marry our rapist.

As I've mentioned, fourteen Latin American penal codes exonerate a rapist who offers to marry the victim and is accepted. In Peru, when Beatriz Merino Lucero, the president of the congressional committee on women, tried to introduce a bill that would eliminate this provision, the judicial committee, a committee composed of men, kept the basic tenet of the law. The only part dropped was a 1991 revision that allowed one of the participants in a gang rape to be exonerated if he offered to marry the victim. If Merino, a Harvard-educated lawyer, were to present her petition to a judicial committee composed more of women, the outcome would have, most likely, been different. This is exactly my point. It's not enough to be satisfied that women are being educated, are in the labor force and in politics. There are women who are lawyers, women who are being trained in the best institutions in the world, women who are fighting to change a system that is unfair. But the rules that prevail are still those proposed and made by men, and what women want and what men want women to want is starkly different. What woman would like to wake up every morning next to the man who raped her?

So this book is not a confession or a memoir. I am not writing it because I am angry at my mother for not liking the life I chose. If I bring myself to open up my thoughts and my experiences, it is because I feel that having spent the first fifteen years of my life growing up as a girl in Barranquilla, experiencing so closely the way men and women relate to each other in a culture suffocated by machismo, marked me indelibly. Spending the next twenty years in the United States has allowed me to step out of the stringent roles that formed me. It is scary to sometimes feel that my grandmother's submissiveness toward my grandfather is latent in me.

What I am proposing in this book has been said before. That Latin American governmental institutions and sexual relationships are tainted by a ubiquitous machismo is hardly a revelation. Thousands of theoretical papers, pamphlets, books, conferences attest to the inequalities of the genders in Latin America. But I know the difference between reading an obscure academic paper or an impenetrable treatise and reading about the experiences of women with names and faces. Before I started this book I had never heard about the First International Conference on Women held in Mexico City in 1975 nor that groups with feminist agendas have been meeting in São Paulo, Tegucigalpa, Bogotá, Havana, and many other Latin American cities since then. Their voices have been heard. In 1979, the United Nations drafted the Convention on the Elimination of All Forms of Discrimination Against Women. In the nineties, the 1992 Earth Summit in Rio de Janeiro, the 1993 Human Rights Conference in Vienna and the 1995 Social Summit in Copenhagen, all addressed women's issues. The culmination of all these progressive initiatives was the 1996 Conference on Women in Beijing.

Despite their immense efforts, their voices and their propositions are rarely heard or embraced by the lady who shops in Miami with her husband's credit card or by the hard-working single mother living in a squatter's home of cardboard and zinc. Neither feels the need to visit the offices that I have visited in São Paulo, in Bogotá, in Managua, and in Quito. Groups like Brazil's CEPIA—which stands for Citizenship, Study, Research, Information, and Action—and Centro de Estudios e Investigaciones de la Mujer Ecuatoriana (CEIME), headed by women who have been able to transform taboos such as domestic violence, rape, and abortion into national issues, are equally foreign to my friends' mothers and to their maids. For all the good faith, studies about gender issues are written in words that are educated, grandiose, and part of a jargon that excludes the average woman, who if raped is afraid to report it, if physically abused at home is scared to seek legal aid, if lying moribund from a clandestine abortion prefers dying to being helped by a medical doctor who might mistreat or denounce her, and upon discovering her partner is HIV-positive will obey his order and not be tested herself.

Women in Latin America are being infected with the AIDS virus at a rising pace, as in Africa and in Asia, where the ratio is reaching one female to one male. The World Health Organization, in conjuction with UNAIDS, the United Nations' AIDS program, estimates that in Brazil the male–female ratio of AIDS cases has dropped from 16:1 in 1986 to 3:1. In the United States, most of the HIV-positive women are Latinas. Most campaigns are targeted to gays and prostitutes. When I went back to The Hispanic AIDS Forum three years after my conversation with Miguelina Maldonado and asked Luis Nieves, the director for an MSM campaign, how successful it was, he said, "I don't think we've had a married man come in yet to our meetings. The subject is waaaay too sensitive."

"How about reaching wives?"

Nieves, a counselor with years of experience, looked at me almost contemptuously. "Sure," he said. "That's going to be real easy."

Millions of dollars have been poured into Latin America with an aim that Luis Nieves knows is as hard to achieve as convincing the Catholic Church to distribute birth control. Pamphlets are being printed. In Brazil, I picked up *Acorda, Adelaide!* (Remember, Adelaide!), which had the format of an illustrated storybook. Two good friends—Nair and Adelaide—are having a coffee and a chat. Adelaide is upset. Her husband Jaime has not been home in months, and she is left to care for their children alone. "I think he is not coming back." She confesses to her friend that she misses him and she is tired of all the work. Nair reminds her that Jaime was never very helpful and that "a husband at home doesn't mean help."

A few months later, the two friends see each other again. Adelaide is feeling better. She has been hanging out with Rubens, whom she has known for years. He is from the neighborhood. Nair asks her if she is taking care of herself: "Remember, Adelaide, I'm talking about AIDS. Even if you have known Rubens a long time, you don't know who he's been with."

"Ah, Nair," Adelaide responds. "How am I going to ask a man that is being so supportive that I want him to use a condom—*fica difícil . . .*"

It is definitely difficult.

The work is commendable; the results are minimal. How many women have actually been able to ask their husbands to use condoms?

A nurse in a family-planning clinic in Vila Kennedy, a Rio de Janeiro favela where *Acorda, Adelaide!* is distributed, was pleasantly surprised at the turnout to her first talk about AIDS. When she asked the fifty women what had motivated them to come, most had the same answer. It was the first time they had received any mail addressed to them. The nurse talked about AIDS and the women listened attentively. When condoms were mentioned, the women shook their heads. One raised her hand. "Could you tell that to our husbands? Mine will kick me out of the house if I suggest something of the sort."

"*Ajá,*" meaning right on, the rest of the women sighed.

The nurse invited the husbands for a chat the following week. Again, she was surprised how many had agreed to accompany their wives. She gave her talk and sent the couples home with condoms. The following week, she invited the women for a follow-up meeting. But this time less than half showed up.

"I am sure, after they were here," she speculates, "the husbands didn't allow them to come back."

To those that did, she asked if they had used the condoms she had given them. Two raised their hands.

Globalization and the rise of AIDS has turned the lens on the empowerment of women, a favorite buzzword of the moment for agencies of the United Nations such as the UNDP and ECOSOC, international lending organizations such as the World Bank and the International Development Bank, large foundations like Rockefeller and Ford, and smaller ones like Panos Institute and the Population Council. One can walk in the remotest village of Bolivia and find a condom stamped with the logo of the UNDP, one can open a glossy brochure of the IDB and see a photograph of a toothless woman with a caption that reads "The face of poverty is the face of a woman." I stopped at a theatre in Copacabana on a random Saturday and was pleasantly surprised to listen to the strong words of Dr. Jonathan Mann, the world's leading AIDS activist, pronouncing, "It was only through AIDS that I realized that a patriarchal society is a threat to public health." The house came down with applause.

But Dr. Mann continues: "It is not through condoms," he says, "that we are going to change anything. We must look at laws." He always refers to the example of the group of women lawyers in Uganda who continue to fight to change property laws. Ugandan law provides that if a couple divorced, all assets, especially land, went to the husband. Women are not allowed to own land, a reason why many women were scared to divorce their husbands even though they knew about their infidelities and the risks they were taking by staying with them. The women lawyers of Uganda continue their legal battle, knowing that when women in Uganda can own land, they are more likely to divorce their unfaithful husbands.

In this day of neoliberalism, when our countries have all their eggs in the basket of market forces and foreign investment, foreign journalists and foreign human rights groups have more impact on local legislation than any local group. If there has been attention to women's issues such as Peru's Shining Path raping women, domestic violence in Brazil, lack of accountability of violence against women in Haiti, it is not because our governments decided they are concerned about women. It is because foreign dollars will not come if they continue to be embarrassed by these reports. It takes the work of poorly funded local nongovernmental organizations and the influence of bigger human rights groups, coupled with reports by foreign journalists, to do something about it. Latin American countries like to say with a mouthful of pride that for the first time in history all of our governments except for Cuba's have been fairly elected. Civil society, open markets, privatizations, the rule of law are the words du jour. This new trend has relegated women's issues to the back burner. During the transitional moments, such as when it was urgent to overcome militarism in Chile, Argentina, and Brazil, women's issues were at the forefront. Today, as Latin America consolidates democracy, cuts the payrolls of bureaucracy, and invites foreign dollars to buy cheap labor, as constitutions get rewritten, as one or two women, one or two blacks, one or two indigenous leaders are made part of *la política*, there is less real concern, less real space for women's issues to be considered.

It is not spelled out that women make up a vital part of the low-skilled, low-paid labor force. To lure foreign capital, our countries are selling the cheapest labor possible. The labor force in these *maquiladoras*—assembling baseballs, T-shirts, and microchips for foreign markets—is eighty percent female. Democracies will never be solidified while women lack real economic independence, not just a job that keeps them poor and second-class citizens according to our customary law and social codes. It is a step in the right direction that Latin American countries are having clean elections, but as long as women are still kept out of the political process, it is a mockery and a falsity to call it democracy. Regardless of Violeta de Chamorro, Noemí Sanín, María Emma Mejía, Rosario Green and Irene Saenz, *la política sigue siendo asunto de hombres.* In 1994, two women ran for the presidency of Peru, six for the vice presidency. But as well-known political analyst Mirko Lauer told the *New York Times*: "These women are not really running as women. They are running as any other politician would. Neither of these women [running for president] has a feminist platform, and they are not putting forward feminist demands. They are running within the macho context."

This book attempts to clarify why the face of poverty is illustrated in IDB brochures as the face of a woman, why more than half of the poor households in Latin America are headed by single mothers, why married women are at higher risk of contracting AIDS than a prostitute, why more than eighty percent of the married women who test HIV-positive were infected through the bi-sexual behavior of their husbands, why the Catholic Church is putting women at risk by forbidding condoms and legal abortions. None of these situations are independent, but they are intrinsically linked with the nature of our culture, our government, and our religion.

If I have a message in this book, it is to lay out an alternative to what our grandmothers and mothers, our teachers and priests wanted us to be, and what the men we are to marry feel most comfortable with. Marriage and motherhood, although important parts of who we are as women, cannot be the sole and total path to our identity as women. Having a choice in whatever we decide to do, from getting married to getting pregnant, can feel as natural and as imperative as going to Mass, to lunch, to the hairdresser. The Virgin Mary and Miss Colombia cannot continue being our role models. We need to introduce an alternative to the dichotomy between a "good woman" and *una mala mujer*; there is something between mother and whore. The definition of "good" need not entail being virginal and submissive. To be self-assured and independent does not mean we are whores. Meanwhile, for starters, I propose that we make our women politicians talk about legalizing abortion, our soap-opera heroines have orgasms, our beauty queens have better hobbies than collecting bathing suits and *tomar el sol*, our love ballads impart messages that give women strength and not tell them to just live for romance. Anything that keeps us from thinking that women don't have to think because men think for us. It is okay—no, it is indispensable—to think.

When I write about this, I feel the sturdiness of my convictions. When I walk into Ana María's life, my whole body wobbles. All the things I feel strongly about and proud of disappear the moment I'm presented with the picture of what I was supposed to become and didn't. Whenever I witness a husband calling his wife from his cellular phone simply to say hello, to ask about the children, to say "I love you" in between his important meetings, I feel I am exaggerating. But it takes about a second to feel reassured when I walk into a mixed gathering and see the men on one side of the room talking about the possibility of a coup or the naming of a new cabinet while the women are on the other side talking about what dirty words their children are learning at school and the youth concerts at the Alliance Française. Then I wonder if they feel as left out as I do.

I'm happy I didn't marry in Barranquilla where a woman is a *quedada*, a spinster, at twenty, and old by twenty-five whether she is a married woman or a whore. A few years back, my favorite relative and his wife invited me to dinner at Steak and Salads, one of the few trendy restaurants in town.

"But you know what it is really called," my kinsman said to me. "Not Steak and Salads but The Flea Market. You know why, right?"

I had no clue.

"Come on, sweetie, pretty simple. It's where the *separadas* and the *divorciadas* come," he said.

"What do divorced and separated women have to do with anything?" I asked.

"What do they sell at the *mercado de las pulgas? Pues,* they sell what has already been used, no?"

His wife laughed, and I was swallowing fire hating a person I had known and loved all my life. Would I too have laughed if I had stayed in Barranquilla, if I had not left when I was fifteen and spent twenty years in a land that has made me into *una mujer liberada*, which is not very different from *libertina*?

I felt fortunate that I had not married José Luis or Arturo. As I said before, I preferred Arturo, but by the time I was fourteen José Luis was *mi novio*, which translates as boyfriend but signifies much more of a formal arrangement. I stopped being Silvana, who I liked being, and became known as *la novia de José Luis*, who I didn't like being. It was pretty much taken for granted that one day we would marry. He was the perfect candidate for a *niña bien*, a *niña del Country*, a good girl like me. He came from a prominent family. We were Conservatives and they were Liberals and it would have been better if the families' politics could have matched, but apart from that there really were no *peros*, no buts. *Al contrario,* few families in Barranquilla qualified better—good, decent people, *lo mejor de lo mejor de Barranquilla, una buena familia cristiana.* His father was one of the most influential political leaders on the Colombian coast, and had also served as minister. And his mother, everyone agreed, was a dear, dear woman, *un amor.*

José Luis and I met because there was no way we could not. He was three years older, no one in Barranquilla goes out with someone their same age, the boy has to be older. We went to the same school, we swam in the same pool and at the same beach, we asked the same waiter at the club for grilled *sanduches de queso.* I was fourteen and I liked having his attention because I knew that he was considered cute by the older girls, especially those from Marymount, the rival school. At seventeen, he not only drove his own car but it was the coolest car in town—a silver race car that his father had bought for him at the car fair in Bogotá, the only one like it in the entire city.

I never asked myself if I liked him. It was enough that he liked me, and that was obvious. Every day after school, he drove by my house playing Barry White's "You're My First, My Last, My Everything" so loudly that it was impossible not to know he was outside. I would be in my room getting ready for my French lesson listening to Barry's deep voice blaring out on the street. One day on the beach he told me he would swim to the farthest rock and back without coming up to catch his breath to show me that I was his girl. I nodded my head and accepted this bizarre—and macho?—proof of his love. At fourteen, I was flattered by his attention and I didn't think I had a choice. It's what happens, what is supposed to happen. A boy sees you and decides to be with you, and you say yes. When I saw a photograph of my parents and his parents sharing champagne at a New Year's Eve party when they were in their early twenties, I thought it was fate. It was romantic like the songs.

Soon after that I was walking into the Country Club holding his hand, which meant we were serious *novios.* I watched him play soccer, waited for his sweaty kiss after the game and for his phone call every night at seven sharp. While he waited for me on Friday nights, my father would ask him to say hello to his father and would remind him that I was to be home by midnight.

José Luis respected my father's curfew more than I did. I asked him to ignore the rule many times, but he made sure I was home five minutes, even a quarter hour, before. He didn't want to be on my father's bad list, but I now know that he was also in a hurry to get rid of me. His friends would be waiting for him to go to El Gusano, the dark dungeonlike nightclub, where privileged young men like him and privileged and important married men would meet once they assured themselves their wives and *novias* were safe at home. Other women were there. The guys in drag who walked up and down the boulevard were also regulars. The place was so dark that it was sometimes hard to know who you were talking or dancing with. Patrons were assured anonymity by the intensity of the darkness. To find a customer a table, the ushers used flashlights.

El Gusano's exterior, a huge green worm made of papier-mâché, sat incongruously next to the imposing arches of the Hotel del Prado and the Art Deco mansions built in the 1920s when Barranquilla was a booming port town at the mouth of the Magdalena River, whose brown waters moved more than eighty percent of the country's commerce. It was in Barranquilla, not in Bogotá, the capital, that the busiest U.S. consulate operated. With the boom came the American ship captains, customs brokers, and representatives of American companies, and Barranquilla went from being a provincial hamlet to a version of the American dream in the tropics. In 1930 it had its own branches of the Rotary Club and the Lions Club and an American Men's Association. The city's first newspaper, the *Old Reliable*, was printed in English.

With a few hundred thousand dollars and the promise of providing sophistication, Karl C. Parrish, an entrepreneur from Boston, arrived in Barranquilla and sold to the up-and-coming merchants and rich landowners a chance for gentrification. He sold them the dream of suburbia, and I was born in the modern and opulent *barrio* with wide avenues, green lawns, large homes, a club with a pool, clay tennis courts, and eighteen holes of golf. We had a majestic hotel, a few churches, and an American school, named after Mr. Parrish, where we learned everything from old textbooks from the United States Department of Defense. When an eccentric resident of the Bario El Prado decided to open a discotheque in the 1970s, El Gusano's big yellow antennas, as high as the spire of the Iglesia de la Inmaculada, looked as if a float from Carnival had been abandoned on the main boulevard of this Latin suburban fantasia and the city's sanitation department had forgotten to remove it.

It was hard to miss El Gusano, especially because it was a place associated with mystery and men. After dropping me off on Friday nights, José Luis's car would remain parked next to the worm's mouth sometimes until very early the next morning. I was so curious about this place that I told him one night I would not go home unless I went inside.

"Your father said midnight, and I will make sure you are home by quarter to."

"But I don't care."

"I do, and you are with me. Anyway, El Gusano is not a place for you."

"Why not?"

"It just isn't and you are not coming tonight."

"I'll never see you again."

I was fierce and I knew those words made José Luis tremble.

"Mi amor, please, I promise I'll take you tomorrow, okay?"

I believed him, but what he meant was he was taking me in the middle of the afternoon. The owner ordered the employees to open up the place for me, and I was escorted inside a damp tunnel that smelled like the closet where my grandmother locked the *caramelos* Kraft, the Venezuelan almonds, and the *jabón de pera* to keep them out of the reach of the maids and her dozen grandchildren. The Worm was an ugly room with aluminum tables, carpet on the walls, chairs with cigarette holes and tacky and dirty upholstery, a bar, and two parquet dance floors.

"¿Contenta?" he said, hugging me as I walked out.

I ran into one of José Luis's Friday night buddies a few years ago. He was with his wife, the girl he married at eighteen because she was pregnant. They introduced me to their children, a teenage boy with long hair and a younger pretty girl, and asked me about mine.

"I don't have any," I replied, by now used to the question.

"You mean, none. Aren't you married yet?"

"No."

"What, then, are you doing in New York? I thought you had married a gringo."

"No," I said. "I just live there."

"Why?"

"I like it."

"What do you do?" he asked.

"I'm a journalist."

"You are what? A journalist? Why there? I mean"—he was truly surprised—"you live in New York, you are a journalist in New York, when all you had to do was marry José Luis and own a media empire?"

For him, my choice made no sense.

I could have been the wife and the mother of the children of an heir or a grand landowner or a future politician, as was in my cards. If I had stayed in Barranquilla, would I be satisfied wearing clothes from Miami, having my hair done weekly, running a house with the help of poor, uneducated women? But how would I have reacted every time my husband told me, sometimes ordered me, where and with whom I was allowed to go? Would I, as a mother taking care of a beautiful home and children, even have known that AIDS was something that needed to cross my mind?

This wife standing in front of me and asking me about my life in New York, has she ever thought that she could be HIV-positive? José Luis and his buddies, let alone their wives, do not realize that the threat of AIDS is closer to them than the slums they try so hard to avoid every time they drive out to the airport to spend a weekend in Bogotá or to take the kids to Disney World and then go shopping in Miami.

One thing that always warms my heart about Barranquilla is that people are really interested to know what you are doing. Acquaintances can be as straightforward—as nosy, opinionated, and obnoxious—as family members. But their sincerity and their *calor*, their warmth, has always touched me.

"I'm writing a book."

"About what?"

I could not bring myself to say that it explains how women like his wife are at higher risk of contracting AIDS than a prostitute, how I think men like him control our lives, how we have the right to be sexual, to have a safe abortion, to know about safe sex, to an education.

I moved to the States before I could get trapped by pregnancy and, unlike my friends, discovered my sexuality while remaining single. That makes me an an oddball back home. Like them, I was surrounded by family and friends who looked and thought alike. I had a privileged upbringing in the land of García Márquez's magical realism, inside a society where men are permitted anything and women are confined to strict, traditional roles. I grew up around women whose lives revolved around the lives of their men, and then around gossip, the importance of last names, and the Church. When I graduated from the University of Michigan, I called my grandmother, bedridden with a very advanced cancer. I knew her days were few. Her body, she told me, was being invaded as fast as the Malvinas, referring to the Falklands, the British islands that the Argentine military had tried to claim that year. To cheer her up, I told her that she could boast in front of her bridge partners that her *nieta* had a university degree.

"I'd rather tell them my granddaughter has a husband," she replied.

I was twenty-one.

Living in the United States put me in touch with women who thought differently from those I had always been surrounded by: women who have careers and who are successful, women who see the world, try to understand it, try sometimes to change it. It was in this country that I learned the jargon of equality, independence, and empowerment. I arrived in Ann Arbor wearing gold Charles Jourdan heels, Calvin Klein jeans, and barrettes on each side of my long hair. The first day of class I wore a flowing yellow gingham dress and found a class filled with students wearing ripped jeans and a professor who cursed his country.

"Fuck U.S. foreign policy," he said, speaking about support for the Shah of Iran. A week later he showed us *Hearts and Minds*, the Pulitzer-winning documentary on Vietnam, and the carpet was taken from under my feet. I was appalled by U.S. involvement, the good United States of America, and fascinated by the possibility of criticism, of confrontation of the status quo. In Ann Arbor, I learned about Latin America, a Latin America that was as foreign as the feel of the winter clothes I had to wear to walk to class in a place whose trees lost leaves, and changed colors. I spoke about Latin America in English, in political science language. I marched to protest U.S. presence in El Salvador. I served as the translator for conferences on labor movements. I helped create a solidarity network with Nicaragua when the Sandinistas took over. But I never questioned the condition of women. I still expected my date to pay for me, as I had been taught.

Slowly I learned that in the United States I had the option of taking care of myself, that paying for myself was not a humiliation as my grandfather suggested. I slowly was able to learn that it was up to me who to kiss and who not to kiss, when to get pregnant and when not to. And it was sitting in the offices of the Hispanic AIDS Forum in Queens, New York, that I made an immediate connection between the letters MSM and my friends back home.

Apart from my own projection of what could have happened to me had I stayed, or my criticism of Arturo as vice-minister, José Luis as the powerful scion, my brother eager to support the Conservative Party, and my childhood girlfriends ready to take on traditional roles, I am most interested in the fact that *en la política* women's issues are relegated, set aside, both by the right and by the left. Women's issues are equally unimportant to the Conservative Party in Colombia, which has no women in its directorate, and to Brazil's Partido dos Trabalhadores, perhaps the most progressive party in Latin America today, a labor party that has a thirty-percent quota for women.

Most Latin American women are not as interested in politics as they are in the rituals of the Catholic Church. The women I knew wore delicate crosses, *medallitas,* rosaries around their necks. They saved, borrowed, played the lottery, whatever it took to pay for a tour to Europe that included a visit to the Vatican. Going to Saint Peter's Square for a Sunday Mass and a benediction by the

Pope was a lifelong dream. Beauty queens are quick to answer that the person they admire the most is the Pope and *mi papá*—obedient daughters to God and to the law, fit to represent the country. But going to Mass, lighting candles, *rezar novenas,* and not eating meat on Fridays during Lent is not going to protect them from getting pregnant, or make a man stop having sex without a condom.

To seek hope in liberation theology is disappointing. In the 1970s, brave priests challenged the orthodoxy of Rome, became political activists denouncing right-wing military dictatorships, and sided with the marginal and the poor. With the concept of *comunidades de base,* base communities, they organized entire neighborhoods to rise against the harsh economic conditions. Women were seminal supporters of the call; as housewives they knew how hard it was to make ends meet. They were encouraged to organize as citizens and demand better conditions for their husbands and for their children. But anything close to demanding better conditions for themselves as women was not only untouched but downright discouraged. In Brazil, Dom Helder Câmara talked about the injustices of poverty but not about domestic violence.

Same goes for leftist politics. Lula, the figurehead of the PT and a metallurgical union organizer, talks about the dangers of privatizations and the structural adjustments of the World Bank but will never be in favor of legal abortions: his alliance with Priests of the Left would be forever severed. Lula will criticize economic policies while supporting the traditional stance of the Church when it comes to women's reproductive rights. Can there be social justice without equality of gender?

It is not surprising that in the seventies, General Augusto Pinochet told women that their duty was to be "mothers of the homeland" and proclaimed that "sacrifice, abnegation, service, honesty, diligence, and responsibility" were to be women's chief characteristics. Millions of Chile's women supported this view along with his repressive and murderous regime. As for the left, it was just as male chauvinist as Pinochet. In Nicaragua, Daniel Ortega promised to fight poverty, but when the state-funded women's agency proposed to legalize abortion, Ortega said that choosing not to give birth was counterrevolutionary and depleted the country of its much needed youth. Would it be any different today?

The situation is not encouraging. Not only are men not interested in giving up more than a few token openings to women, but in important governmental positions one sees only women who are not ready to be outspoken about women's issues. When *Mujer* asked Noemí Sanín, Colombia's presidential candidate, what she thought about abortion, her answer is not only ambiguous and full of hyperbole but basically pro-life: "I respect life in whatever form, but I believe that abortion should not be penalized by law or with prison: the woman who aborts suffers so much that it is punishment enough."

I am aware that all this can be described as the lament of a bourgeois girl who traveled a little and became somewhat liberated. My words can be dismissed as the rantings of privilege. Poor and working-class women, mestizas and mulattas, are exploited by a capitalist system, by a privileged class of which I, by virtue of birth, am a member. But regardless of these distinctions, as women we all live within the confines of the structure of patriarchal domination. Regardless of our position in a society divided by class, we as Latin American women know domestic violence, economic dependence, sexual aggression, discrimination in the workplace, lack of reproductive choice, and clandestine abortions. Soon we are also going to know how vulnerable we are to AIDS.

In the age of AIDS, men's control over their women's lives is literally life-threatening for many wives. In Mexico City, Rio de Janeiro, and Bogotá I've met young widows who knew their husbands had AIDS only after their deaths. A brave nurse in Bogotá explained to me how difficult it was for her to convince women to get themselves tested. Usually once the husbands find out they are HIV-positive they "do not even allow them to go to the hospital by themselves." Like the *de* after Ana María's name, commonly used verbs such as "to ask for permission" and "to allow" have felt as uncomfortable and as wrong as when José Luis would ask me to change my clothes. When I refused to wear a longer skirt, my punishment was José Luis's anger. Today, to have to do something "because I say so" endangers more than a woman's independence or sense of self, such submissiveness may endanger her life.

II.
Makers of Angels

*Unto the woman he said, I will greatly multiply thy sorrow
and thy conception;
in sorrow thou shalt bring forth children;
and thy desire shall be to thy husband,
and he shall rule over thee.*

—Genesis 3:16

Josefa got out of bed slowly so as not to wake her husband. She tiptoed to the kitchen as she has done every morning since they started living together more than twenty-five years ago, and put the coffeepot on the front burner of the gas stove. It was not yet six in the morning. Outside the window that faces the unpaved street she could see the other women who, like her, were getting their husbands ready for another day of hard work and low pay. From Monday to Friday, all mornings begin in the same way for the married women of the *periferia*, the poor neighborhoods far removed from the center of prosperous and polluted São Paulo: brewing coffee for their unfaithful men.

This morning Jose, as most everyone calls Josefa, made the coffee particularly strong and mixed in the herbal brew given to her by one of her *comães* down the street whose husband also drinks. The woman told her the concoction makes men stop drinking. As Josefa waited for her husband to come and grab the coffee from her hand the way he usually does, without saying a word to her, she decided not to say anything about the fact that he arrived very late and very drunk the night before. Why cause an uproar? It doesn't change anything.

She used to confront him, years back, when he would stay out *all* night and it would still hurt her to find out that he had been drinking—drinking at brothels.

"I would talk to him one day, and the next day he was doing the same thing," she says. "So what's the use?"

At forty-six, Josefa looks tough, worn out yet somehow ageless and strong. Her body is squat, her face is sad, but she seems to need no one. Black eyeliner is stuck in between the creases of her leathery crow's feet, her lipstick is smudged, and the black roots of her hair predominate over the badly dyed blond. She straddles the metal chair she is sitting on in her daughter Mariana's cramped bedroom. Grandchildren hover around her.

I came to her house that morning to talk not to her but to her nineteen-year-old daughter about a self-induced abortion but, four hours later, I am still sitting on Mariana's bed listening to Josefa tell me about her married life. As she talks I can sense she has rarely spoken so openly to anyone about the life she has led for so many years. She holds on to the granddaughter who lost her father to AIDS a year ago.

"Now I just want to do everything right so *he* can't talk."

"He" is Mario—the man she calls her *marido* although they are not legally or religiously married, her common-law husband whose shirts she's been ironing for almost three decades. In his pockets she has always found other women's phone numbers. Recently she discovered the wrapper from a condom as she picked up his shirt from the floor. Years ago the phone numbers made her angry and sad. Now when she stares at the torn-open wrappers in her hand, she feels relief. Ever since the family-planning clinic down the street, where her elder daughter works, started talking about AIDS, she knows how hard it is for the other women of the neighborhood to get their husbands to use condoms. At least now—after their son died from the virus—Mario is being careful.

I am always surprised to see how AIDS prevention campaigns in Brazil have really been successful in their outreach. Josefa talks about AIDS and condoms with the same familiarity as she would talk about the feijoada she is making for dinner. Yet Josefa's story saddens me, in fact it infuriates me. I know it is useless for her to know about the risk of AIDS. It is not up to her but to her husband to decide to use a condom. And her husband like most men will not listen to what he does not want to listen to, and she will not insist on anything, even if it hurts, even if it might kill her. It is more important not to create a fuss than to do otherwise—anything so that "he can't talk." She could leave him but she never will.

"Where to?" says Josefa, her rough hands softly touching her granddaughter's dark ringlets. "You get used to feeling comfortable with everything." And she is the happiest now, she tells me since she "became frigid, more than *fifteen* years ago."

I subtract in my mind: If she is forty-six today, that means Josefa stopped feeling sexual pleasure when she had just turned thirty years old.

Josefa's story does not surprise me. Having grown up in Latin America, I have been hearing variations of her story all my life. Women who rely on resignation, votive candles and *rogos ao Senhor* to cope with mistreatment seem to be as present in the slums of Brazil as they are inside the large homes of my childhood in Barranquilla. The main difference is that while women like Josefa are miserable in voiceless poverty, in my world women are miserable in luxury. They might not stand in front of the stove stirring a pot of black beans or ironing shirts. They hire poor women to do that. Still, their attitude is the same—being servile to their rich and powerful husbands who, chances are high, are as unfaithful and as difficult to talk to as Josefa's poor, half-literate Coca-Cola delivery-truck driver.

What does surprise me, however, is to find that both the privileged and the dispossessed are not only resigned but quite content with the way things are. Marriages in which husband and wife barely speak about intimacy last thirty, forty, fifty years. Marriages in which men leave other women's phone numbers in their pockets, carouse in public with women other than their wives, keep a *querida*, a mistress, are common. Men are simply expected to be unfaithful, women to look the other way. In 1994, *Semana,* the same magazine that conducted a survey showing that three quarters of Colombian men have been unfaithful to their wives, conducted another survey about the way women see their lives. Eighty percent of the women were comfortable being house-wives and being financially dependent on their husbands. They wanted to continue spending their time, the survey concluded, worrying about the home, the children, buying clothes, and go-ing to the beauty salon, in that order. When asked if they were sexually satisfied, they responded that that was something they simply did not think about: Twenty percent said sex is of *no* im-portance to them. Yet thirty percent of them said they felt sexu-ally unsatisfied.

The sad truth is that I hear some variation of Josefa's story from almost every woman I talk to for more than ten minutes in Latin America. Add or subtract a few details, the stories told by any of the women who live down this dusty row of cement houses will be virtually the same. And I will bet that if I were to spend a morning with the women living in the rich homes of the Avenida Paulista, the circumstantial information would differ, but many would confess difficulties talking to their husbands and not feel-ing loved, listened to, respected, or sexually satisfied. The men expect their wives to feed them, take care of their homes, make sure their shirts are pressed—by them or by hired help—while they have flings, frequent brothels with their friends, and have sex outside of their marriage, many of them, as I have recently understood, with other men.

I have spoken with very few women in Latin America, rich or poor, who are genuinely satisfied with their lives or with their re-lationships with their men. But few do anything to change their situation. We are brought up to gratefully assume the role of deli-cate invalids from the day we are born girls. We are raised to want to be asexual second-class citizens. To want anything else—a profession, a fair paycheck, a role in government, a good educa-tion, the right to choose when to give birth and when not to, when to have sex and when not to, to want good sex, communication, respect, and love—makes us undesirable, unmarriageable. How could you? *No le queda bien a una mujer*—it does not look good in a woman. This is the lesson I was taught in Barranquilla. But to find out that it is the same lesson that Josefa learned in Brazil was surprising.

Brazil, I thought, is different, not as backward as my Barranquilla. It is billed as having the most sensual women on the planet. The first time I arrived in Rio de Janeiro, I wanted to be a *carioca*, a woman from Rio—women the color of chocolate truffles who prance down Ipanema and Copacabana with a self-assuredness that I had never seen in a woman, not even in New York. These women were sensual and smart, and not afraid of displaying either. These women, I assumed, know what they want. They flirt, make a move, take a stand, show off their bodies, and say what's on their mind—and they are feminine. At a newstand near the beach, I bought *Elle* magazine in Portuguese and read an interview with Marta Suplicy, a congresswoman and sexologist who writes how-to best-sellers about sex and talks frequently about orgasms and condoms on national television. Suplicy has the face of a rich, educated woman and the attitude of a woman who knows what she wants and can ask for it. She is asked about AIDS-prevention and the risk the disease poses for women. Suplicy does not hold back and her answers are myth-breaking, straightforward, and to the point: "Prevention work must face many cultural obstacles, many myths." She talks about the need to face the reality of unfaithful marriages and the difficulty of bringing up the subject of condoms in a population that expects women to be submissive. "How to tell someone who you've been with for twelve, twenty years that it is best to use a condom? How many couples have that honesty?"

I have not heard any Colombian women in office speak so directly, I thought to myself, regretting not having been fifteen in Rio, where I could have worn tiny bathing suits and read my Simone de Beauvoir. But as I sat in Josefa's house, I felt far removed from Marta Suplicy, the sensuousness of the samba and the *tangas*, the tiny bikinis on the beach. Josefa, loving and maternal, living in the most sensuous country in the world, had never heard of Marta Suplicy. She had much more in common with a housewife in a *barrio bajo* of Barranquilla than with the women of Ipanema's beach.

Those few like Marta Suplicy who want to change or challenge the way things are have to work with the frustration of knowing that their concerns fall on deaf ears, or that they are preaching to the converted. During the travels for this book, in every major Latin capital I found I visited small-staffed nongovernmental organizations—NGOs, as they are referred to in their isolated world—run by women as impressive as Marta Suplicy, usually funded by foreign foundations: CEPIA in Brazil, CLADEM in Peru, CEIME in Ecuador, thousands more that put out important literature about domestic violence and gender inequality. In Quito neon billboards on every main avenue denounce domestic violence. In Brazil AIDS awareness campaigns are seen on daytime television and in teen magazines, main newspapers, and radio spots. In Jackson Heights, Queens, the director for the MSM project gave me a small brown envelope containing a tube of lubricant and three condoms—one red, one green, one mint-flavored. In Barranquilla, a young epidemiologist handed me a bumper sticker: MY PARTNER AND I USE CONDOMS. Dr. Alejandro Haag is very proud of his work, as he should be, yet I have a feeling that the fate of those bumper stickers, as with the rest of the attempts to shock the status quo in hopes of creating a change, will be the same as my mom's friend Alicia.

Whenever people talk about her, they always start the story by saying she is a bit of a troublemaker. *Cosmopolitan* magazine, with its covers of sexy women showing cleavage and its articles on having orgasms instead of faking them, arrived in Barranquilla sometime in the mid-seventies. With the first issue came a free bumper sticker that read *YO SOY ESA CHICA COSMO*—enticing women to come out of the closet with their sexuality. Before *Cosmo* hit the stands, women like Alicia had *Vanidades* and *Buenhogar*—pages filled with recipes, the latest in *haute-couture* from Paris, and gossip about European royalty.

To read *Cosmo* was to announce that you thought about sex, that you might even like it. In Barranquilla that was unladylike, vulgar. Alicia bought the magazine and pasted the sticker on her mustard-colored Renault. When her husband saw it, he threatened divorce if she thought of driving around Barranquilla "selling" herself like that. The sticker was of course removed.

A few years later, when her husband fell into financial trouble, Alicia didn't bat an eyelash, just picked up a pen, a pad, a phone, and her car—without the sticker—and became one of the first married upper-class women in Barranquilla to work, to join *el mundo de los negocios*. In a few years she owned one of the most successful advertising agencies in the city. She tells a million stories about how men, men who knew her husband well, could not resist making a pass at her. If she worked outside the home, if she kept an appointment book for meetings, if she was *atrevida* enough to go to a meeting at a man's office alone, it was implied that she was looking for something—meaning sex. She once walked into the office of a man she knew well—she had been to dinner parties at his home with her husband—only to find a copy of *Playboy* on his desk, splayed at the centerfold. She walked out and lost the account. Her success in business, her brashness, her attempt to confront tradition by daring to drive with the bumper sticker never made her comfortable enough, however, to talk to her daughter openly about sex. She had had to marry because she was pregnant. I think her putting on the sticker was more a sign of her naughtiness than of acknowledging her sexuality.

Today, many of Barranquilla's wives work. Friends of my mother own shops and small businesses: Alicia owns a gourmet shop; Carmen manufactures linen clothes; Gertrudis started a fast-food chain. Still, one hears the same attitude that Alicia encountered almost thirty years ago. In 1992, a male doctor, prominent enough to have been awarded the National Prize of Medicine, said while being interviewed on the radio that women who worked are "more inclined to homosexualism and masturbation." He meant both of these as evils.

As I have said, I did not go searching for Josefa's story. I did not come to her house to hear her words of discontent about her life as a wife. I walked into her living room one morning in July 1995, looking for her daughter Mariana, to talk about Mariana's self-induced abortion. I had been taken aback when I learned that women in Latin America have, on an average, more abortions than women in the United States. Knowing that abortions are expensive and illegal—punishable by prison—in every Latin American country with the exception of Cuba, I cringed at the thought of what it meant to be eighteen, poor, pregnant, and wanting an abortion.

The report, published by the Allan Guttmacher Institute in New York, stated that four million abortions are performed clandestinely each year in Latin America. According to their estimates, about four abortions occur for every ten live births in Brazil, Colombia, Peru, and the Dominican Republic. In Chile the levels are substantially higher—close to six abortions for every ten births. By comparison, estimates for the mid 1980s in countries where abortion is legal show that of women ages fifteen to forty-four, 0.5 percent have abortions in the Netherlands, 1.2 percent in Canada. 1.4 percent in England and Wales, 2.7 percent in the United States. The difference was enormous.

In Peru the penal code states that "a woman who causes an abortion, or consciously allows someone else to practice one, will be punished with no more than two years of her liberty or with community service for 104 days." In Colombia she can get up to four years in prison. But scarier than the legal punishment was the list of methods used to have them: knitting needles, clothes hooks, spoons, or umbrella rods inserted into the vagina. Women of all ages take a wide range of pharmaceuticals and folk medicines. The list ranges from effective and dangerous to ridiculous and dangerous: high doses of estrogen; laxatives; marijuana mixed with oak and avocado or parsley and coriander. They take veterinary prostaglandins or inject muscle relaxants, swallow bleach or cheap hair dye or laundry bluing mixed with urine. They will use anything they can afford or get their hands on to terminate an unwanted pregnancy. Many dance and drink for days. Some pray. Others make themselves fall intentionally from roofs, staircases, trees. The last item on the list sent a chill down my spine: "Voluntary blows by the husband in the stomach."

I remember the first time I heard about abortions—although the word was never used. I must have been twelve or thirteen, and I noticed that Ana, our maid at the time, had not brought up to my room the fruit juice I had before running out to school every morning. I could tell something was terribly wrong, for she was sick in bed. In Barranquilla, maids are never sick, or, if they are, they are definitely not allowed to linger in bed. When I went downstairs I saw my mother talking to Ana's husband, who also worked in our house, keeping up my mother's roses and the bougainvillea and the little red flowers she called *novios*, lovers. I couldn't tell what they were talking about, but I knew it was serious and I had best leave the kitchen.

When I returned from school that day, Ana and her husband were gone. My parents went out that evening, so the cook oversaw our dinner. She didn't exactly sit at our table—the help never did—but she was close enough to make sure we finished all the food she had served in our plates. I asked her if she knew where Ana had gone.

Back to her *pueblo*, she said.

"Why?" I asked. I knew my mother liked Ana a lot and wanted to keep her so much that when she married the gardener from down the block, she gave him a job, bought them a double bed, and allowed them to keep the maid's room to themselves. The cook moved her cot to the sewing room off the kitchen.

The cook told me that my mother was talking to the gardener because she wanted to know if Ana had lied when my mother asked her if she was feeling sick because she was pregnant. When she couldn't get out of bed the next morning and she refused to see a doctor, my mother grew suspicious. Ana said it was only *gripa*. Her husband said he didn't know what was wrong with her. I remember there was a lot of talk about a Coca-Cola bottle. The cook had told my mother she had seen him take one from the case in the *despensa*. An empty bottle had been found in their room.

When my mother questioned her husband about the bottle, he filled his answer with empty pride but provided my mother with no leads: "*Usted verá si me cree* but if you want us to pay for the Coca-Cola, *descuéntemela,* take it from my salary."

I never understood what the fuss was over a Coke. Couldn't my mother stop counting the number of bottles left in the case? Why bother if Ana or her husband had taken one without permission? Couldn't she stop questioning the maids about the rice, the coffee, and the Coca-Colas kept under key? Years later I figured out that my mother's inquiry was triggered by the probability that Ana had spurted the gas from the Coke inside her vagina in an attempt to end a pregnancy.

I never knew the details of Ana's abortion—I never saw her

again—but I now know that the use of bottles containing gaseous liquids is a common method among maids in Colombia. Was Ana afraid she would lose her job if she decided to continue her pregnancy? Many families do not allow their servants to keep their jobs if they get pregnant. Did her husband help her, or force her, to use the bottle?

The second time abortions came up for me, it had the same mysterious overtone. All I could make of what I heard was that it involved babies and bodies and that it was bad, very bad—not very different from my perception of sex. The girl in question must have been fourteen or fifteen and everyone—the older girls at school, the ladies that played bridge every afternoon at the Country Club, *las viejas chismosas* whose tongues were the thermometers of a girl's reputation—everyone was talking about this one girl. I didn't know her personally but I knew exactly who she was. Her brother was in my class and I had seen her at the club, always holding hands with her boyfriend, the boy everyone blamed for what was happening to her. She was one of the most popular girls in Barranquilla because if you have eyes like her eyes, oval and blue and shaped like cats' eyes, everyone knows who you are.

The story, as I recall it, was that she was pregnant—pregnant being a bad thing. She was such a nice girl, I remember thinking, protected by those pristine eyes, how could she have done anything bad or wrong? I was confused by all the versions. I heard that her boyfriend had taken her to an empty apartment and had taken advantage of her—advantage meaning sex. Others said he had taken her to a party, had given her a drink with *burundanga*, a powder that made her lose consciousness, and then had taken advantage of her. Most everyone blamed him. Some said he might even be put in jail. Many blamed her mother for not having been strict enough with her, *la tenía suelta de madrina*. She didn't have a curfew like we all did and she was allowed to go out with her boyfriend everywhere.

None of the versions I heard, however, considered that they were two young kids in love—always holding hands, sometimes they dressed alike—and that they had allowed their bodies to express that feeling. If she had gotten pregnant, it could also be that her boyfriend had not forced her to do anything she did not want to do, that they were both following their desires. Their mistake was they had not used birth control. But how could they? At fifteen, no one I knew had a mother who talked straight about how our bodies really functioned, or how to avoid a pregnancy. When we started menstruating, we were given a box of sanitary napkins and told that now that we were señoritas we had to be careful around boys, they could wrong us, do us *una maldad*. Visits to gynecologists were unheard of, and sex education at school consisted of a boring film showing cells and eggs and sperm, not bodies. Birth control was not only beyond our realm—I don't think I even knew it existed until I came to the United States.

I knew boys kept something in their wallets that they used when they went *donde las putas*. I remember my friend Francisco's face turned blue when I took his wallet and asked him if I could look through it. Enticed by his panicked face, I ran with it. I found his school ID, his club card, Bazooka bubble gum, his karate lesson registration card, and a small square of sealed plastic. I had never seen a package like that before, but by his reaction I knew I had found what I was looking for. Still, I did not know what it was used for. All I knew was that it was something only for boys, something that made them giggle whenever it was mentioned between them but had nothing to do with *niñas bien*, good girls like me. If good girls don't behave, *si no se hacen respetar,* boys will treat them like a *cualquiera*, like one of the girls they find at Estelita Reyes's—the brothel where their fathers, their cousins, their uncles take them to make machos out of them—or at El Gusano. By the time they turn fifteen, most of my friends had been there.

If a girl does not behave, she will be punished like the pretty girl with the blue eyes who had to go to Miami where they have special operations, where they can do something if something like this happens to her, something that will make her not be pregnant anymore. After Miami, I heard her parents took her to Disney World.

My new classmates at the Academy of the Sacred Heart were everything my mother's friends had warned her about. They not only had sex, they shared stories about it. They talked about "my pills" and about "my diaphragm" and I had never seen either. They spoke about abortions with little mystery. I was confused with all this information. It was so different from the secrecy that had surrounded me, the mystery associated with sex as sin and as something exclusively male.

I made friends with these girls, girls who in Barranquilla would have had the worst reputation, girls who if they lived there my mother would not have allowed me to invite over. That summer they came back with me. Overnight my house became as popular as a summertime street fair. The doorbell rang incessantly, boys I knew, boys I had heard about, boys I had never ever seen, all courting my friends the gringas, asking them out every night. They were taken to El Gusano, the infamous discotheque my father and my boyfriend would not allow me to set foot in. Laura and Pam were having a ball at first, but sometimes they came home surprised at what had happened. Dates here are very different, they said.

"How?" I asked.

Laura was driven to an unlit and lonely road that lies outside the city, and asked to duck under the dashboard. I had never been on this road and I didn't really know where it was, but the lore of this excursion is as well known as the sex that hangs between the legs of the large women on the Boulevard del Prado. As soon as Laura started talking, I knew where she had been.

La Carretera de los Locos, the Road of the Madmen, is right up with Estela Reyes's brothel on the list of things that boys go to and girls don't. Where Barranquilla ends, a dark two-lane road leads to a string of hidden-away motels. Unlike the Holiday Inns along American highways, these motels—Hawaii, Oasis, Maracaná named after the famous Brazilian soccer stadium—require no lobby check-in and most take no credit cards. They are there to provide guests not with comforts but with secrecy. They do not offer free cable, just anonymity. Guests go directly to their rooms without leaving their cars, by sliding into the first open garage. Doors shut immediately after the car enters, allowing the passengers to walk into the adjoining room without ever encountering a single soul. Here rooms are rented not by the night but by the *rato*, for the while, as long as it takes, within the boundaries of reason; it could be an hour, twenty minutes, maybe more.

The only road that leads to the illicit world of Juan Mina, as the nearby hamlet is called, is the one Laura described to me. La Carretera de los Locos owes its name to the fact that men are seen driving alone, late at night, talking to themselves. Their escorts, whoever they might be—girlfriends, mistresses, gringas in town for a summer vacation, prostitutes, men in drag, other men, wives of other men—hide in the footwell to avoid being seen on their way to sin. No boy in Barranquilla ever suggested taking me there, but it was just assumed that *las gringas lo dan*, they put out.

Abortions have always been available to the rich in Latin America, but always cloaked in an air of mystery, never ever called by its name. In Barranquilla, the girl with the blue eyes had a special operation, not an abortion. At the Clínica María Auxiliadora, located behind the old soccer stadium, they do *raspes*, "scrapes," not abortions. As far back as the early parts of the nineteenth century in Brazil, newspapers in the northeastern city of Recife carried ads announcing the services of midwives who knew what to do in case the perfumed ladies got pregnant from an illicit or unconfessable love tryst. For the refined dames, for whom religion would most certainly get in the way, these *curanderas* referred to themselves as "makers of angels."

I knew the abortions were performed but I thought they were few and far between, possible only to women like me who can pay at least five hundred dollars—about five minimum salaries— to a respectable gynecologist or who can afford to fly to Miami for the weekend. In Panama, a prominent female gynecologist serving an upper-class clientele will say she "does not have a moral problem, I just don't want to lose my license." She will, however, make the phone call and arrange for an appointment with a doctor who will perform the operation. A friend told me the other day that a woman in Barranquilla is charging up to two thousand dollars for a D&C.

I thought that to decide to end a pregnancy was an alternative considered by women with a certain degree of education, preferably acquired abroad, and access to quick cash. I could count on the fingers of one hand women I knew who I thought would consider having an abortion. Instead, a few months ago, a friend from Barranquilla confessed to me that she had had one—at age 14.

"How did you know where to go?" I asked.

"My maid knew and she was my confidante. She was always helping me to escape to go see my boyfriend, so when it happened I went and told her," she said. "There was no one else I knew that I could ask."

"Your mother?"

"My mother cried the day she found out I was not a virgin. She had read it in a letter I had sent to a friend. 'How can you do this to me?' she bawled one day as she was driving me back from school."

The maid told her to go to the house behind the zoo, that it was where she had gone to have hers.

"All I remember is the heat and the lion's roar coming in through the open window."

The Guttmacher Institute study reports that like my friend in Barranquilla, a woman in Bogotá can get a clandestine but a safe abortion for forty-four dollars, a reasonable price for a middle-class woman, say a woman whose lover works or who works herself as a secretary, a bank teller, or an accountant. Advertisements are widely displayed in major newspapers. They are not as blunt as the ones seen in New York City subways, and they are much less allegorical than they were in the 1800s in Brazil, but there they are next to the ads that guarantee riches or the return of a loved one through witchcraft: Pregnant? Immediate solution—American Method—no pain—economical—read one.

The message is loud and clear. If a woman wants to have an abortion in Latin America, she will, regardless of its being illegal and forbidden by the Church. Nothing will stop a woman who is desperate to end an unwanted pregnancy—not the law, not her father, her husband or her God. The possibility of going to jail does not stop a woman from drinking formaldehyde in the hope of aborting. Being punished by God does not either. The need to void her uterus is stronger than the risks she can cause her body. The report estimates that fifty to sixty percent of women obtaining abortions from untrained practitioners or inducing the abortion themselves will experience complications. As expected, poor rural women who have abortions are at higher risk of health complications than are poor urban women—more than half of poor rural women, and about four in ten poor urban women. Barely more than one in ten middle-class and rich women will experience complications. This is not surprising: Most of them have safe and complete curettages. It is the poor who are inserting the needles, or wires, who are drinking chlorine or kettles of calabash tea.

"As long as the rich can have safe abortions, abortion will continue being criminalized," Jacqueline Pitanguy, who led a campaign to decriminalize abortion in Brazil in 1986, explained to me. "It is not the wives or the daughters of the senators who will die from complications of an abortion. They can go to Miami."

I was in Mariana's bedroom that morning because I knew she could never afford to fly to Miami. But when she knew she was pregnant, she knew she would do whatever it took not to be.

When I first talked to her on the phone, I did not know how to tell her why I was calling her. I was so nervous that I contemplated telling her it was about the angel she had made. I simply told her my name and asked her if Barbara, the nurse at the family-planning clinic where her sister works, had told her that I wanted to visit her. She said she had.

"When can I see you?" I asked.

"Oh, whenever you want," she said cheerfully.

"Tomorrow morning?"

"Sure, come by my house tomorrow. Ten, eleven, whenever, I'm always here."

Did she understand I was going to ask her about her abortion? Her tone, her friendliness, her readiness to meet seemed as if I was asking her out for an ice cream.

I knocked on the aluminum door which corresponded to the address she had given me. I was expecting Mariana to look like a teenager but she looked matronly, dressed as if to play a middle-aged housewife in her high school play. She held a baby in her arms. Her hair was dirty, up in a ponytail. Her hips, under the long skirt, were wide. She greeted me with a big smile and guided me, dragging her rubber flip-flops, to her bedroom. As we passed the kitchen, she introduced me to her mother and I said a quick hello to a woman overseeing a cauldron of black beans. At that point, I had no inkling that I would end up talking to her too.

We walked into an adjacent room which had comforts I did not expect to find in a home of a poor neighborhood: a color television, a nice stereo system, a big wooden armoire, a double bed, baby toys, and lots of clothes.

"Sit," Mariana said, pointing to the bed.

She took off her red and white slippers and lay on the left side of the bed.

"Pretty room," I said to open the conversation, and sat on the right side.

"Yeah, I live in this room with my husband and my baby. But it's my mother's house. Upstairs there's my mother and father, my sister and the grandchildren."

"You're married?" I asked, confused.

"Well, not *married*, but Michel's father and I live together since Michel was born," she said.

"Michel is your son?" I asked, thinking that maybe I was in the wrong house.

"He is," she said. "But I know you want to talk about that thing I did before he was born, right, the *aborto, né*?"

Her smile never left her face.

"Yes, the abortion." It was the first time I could say the word myself, and only after she had said it first.

She didn't seem to mind that I, a complete stranger, someone she had never seen, someone who does not even speak her language well, was there to discuss such an intimate experience. Mariana started talking to me as if she were chatting to her best friend, while she changed Michel's diapers.

Those days when she didn't know if she was or wasn't were horrible, she remembers. She was always taking out the calendar she kept folded in her wallet to keep track of her periods. She kept counting the number of days since she had last made love to her boyfriend—who is not Michel's father—praying at school and quietly in her bed: Please, God, don't let me be pregnant. She had learned about counting days, about the *tabelinha*, at school. Following the rhythm method, trying to avoid the days she thought were "dangerous," was the only way she could continue to have sex without buying contraception she could not afford.

There are thousands of free family-planning clinics in Brazil. But even if she had wanted to go to one, she didn't know how to find one and she didn't know who to ask. Certainly not her mother. There was one half a mile down the road from her house, but she had no idea it was there until her elder sister started working there. Plus, it had never occurred to her that she needed to know more than she knew. She had been counting days for more than three years when she started to have sex at fifteen. She had sex on the good days and she didn't on the bad ones. It had never failed. She always got her period on time.

This time, days passed and nothing came. Getting her late period became an obsession. She would run to the bathroom and look at her underwear, hoping for an oval stain. She would unfold the chart, which by then was dirty and creased, over and over, twenty, thirty times a day. She stared at the chart and at her panties, hoping that doing this would somehow make her enlarged breasts go away. No one had ever told her how risky the *tabelinha* is. But then, no one had ever talked to her about sex.

All she could think about was how a pregnancy would get in the way of the biggest opportunity of her life. She was a contestant in the Concurso por la Garota Mais Linda do Sul do São Paulo—the contest for the most beautiful girl of southern São Paulo, the local beauty pageant for the daughters of the Brazilian poor. And like most girls her age, rich or poor, Mariana's dream was to be a beauty queen.

It would have been hard for her to be one. Honestly, her chances were slim. At eighteen, she had the firmness and freshness of youth, she had beautiful olive skin and long healthy hair, but her looks were not enough to pull her out of the slums. Yet Mariana felt her dream was attainable every time she stood in front of the mirror fixing her hair. When she wore the black lycra swimsuit with the high-heeled shoes, she felt anything was possible. If she were pregnant, however, she could no longer wear it. She would have to give up the contest, and with it the hope of ever living in a street with a paved road. A pregnancy would ruin her body, and having a perfect body was the only way she knew for a woman to become rich or marry rich.

She was already feeling the changes. Her breasts felt squeezed under the slinky swimsuit.

The only person Mariana confided in was another contestant. The thought of telling her boyfriend scared her. He could run away and she would lose him—she knew men run away when things like this happen. Or he could demand that she have the baby, and that would trap her into an existence like her mother's. Again, she would see the end to her dream, stuck with a poor husband who worked menial jobs like her father. Mariana was desperate to find a way to ensure that everything was not over for her. She couldn't be pregnant, she kept saying to herself. Her breasts continued to swell and feel tender, and the last time she had her period was three months earlier. It was time to ask her friend at the pageant for what she had promised to give her.

"Tonight you take two pills with water and the other two you put inside you."

That night Mariana waited for everyone to retire to their bedrooms. When she was sure all the lights had been turned off, she tiptoed to the bathroom, swallowed the two pills with water from the sink, slipped her underwear down to her ankles, and inserted the remaining pills way up her vagina. She tiptoed back to her room, making sure she did not waken her sister who slept in the twin bed next to hers. She felt relieved when she got into bed, thinking she would finally fall asleep easily. It was the first night in many that she would not lie awake until dawn, holding her sore breasts, feeling desperately trapped. After tomorrow, her dream would be possible again. All she had to do was wait six hours for the pills to have their effect.

She awoke in the middle of the night from the pain in her abdomen. She felt her belly contracting the same way it did when she started her period, except this time it was impossible to get up from the bed. She felt the moistness of blood between her legs. If she didn't hurry to the bathroom, she was going to tint the white sheets cardinal red, and her mother might get suspicious. Normal periods don't stain this much.

The amount of misoprostol, the active ingredient in the drug, inside her body caused the muscles of her uterus to contract so strongly and dilate her vagina so widely that what was inside of her came right out. Mariana had taken two hundred grams of Cytotec, a medicine prescribed to treat gastric and duodenal ulcers, but in countries like Brazil, Colombia, and the Dominican Republic, women discovered it had other uses.

When the drug was introduced on the Brazilian market in 1986, women were its biggest buyers. By 1989, sixteen million pills were sold over the counter in pharmacies across the country. Of all the methods available, this was the best—a little costly for the very poor, at about $40 to $80 for the needed dosage—but there were no immediate side effects. There was a chance the pills would not do the entire job and clean up the uterus completely. In fact, a study reported that up to forty-five percent of the women checking into Brazilian hospitals were there because of complications from Cytotec. But it was better than inserting a stalk from a papaya tree or a piece of barbed wire.

The government caught on and embarked on a national campaign to put an end to the use of Cytotec. In an effort to stop women from buying it, newspapers wrote articles claiming that women who took the pills gave birth to babies without feet or babies with deformed mouths who would never be able to talk or to even smile. But that did not deter millions of women to continue using it—thirty-five percent of all sales were still from women who used it as an abortifacient. That same year, the Brazilian government decided to prohibit the over-the-counter sale of the drug. In 1992, sales of Cytotec still amounted to $100 million a year regardless.

When Mariana got pregnant in 1993, Cytotec was illegal, yet it had not been that hard for her to get some. She was lucky that her friend had given it to her. She could never have afforded it. Four pills can run up to forty dollars in São Paulo's slums.

Mariana felt the hemorrhaging start, tiptoed back to the bathroom, and squatted open-legged in the dark, afraid to turn the lights on, feeling the pulpy matter pass between her legs. Then, kneeling in front of the toilet, she stuck her hand in the bowl, groping with her fingers for the mass she needed to put inside the plastic bag. When she thought she had removed everything and all that was left was water in the bowl, she tied the plastic bag, went to the kitchen, and threw the bag in the trash.

The next morning, her sister noticed the sheets and the mess in the bathroom. She walked over and sat on Mariana's bed.

"*Tudo bem?*" she asked.

Mariana was trembling, soaked in sweat, tears, and blood. She spent three days like that. When the bleeding and the fever left, the tears continued. Her sister suggested that she go to the doctor but she was afraid. She had heard that doctors were mean when they found out you had taken Cytotec.

"I was scared. The doctors are very cold," she said, "very cold. Men doctors. They give no attention. They would give me attention if I were not pregnant, but in my case they would have known why I was there, and they don't give you a lot of attention. If you are feeling pain they let you feel pain so that you get conscious of what you did. *Entende,* they don't forgive. If we don't want the child, we are assassins."

"Do *you* think you are?" I asked.

"I didn't used to think like this, but having an abortion is very disturbing. A person feels inferior after they have an abortion. I feel I'm inferior. I've changed very much. Look."

She hands me a framed five-by-seven photograph that hangs on the otherwise empty walls of her bedroom. It is a photo of her taken during the pageant, wearing the black swimsuit, the heels, the makeup—her passport out.

"I always looked sexy before, but now I don't worry about it like I did before I had the baby."

"When did you have Michel?"

A few months after she had the abortion, she felt ready to leave her house again and decided to go back to her eighth-grade class. There she met Andrè, and they started going out together.

"Then, right away, I became that way again," she says, making a balloon out of her stomach, meaning she had gotten pregnant.

"But weren't you being careful?"

"I was."

"What were you using?"

"Same thing," she says, with the same complacency with which she told me about her abortion. "A *tabelinha.*"

During our conversation, she had fed Michel his bottle, and she was now holding him, patting his back to let him burp. "I wanted to be a model. Now I don't leave the house. I stay with the baby. If I leave him, he might get sick. I don't even take him out to the sun. What if he gets sick?"

For Mariana, there were two choices: glamorous model or dedicated mother. She tried the first and failed. So she exchanged her sexy swimsuits for big T-shirts and comfortable drawstring skirts that show the forty pounds she has put on. Of her dream, of her youth, of her sensuality, all that is left is the picture on the wall—which her husband, an 18-year-old messenger, hates to see and makes her take down every time a friend of his comes to visit. In his opinion, Mariana must act like a mother and not feel sexy.

I ask her if she uses birth control or condoms now. She laughs and says she knows how important it is to use them but André refuses to use them. "He says they are very bad, *muito ruin,* and he gets angry now when I bring it up, so I don't want to make him mad. He is good to me and to Michel, and I feel lucky I now have my baby even after having done such an awful thing.

"But talk to my mother," she says in the same monotone in which she has told all this. "She's had eight."

Josefa comes in, wiping her hands on her black leggings. A cluster of boys and girls ages two to nine come in with her.

"She wants to know about your abortions," Mariana says, pointing at me.

Josefa sits on the metal chair and, shrugging her shoulders, says, "Oh, that."

She straddles the chair. "It's because of that that I'm having all these health problems. The doctor thinks I have to have my uterus removed, but I missed my appointment last week, too busy, too much to do. Who's going to cook lunch if I go to the doctor? Whose going to give these creatures their food?"

She takes a crumpled tissue from under her sweatshirt and, holding her granddaughter's nose, asks her to blow. "She's been sick all week." She tells the child to throw out the tissue, and turns to me. "What did you want to know?"

"Eight, really?" I ask. "You've had eight abortions?"

"I think eight. Or nine, I don't know exactly, but in any case many, many."

How, when, why—I have a flurry of questions, but she gives me no time to ask. I had wanted to explain who I am and why I am there, but the cork has been popped. She has already started talking. I will only get up from Mariana's bed four hours later.

"I met Mariana's father," she says referring to the man we already know is unfaithful and insensitive. "I didn't have much experience. We were both young, around eighteen, we didn't behave well, and I got pregnant. I had no luck, every time I took *um passo em falso*, it would happen. I would get pregnant. The first time I was so desperate, someone told me to use the branch of a tree, so I got the *cabo de mamão*, and I did it like that."

She points between her legs.

"I started bleeding, but that didn't resolve the problem—just made me more desperate, and I didn't know what to do. I was alone, no family. I had just arrived from Ribeirão Preto."

"And Mario, your husband, what did he do?"

"I knew I couldn't talk to him so I didn't say much. I wanted to get it over with. When the papaya stalk didn't work, I just got a piece of wire."

She points again between her legs.

"It still didn't work—I knew it hadn't all come out—so I put in the rubber tube with the wire inside again and again. I think that's when I perforated everything. I remember I started having fever, fever, fever."

Her friends, not her husband, wrapped her in ice and took her to a hospital.

"Did your husband know?"

"My husband?" she repeats after me as if I had asked the stupidest question. "Oh, he knew but he didn't care. They never do. If it wasn't for my friends I would have died."

After that she got pregnant many times—as she said, every time she took a false step, a euphemism for having sex. When it was time to terminate a pregnancy, she would sometimes do it herself. Other times, she would go and have it done by a *partera*, a midwife. But sometimes the *partera* wouldn't finish the job either and she would spend entire nights sweating a fever, and hemorrhaging alone. I have restrained myself from mentioning her husband again, but she keeps telling me that each time she was alone. I ask about him again.

"Where was he?"

"Meu marido—pfff, mia filha," she says and exhales loudly, "he doesn't say anything about anything. He is, you know, one of those men who doesn't worry about anything, that's his type. He is a neutral person. For him, when it comes to me, one way or the other is okay with him, it's the same for him. I did all these things for him, to help him, I've worked for twenty-five years, you saw what I went through. It's a very hard life, getting pregnant, searching for abortions, working, working. I worked to help him. Today, I don't have health, I destroyed my health, maybe I lose my uterus from so much *extravagância*, but he doesn't care, he doesn't worry about a thing. He never has. That's why I tell Mariana to be careful. That boy Andrè is now young, but with men it's always the same."

Josefa continues to speak about her husband, a man she still shares a bed with, with scorn, bitterness, and regret. She remembers being bathed in sweat from high fevers, sometimes not really caring if she would survive. He was seldom around. He could not keep a job because of his drinking, and she knew he was unfaithful since day one because "men in general do it but they do it hiding it, and mine just does it like that, *assim, muito cara de pau.*"

But she never said a word to him about his behavior, about his lack of concern, about his shameless unfaithfulness. She resigned herself like most women in Latin America to finding solace in the belief that, after all, "men, *filha mia,* are men." Like most of the women I grew up with, she has been able to withhold any need or desire to communicate her happiness or unhappiness, her anger and her hurt, to the man she has shared her life with since they met in 1964, the year of the inception of the military dictatorship that would reign over Brazil until 1985.

She was seventeen, a country girl who traveled to São Paulo the moment she heard about the military promise to make Brazilians rich. Like the authoritarian regimes that sprung up in the rest of the Southern Cone in the seventies—Chile and Uruguay in 1973, Argentina in 1976—the military promised to get rid of poverty and communism. Offering to turn their countries into rich nations, into great powers through modernization, they resorted to torturing and killing those who got in the way. With economic growth came the *desaparecidos*, Argentina's Dirty War, Chile's roundups at the National Stadium, and Brazil's institutionalized tortures.

Unequivocally, Brazil was modernized. In a few years the generals put Brazil on the map as the eighth largest economy. Brazil had the largest economic growth in the Third World. It stopped being an underdeveloped country and became a world power complete with nuclear weapons. São Paulo—where Josefa lived in a cinderblock house with her aunt—became the messy epicenter for what the government referred to as Brazil's economic miracle. Skyscrapers, shopping centers, expensive residential areas, twenty-six thousand new roads, a maze of factories sprung from São Paulo's swamplands.

More than half of the country's important companies settled in São Paulo, creating an enormous demand for labor. Josefa joined the mass migration, coming with the rush from the provincial city of Ribeirão Preto, about 190 miles north of São Paulo. Mario, the man who would become her common-law husband, was already there, one of the more than fifteen million unskilled industrial wage earners, construction workers, or odd-job men that were to make the military's miracle possible. Josefa met Mario at the open-air market near Campo Limpo where she sometimes begged for food and he worked as a street vendor selling rope, gift-wrapping paper, and Durex glue.

One afternoon he invited her to have a *pamonha*, a popular fried bread. She was hungry and accepted. They had fun, and eventually he left the woman he was living with. Josefa moved in with his parents when she got pregnant for the fourth time. "I didn't want to have another abortion," she tells me.

Josefa is talking to me about her life in the mid-seventies when the military was in the height of power, when there was work for the unskilled but there was an inflation rate that made the price of milk double in less than twenty-four hours. A poll taken in 1975 showed that a family of five, two parents and three children, could not survive on the salaries of two adults making minimum wage. Josefa had a family of four and a husband who did not work. She could barely make ends meet. But much to my surprise, Josefa complains about her husband and talks about the military with nostalgia.

"They not only promised things like politicians do anyway but they got them done," she says matter-of-factly. "I worked hard— I could always find a job. He never could keep his, but there was work. He was just lazy and always drunk, but there was work because it was not like it is now. There was employment then. Not like now."

In a way, she is right. Brazilians lived with an economy that grew ten percent per year. But the work she is referring to is the type of work that provided most Brazilians, especially the millions who migrated to the cities, with a daily meal of beans and rice, a home with no water or sewage, and stolen electricity to watch the television bought on a layaway plan. *Carne seca,* a dried cured inexpensive meat, was only affordable maybe twice a week for families like Josefa's. But the neon lights of the city made this life more alluring than working the small patch of land her parents owned in rural Ribeirão Preto.

The labor rush made paychecks accessible to women as they entered the workforce. If in 1970 the labor force was thirteen percent female, by 1985 the figure was almost forty percent. But women worked the most monotonous and poorly paid jobs, and the policies implemented to hire women were outright discriminatory. Brazilian law requires companies which employ more than thirty women over sixteen years of age to have an on-site day care center. In 1970, of the 36,000 companies that should have had them, only eighteen did. In order to avoid complying with the law, companies decided instead not to hire pregnant women. If a woman got pregnant while working, she was fired. It was common practice for companies to ask their female employees for a letter of resignation to be kept on file in case she missed her period one month. Many companies kept track of the menstruation cycles for each female employee, requiring her to go and report her first day of bleeding.

Josefa's answer about the military still troubles me. I remind her that, while there was employment, there was also inflation and unaffordable prices. Josefa nods with the conviction of someone who knows just how hard it is to make ends meet on the minimal salaries imposed by the so-called economic miracle. Hoping that she will retract her admiration for the military, I also remind her of the arbitrary arrests, the detentions, the torture, and the murders. She nods, but this time it is a blank nod. If talking about economic hardship struck a chord with her, this means nothing. She supported, and misses, a system that would kill her without a second thought, and one that believes women's roles should be exactly those that have made her miserable.

Why should I be surprised to find that Josefa believes in the conservative values of church and government that have kept her in the place she occupies today? Can I make her understand that her uterus has been ruined as a result of the policies she supports? Why is it surprising to me that she, like most women I know, are conservative to the point that they are ready to support murderous regimes? God, family, private property, and *la patria* seem to be values with which Latin women can identify. Don't they realize that that's what's keeping them miserable, sweating at night bathed in blood from dangerous abortions and sexually exploited.

I remind myself of the experience of Salvador Allende in Chile when he tried to introduce a progressive agenda for women— legalizing divorce and providing maternity leave and equal rights for children born out of wedlock. And how Augusto Pinochet's opposition was able to manipulate women to organize and help overthrow Allende's government in 1973. Pinochet's leadership, mostly male, masterminded the creation of Poder Femenino, Feminine Power, an organization of conservative housewives, professionals, and businesswomen, to oppose Allende's allegedly "Marxist" reforms. As an observer of the movement explains, the men knew exactly what to do to get results from Poder Femenino: "The women must be made to feel they are organizing themselves, that they play an important role. They are very cooperative and don't question the way men do."

She continues: "Women are the most effective weapon you have in politics. They have time and they have a great deal of capacity to display emotion and to mobilize quickly. For example, if you want to spread a rumor like 'the President has a drinking problem,' or 'he had a slight heart attack,' you use women. The next day it is around the country."

Poder Femenino organized "marches of the empty pots," in which they would demonstrate, pounding on pots and pans. Allende was overthrown five days after the largest "feminine" rally Santiago has ever seen.

Women may well be the "most effective weapon" in politics. Unfortunately, Poder Femenino chose to support not Allende but Pinochet, who saw women as "carriers of patriotic values," "pillars of the nation," and "defenders of the moral order." In just a few months Pinochet undid the work Allende's government had begun during his three years in power. Instead, Pinochet created the National Secretariat of Women, whose job was to restore the "values of the family and the fatherland" that the Allende government had "desecrated." He named his wife as the director.

In Argentina and in Uruguay there were also movements like Poder Femenino. And in Brazil they had names like Feminine Civic Unity, or March with God for Family and Freedom, women's groups that supported the same conservative crusade. In 1975, the president of one of these groups explained the role of women in the fight against communism: "I am the granddaughter, the niece, and the sister of a general. If women don't get involved, this can be bad. As women, we must be obedient."

The granddaughter of a general did not have to worry about low wages, high prices, lack of child care, or the persecution and disappearances of their husbands, their children, their friends, and their brothers. The women in the *bairros* where Josefa lived did. Like the Mothers of the Plaza de Mayo in Argentina, and the Chilean Association of the Relatives of the Disappeared, Brazilian women were, also, the first to denounce the disappearance of their husbands, their children, their friends, and their brothers.

Many women joined clandestine groups and some took up arms—"they used us in transporting the arms," Clio, a former guerrilla member tells me. "We would hide them in our mini-skirts. They, the leaders, knew that it was easier for us women to distract the policemen." But mostly, the women who organized against the regime were not the young university students like Clio, who were reading Marx, Engels, and Che. They were Catholic housewives and mothers who were distressed about the dire eco-nomics of their homes, about how to feed their children and their husbands, and not about the armed struggle. With the help of priests and nuns engaged in what came to be known as liberation theology, these women became "militant mothers," demanding their rights when it came to domestic work, education for their children, and discrimination in the workforce. The meetings were taking place very close to where Josefa lived, but she never heard of them.

I ask Josefa if she remembers the *movimentos de mulheres*, as these organized actions advocating the right to better conditions of life and work became known. Does she remember, I ask, the meetings organized by the church, which were taking place right under her nose.

"Movimentos de mulheres?" she repeats, and stops to think.

Interviews are difficult. Josefa doesn't want to give a wrong an-swer, and how do I let her know there isn't such a thing?

"Ah, *sim, sim,* there was a lot of *movimento*." She snaps her fin-gers as if not to let the right answer fly away. "There were many *mulheres*." Her voice acquires that tone of complicity that comes when one thinks one recognizes an ally. "Ah, *sim,* there was a lot of *prostituição*."

I knew then that, no, Josefa had no idea what I was talking about, and that it was naive of me to try and engage her in a feminist dialogue. Shouldn't I stop holding her responsible? She was too busy making ends meet, supporting her husband and taking care of her children. Civil liberties and political repres-sion were not things she had time to be concerned with. Would I, if I had to worry about my husband keeping his job, coming home drunk or not at all, crawling into my bed after having paid for sex?

She worked as a beautician, bleaching and straightening curly hair, while she took care of her three daughters and her son and a husband who made her unhappy. She had no time to go to Sunday Mass, where the sermons became the seeds of opposition to the government. The priests provided a place in the neighborhood churches for the women to go talk, but Josefa never showed up.

It was 1975, the United Nation had declared it the Decade of Women, and international funding was available for the priests and nuns to encourage these meeting where women could discuss their economic situation, to organize marches, to write angry letters of protest to the government. What began as groups of neighborhood women gathering in the basements of community churches emerged into a cohesive, broad-based group—O Movimento do Custo de Vida, the Cost-of-Living Movement. In three years, the movement had organizers all over São Paulo. In an effort to get General Geisel's government to respond to its demands, it started a campaign to collect one million signatures. They drafted what became known as the Carta das Mães da Periferia de Sao Paulo. Reading it today is like listening to Josefa's laments: "We are desperate *mães de familia*, and more than anyone we feel the price of food, of medicine, school, clothes, shoes, household goods, and rent. We are tired of this exploitation.

"In order for us to survive," the letter continues, "the father of the house is in need of working many extra hours and never gets to see the kids. The mother also works. Many children of school age need to do odd jobs. . . . This is all damaging our families. . . . To support all this, we women need to work but we have no day care center."

The women also demanded a control of the cost of living, and asked for higher salaries, better health centers, schooling for their children, running water, transportation, and electricity. More than 1.3 million Brazilians signed the petition. Josefa did not. She does not even remember the march on April 27, the one where thousands of organizations took to the Praça da Se after the government tried to dismiss the Carta by suggesting that the more than a million signatures were false.

Despite the hardships, the Movimento gained important benefits. It succeeded in getting the government to create *creches*, day care centers where women could safely leave their children while they went to work. Considering that eighty percent of households in Brazilian favelas are headed by women, this was a great triumph for the women's movements. Josefa tells me that she did send her children to the *creches* after the law passed in 1978, but she just had no idea how they had started.

"But Josefa, you never heard about these women's meetings?" I ask her. "It happened right here. What were you doing in 1978?"

"*Oi, mia filha,* I was working. I've always been working, working, working. I had the children. Since I met Mario, my life has been *uma vida muito sofrida.*"

In 1978 Josefa was not even thirty years old, and yet she described her life as a life of suffering, an expression I heard frequently on the lips of the women who surrounded me. As much as the Catholic Church encourages it, I hate this resignation, common among devout women. They think suffering comes with the package of being married, of being woman. Furthermore, the more suffering you take, the better woman you are. A life of suffering can make you into *uma santa* even. Although it is a high form of praise for a woman in my culture, I do not aspire to be identified with sainthood. This mixture of mother and wife, of martyr and hero, is the desirable state in these lands. Josefa met every qualification to be the perfect *santa*.

She has "worked, worked, worked"—at least ten hours a day since she arrived in São Paulo, still a girl. By her twenty-first birthday, she was *dedicada a la família,* taking care of her home and the children she bore in the city. She had been a mother before—at twelve when she was still living in Ribeirão Preto. She had twins, she tells me, but she left them with her parents, who grew corn on a small plot of land. That's when she came to São Paulo to work with her aunt.

As I sit in New York listening to Josefa's voice on my tape recorder telling me about the twins she had when she was twelve, I start to wonder whether Josefa came to São Paulo like the millions of peasants who left the land lured by the metallic hope of modernization or because she was running away from a rapist, the father of the two children she had left behind. Who was the father? Most likely, she grew up with a stepfather who sexually abused her until the day she got pregnant. This is no uncommon scenario in Latin America. Young boys and girls are often sexually molested, raped by members of their family. The most common perpetrator is the mother's new husband. When the new couple start having children of their own, those from previous marriages are sent away to other relatives or to an orphanage or, more commonly, are simply thrown out or abandoned. A Latin macho does not take care of the children of another man—it would make him less of a man. It is not surprising that Latin America has the highest number of street children in the world. And still the Catholic Church makes the termination of unwanted pregnancies the gravest of sins.

Josefa was lucky she was not thrown out on the streets. She came to live in São Paulo with her aunt, who worked in a restaurant. The aunt found her a job cleaning tables there and gave her a cot in her one-room cinderblock house. But to her aunt's surprise, Josefa quickly got tired of clearing away leftover food. She had noticed how women in the city looked different from those back home in Ribeirão Preto. They looked more like the women she had always admired in the soap operas. They had long, flowing blond hair. In the city she found out that black hair could became blond and frizzy hair could become straight. She wanted to learn how to resemble those women, so she decided to become a hairdresser.

"You are here to work," said her aunt. "If you're going to study, you can't do it in my house."

Josefa made a deal with the owner of the beauty school near the favela where her aunt lived. After the school closed, she cleaned it. In exchange, she could attend free classes. A friend she met at the beauty school offered her a place to sleep, but some nights she cleaned until midnight. When it was too late to knock at her friend's door, she would sleep outside her friend's building or in the school's bathtub. Never did she think of returning to her family in Ribeirão Preto, not even when it was winter in São Paulo and the only way to keep warm was by wrapping herself in her apron at night. By then she had already had the three abortions, and by the fourth time she got pregnant Mario decided to leave his other woman and have this baby with her.

That was also the last time she remembers doing anything fun. "I haven't been to the beach in more than twenty years," she tells me, pointing at the palm tree–lined beach on her black T-shirt.

Maria Amelia de Almeida Teles, known to everyone as Amelinha, went to many of the meetings that Josefa never attended. She went to fight not only for *creches* and lower prices; she would storm in to talk about repressed sexuality, about the right to sexual pleasure, about pregnancy, birth control, menopause, about women who work double in one day as wife and laborer. She would go to tell the women that they had a right to demand being treated with respect, to tell them that they could do something more than just accept a life like the one Josefa describes.

Whenever Amelinha, small and feisty, showed up, the priests trembled. And both the political opposition and the clergy would beg Amelinha to stop—in the name of the worker's movement, they would tell her. "It is a deviation from class struggle. What the proletariat needs is to be united to oppose the military regime. Why talk about sexuality if people have nowhere to live and nothing to eat?"

But for Amelinha, it was essential to include an open talk about the condition of women. She wanted to revolutionize the *movimentos de mulheres.* "The fight is not only to demand better work conditions but also to make women the protagonists of their own lives. We must stop letting men do everything while we just applaud," she wrote in *Brasil Mulher*, one of the more radical of the handful of magazines advocating women's issues, which had been started with the dollars available after the UN's declared Decade of the Woman in 1975.

Women's rights *was* the hot issue of the moment. Betty Friedan visited Brazil. But the editors of *Brasil Mulher* and others, like *Mulher Accion* and *Nos Mulher*, were reluctant to publish anything other than articles about the safe issues: the *creches*, the need to start collective laundries and affordable eateries so that women could join civil society as freely as men did. The motto— "We want men to recognize that the house they live in and the children they have are also theirs"—was safe to both the church and the political opposition to the dictatorship. And to the dictatorship they posed no threat. Women were the only group allowed to meet. In the government's military minds, who could be threatened by a bunch of women gathered in a basement?

"We feminists made an alliance with the church, and the church supported us because of the dictatorship, but they supported us as long as we were well behaved. You could raise the question of abortion, but when you did you were kicked out of the meeting," Amelinha recalls almost twenty years later, sitting behind a big computer screen in her office surrounded by posters and mementos of those days: the fist of the Black Panthers; piles of back copies of defunct women's magazines; pastel-colored posters of elongated and ethereal women; other more political ones, like the one that says that children are not only the responsibility of mothers; another more direct one that shows that the A of the ABC stands for Abortion.

Amelinha recounts how it was almost impossible to read an article in any of the so-called women's journals that was related to sexuality or birth control, about sexual pleasure, that were not tied to reproduction. But, slowly, space started to open. *Nos Mulher* dared write in 1976 that the "sexual lives of women are not just to please their husbands and to procreate. Sexuality is more than that. It is an endless fountain of physical and psychological pleasures, which also brings enrichment and affection."

I cannot picture Amelinha using such saccharine pop-psychology jargon, but this was the message she wanted to get across at the meetings. It was difficult for her to bring up. Not only were the priests ready to kick her out but the women were embarrassed to speak. Whenever she would talk about these things in front of the priests, the women would clam up. But when the priests weren't there, they were more open. And when they talked they started to realize that the majority of the women were not having sexual pleasure and that they felt "inferior to men, that because they were married, they were in the obligation of *dar*"—which simply means to give but in the machismo-laced sexual context means to put out.

Talking leads to thinking, to questioning. Soon the women were coming to a conclusion for themselves: It does not need to be like this. When they did, many started losing the support of their husbands, who thought it was one thing to talk about the problems of the neighborhood but another to talk about sexual pleasure. "My husband thinks this is all *putaria*," one of the participants told Amelinha then—slutty stuff. He didn't want her to attend after that.

Amelinha also recalls a meeting in the *bairro* of Sapopemba around that time, 1978 or so, where women started talking about their lack of freedom. "And what freedom does a woman want to have?" she recalls one of the women asking. "We are not talking about the same freedom as the men who go around from bar to bar, drinking and meddling with every woman's skirt that crosses his sight. We want a different freedom. We want a freedom that would allow us to live without the prejudice against us as women."

But Amelinha learned that to transform the agenda of the women's movement, to have them include the fight against discrimination and the subservience of women as well as the fight for economic reform would be impossible. The *movimentos* were linked to the church and to the political opposition. Those groups would never allow it.

Other feminist fighters were feeling Amelinha's frustration, and in 1980 the women's movement experienced its first real division. During the Second Congress of Paulista Women, while 4,000 women representing 52 different groups met for two days to talk about the future of the movement, about 150 women decided to concentrate on two specific areas: domestic violence and birth control. For them, women's issues came before political issues. To be effective, Amelinha knew she needed to abandon politics.

Eighteen years later, she heads the União de Mulheres de São Paulo, whose mandate revolves around two main campaigns: to stop the impunity with which crimes of passion are committed and to legalize abortion. She is still as caustic and as subversive as she was in the seventies. She has not changed her discourse, she has changed her audience. Instead of being an active member of the Communist Party or the PT, which was a child of the marriage between the unions and liberation theology, she now writes books, lectures, attends conferences, and travels to the countryside to talk to women, mostly wives, about their sexual lives. She gives me a copy of the book she wrote for her road trips: *Breve história do feminismo no Brasil,* an accessible, informative little manual she hands out to the women who attend her workshops.

"Do the women read it? Do they get it?" I ask.

"Ah, *mia filha,* when we are talking to them it is not absurd, it is not abstract. It is not like with the men, where these things are abstractions because it is not something they live personally. Women know what you are talking about when you talk about repressed sexuality, about pregnancy, birth control, menopause, or about doing double work in one day. The women feel what you are talking about."

Along with her book, Amelinha also gives me a copy of the Union's latest poster, a photomontage of a pregnant pope which says IF MEN COULD GET PREGNANT, ABORTION WOULD BE A HUMAN RIGHT.

"Things are getting worse in the church," she tells me. That week, the National Conference of Bishops of Brazil (CNBB) had elected a new president, and for the first time in twenty-four years it was not a friend of the PT, not a friend of liberation theology, but a friend of the conservatives, a vociferous and loyal follower of old-style Vatican Catholicism. That Dom Lucas Moreira Neves believes that television is an evil tool and that Afro-Brazilian religions are things of the devil is not as dangerous for women as the fact that he believes that condoms are not a way to fight AIDS and is vehemently opposed to divorce, extramarital sex, and all forms of birth control except abstinence. According to the issue of *Veja* that week, the archbishop believes that the worst illness of our century is not AIDS but hedonism and that the cure for it is prayer, sacrifice, and penitence.

For Amelinha's campaign to decriminalize abortion, Dom Lucas's election as head of the CNBB is ill fated. "The church has a way of working, a scheme, an *eminencia parda,* you know what it is, the person who acts in hiding, not straightforward. And if the progressives"—she means the priests of liberation theology, the friends of Lula's PT—"act that way, can you imagine what the reactionaries can do? Worse, much worse. The church is power. Here in Brazil, the church occupies the same place as the state."

In 1880, more than one hundred years ago, Soledad de Samper, a privileged Colombian woman, wrote: "A woman's heart is composed in equal parts of candor, poetry, idealism of feeling, and resignation. It has four epochs in its lifetime: during childhood it vegetates and suffers; during adolescence it dreams and suffers; during youth it loves and suffers; and in old age it understands and suffers."

Sadly, if suffering was a constant in the hearts of Latin American women a century ago, it is not much different today. At forty-six, Josefa is about to lose her uterus, she has cast aside all sexual feeling, and she now spends her days taking care of grandchildren and husband—understanding and suffering. At forty-six, she is in the last stage of a Latin woman's life.

Josefa reports that the last time she went out and had fun with her husband was about the same time she last went to the beach. The evening ended in a fight. He invited her out to get *pamonhas*, but once at the restaurant he started flirting with the waitress. Josefa shouted at him and he shouted back. Though Josefa and Mario have three children, the last time he kissed her was sometime before Mariana's older sister was born. But Josefa continues to have sex with Mario whenever he insists. It's about once a week now. She prefers to close her eyes and bear it rather than to tell him that she stopped feeling pleasure in sex at about the same time he last kissed her. She says one gets used to loveless sex too.

"I used to say no, but to avoid a big fight inside the house, I end up doing it," she says. "I don't want the children to hear a fight." In Latin America, sex for a married man is a right, for his wife it is an obligation. To say no is not an option, but praying for him to climax quickly is.

In some ways, she says, her life is much better now that she focuses only on her home and her children. "Things are better now that I'm frigid," she says. Mario, her partner for more than half her life, her only real lover, has become merely the man she shares a house with. She tolerates him because where else would she go?

And he gives her the paycheck he earns driving a delivery truck for Coca-Cola. With that money, she bought herself a fifteen-year-old two-door Fiat that she uses to take Mario to work every morning and to pick him up at the end of the day—if he's not going out with his friends.

Two years ago she was able to stop working outside the home, and now she "only" has to deal with the housework, cooking the three meals, taking care of her husband, her two adult daughters, a son-in-law, and the grandchildren who live with her. Her biggest satisfaction has been being able, with Mario's check, to expand the one-bedroom cement house into a duplex with an outside patio she built herself. Mario did not lay a single stone. While she spent every Saturday for seven years going to the quarry to pick up slabs of green, black, and pink stone, he was "out with his friends."

"And you know what that means," she says to me as she shows me around. She might not be proud of her life, but she is sure proud of her possessions. In addition to her fancy patio, she has a nineteen-inch color Sony Trinitron, a washer, a dryer, a leather-covered Bible, a framed picture of Ayrton Senna, the race car driver who brought Brazil to a standstill when he died in 1994, porcelain puppies and elephants and circus ladies with lacy hats, plus an impressive array of pots and pans.

She knows that her husband has always praised her as a perfect wife, an excellent housekeeper, and a good mother too. A prostitute told her that. But this same woman also told Josefa that she did not sexually satisfy her husband. Josefa wanted to run away, to disappear. She was still at that stage that Soledad de Samper said "loves and suffers." She loved Mario, she still felt passionate about him, when she learned this.

She went to see the piranha, she tells me, referring to the prostitute, after she found insect bites all over her inner thighs. She remembers her whole body had itched, so she locked herself in the bathroom and lifted her skirt. Her groin was covered with pimples. She removed her underwear and felt desperate as she saw lice walking her pubes. She rapidly dressed and, scared, went to show Mario what she had found.

"Mario, look, I'm full of these critters."

"You're joking," he said. "I am sure I don't have them."

"If you don't have them, how is it that I do?" she said. "Take off your pants, you are going to show me."

Each pubic hair on his body had five or six larvae.

"Oh, you know what it is, I must have sat on João's bed."

She shaved his body, rubbed it with gasoline, bathed him, and scrubbed him with lice-killing medicine. Josefa believed that Mario had gotten the crabs from his colleague João. It was possible, she thought. Mario had found a job reading water registers, and she had a notion that water attracts all kinds of funny bugs. What she didn't realize was that water meters are not near the water. Only later, showing the scabs to a woman from the *bairro*, did she learn the truth. Her neighbor told her that a woman who lived above the luncheonette down the street and who worked as a prostitute had become Mario's mistress.

Josefa's first impulse was to leave for good, but her daughters were one and two and she had no family around except him. She couldn't think of anywhere to go, so she stayed despite her hurt. She felt sickened and, knowing that she could not talk with him, she went to talk to the prostitute.

The prostitute told her the problem was that because she didn't let Mario *fazer tudo*, do everything, he had to seek other women who did, women who get paid for sex.

"The women of the street, they do anything the guy wants," says Josefa when I ask her to explain *fazer tudo*. "But the woman inside the house is different, she likes things more simple. But Mario, he is this kind of man, he's like an animal. The things that I don't like and that you probably don't like, he likes."

I knew what she was referring to, but for the record I needed to have her say it. I don't want to be accused of making this up.

"Like what?" I asked, feeling I was using her.

She looked at me. "You know," she said, turning her face and her hand toward her back. "To get women from behind. This kind of thing that I never accepted."

"Has he always wanted that?" I felt as slimy as the prostitute who told her she gave her husband no *tesão*, no arousal.

"Always, always."

Anal intercourse is one of those subjects that are rarely discussed. But it seems that in Latin America it is practiced with much more frequency than it is talked about. Brazil, of course, advanced as it is in the field of human sexuality, had done statistical surveys. A 1983 study based on five thousand interviews of men and women throughout Brazil found that more than five percent of those interviewed in Rio de Janeiro and forty percent in the rest of Brazil practice anal intercourse, at least occasionally. Unfortunately, the study does not show how often it happens between *marido e mulher*. My guess is that it rarely does. As in the case of Josefa's household, it is reserved for outside the home. Her husband goes out to look for a woman who will abandon sexual taboos, generally for money. Women, especially housewives in Latin America, have very strict ideas about what a wife's sexual activity should include. Anal sex is not considered *decente*, ladylike. Furthermore, Josefa reminds me it is condemned by the Church.

Very few Latin American women are encouraged to explore their bodies, to understand their sexuality. We as girls start feeling funny chills up and down our spine, in between our legs maybe showering, or touching in a certain way, but we don't know who to ask. We only know not to ask. When I started menstruating, my grandmother told me I was now a *señorita*, and that I had to be very careful with boys, but she didn't tell me what that meant. Meanwhile, boys my age were being taken to bordellos by their older brothers or cousins on Friday afternoons after school.

Dr. Bernardo Camacho, the Colombian doctor working with AIDS patients in Bogotá, gave me one of the most succinct explanations of sexuality in Latin America: "In our society, women attach punitive attitudes to their sexuality. They associate sex with sin, so they carry a negative emotional burden. For a man, sex is the opposite. He thinks he has the right to all, so he never searches for a point of equilibrium. Our society does not allow an adjusted sexual development, and so it is one of great distortions."

The nurse at the family-planning clinic who put me in touch with Mariana and her mother told me the story of the seventy-year-old widow who had adopted three children because she thought she was infertile. Her husband had had children before. When the nurse examined her, she realized the woman's hymen was intact. She asked the widow if she had had sexual relations with her husband.

"Yes," the widow replied.

She had only had anal sex all her life. And her husband was inconsiderate enough never to tell her.

I had arrived prepared to be careful and solemn when talking to a young woman about such a very personal and delicate issue. I didn't expect her to bring it up herself, almost giddily and right away, but I'm always surprised at Brazilians' complicated and tricky openness. It is a culture that invites anyone to follow the example of the omnipresent statue of the Corcovado, the Christ Redeemer, who stands tall overlooking Rio de Janeiro with open arms, embracing all that happens under his feet: the beautiful and the ugly, the clean and the corrupt, the peaceful and the violent, the black and the white, the rich and the poor. Brazil, for me, has always been confusing for the same reasons Colombia has not. While Colombia is straightforward in its oppression and in its repression of women, Brazil is blurry. For Brazilians, their society represents the closest approximation to a perfectly undiscriminating, multicultural democracy—an image that, for me, has never quite stood up to the reality. But it is easy to be fooled. Brazil is extremely seductive.

The first time I visited Brazil, in 1991, I fell in love with the warmth and approachability of everyone, the candor of Carnival and of Candomble, the beauty of Brazilians' smiles, the vibrancy of the civil society, the twenty-five hundred organizations dedicated to women's rights, the stamina and the strength oozing out of the women walking down the busy streets, their fluid movement, their playfulness, their deep attachment to their bodies—particularly their round buttocks, be they dressed or not. Brazilian women expose their bodies naturally and not only when wearing the tiny *tanga* and the tinier *seda dental* on the beaches of Ipanema. That women wear revealing clothes to work is so standard that a law was passed in April 1995 prohibiting women who work at the state courthouses of São Paulo from wearing bare midriffs and halters. Regardless of how undressed they are, they seem to carry a certain assertiveness that differs from the stereotype of the defenseless Latin American woman who wears ultratight clothes and high stilettos. Or so I thought.

It was confusing, with the image of openness and, more than the image, the feeling I got from being in Brazil that first time, to learn that women are as mistreated, as abused, physically and verbally, and that men are as macho-minded as they are in more conservative Colombia. It was frustrating to find out that, just like in my Barranquilla, men dance during the three days of Carnival, they drink and dress up like women, while their wives, women like Josefa and her daughter Mariana, stay home. The sensuous women exposing their sweaty torsos and round thighs, moving to the sound of the *batucadas* in the Sambodromo, are a minority.

Brazil's sensuality is a double-edged sword for women. The air smells of passion, and sex talk is candid on television. Marta Suplicy, the psychotherapist and sexologist with great interest in gender equality, can be elected to Congress. A nun can insist that abortion is not a crime. After the fall of the military government in 1985, a special federal agency for women's rights was created: the National Council for Women's Rights (CNDM). Its aim was to "promote in political circles the elimination of discrimination against women, guaranteeing conditions of freedom and equal rights as well as their full participation in political, economic, and cultural activities." In a country where abortion is a crime and a sin, it was bold of the newly elected government to name Jacqueline Pitanguy, an ardent and vociferous pro-abortion activist, as the CNDM's first president. But the openness to women's issues that the political opposition to the military so proudly proclaimed underscored the reality of how men and women relate to each other on a more simple level. President Jose Sarney's government allowed for certain advances, yet day-to-day a wide gap persists between the place of men and that of women. In Brazil, as in less progressive Honduras, more than sixty percent of women are the victims of some sort of domestic violence.

The government could have intended to create the CNDM merely as a political showcase. After all, the feminine electorate and organized female constituencies had played a pivotal role in the fight against the dictatorship. Parties of the opposition had to pay the women back. But these feminist inroads into formal politics translated into gaining access to policy. The CNDM intervened in favor of women in areas such as agrarian reform, day care center policy, and antisexist educational reforms. During the rewriting of the constitution, the CNDM was able to develop a women's agenda for inclusion in the document. The "Letter from Women to the Constituent Assembly" called for democratization of both public and private life. Women understood that the new place that was opening up for them in the democratic transition had to come hand in hand with a new reality in their private lives. "For us women," they wrote to the Assembly, "the full exercise of citizenship means, yes, the right to representation, a voice and a role in public life, but at the same time, it also implies dignity in daily life, which the law can inspire and should ensure, the right to education, to health, to security, to a family life free of trauma."

The demands were heard and the Constitution of 1989 was a breakthrough for women. As far as women's rights go, Brazil has one of the most advanced constitutions in the world. Amelinha considers that the women's groups were triumphant in all of their demands—"I will say in all except abortion."

For example, women can now work the night shifts, and they are free to work in an unhealthy environment if they choose to—night work and mining previously were banned. Men now share the responsibility for bringing up newborn children and are entitled to paternity leave. Paid maternity leave was extended from three to four months. The state must provide free day care, the so-called *creches*, for children up to age six. The issue of sexual and domestic violence was firmly confronted by the federal government when it launched a national campaign and established the women precincts. Men were no longer accorded *chefia*, dominion over the family. Until the new constitution, husbands had been the managers of all family assets and had had the legal right to decide where and how the family should live.

For Jacqueline Pitanguy, to get men to give away this right was among the greatest achievements. "It is a cultural thing," she says, sitting in a pretty rattan chair on the balcony of her office in Rio de Janeiro. Soon after these *logros*, these achievements, Pitanguy resigned as director of the CNDM. When she embarked on a national campaign to legalize abortion, she realized that the CNDM was more makeup than substance. When a new minister of justice, under whose mandate the CNDM fell, was appointed in 1989, Pitanguy's initiatives were blocked. "There is no way to resist from inside," says Pitanguy, an attractive, blond-haired woman dressed in silk who has the same self-assuredness as Marta Suplicy, the attitude that comes with higher education, trips abroad, and a privileged upbringing. "If you stay, you get coopted." So she left.

Today, she heads CEPIA, a nongovernmental group whose acronym stands for Citizenship, Study, Research, Information, and Action. The group publishes reports, conducts nationwide surveys and studies of judicial response to crimes against women, and evaluates possible strategies for the expansion of their reproductive rights. Her spacious office, overlooking the ocean and the Pão de Açúcar, has the same feel one gets from talking to her— organized, thoughtful, and committed. Like her voice, the phones and the faxes ring constantly but softly. Like the silk skirt under the blue blazer, the covers of the reports that the staff hand me are colorful yet serious and tasteful.

"Were you surprised?" I ask her. "Were you disappointed with what happened with the CNDM?"

"No, not at all. We were conscious that we had a political window of opportunity there, and we needed to use it as fast as we could."

Regardless of the new constitution, men are, by far, the absolute rulers of the country, of its institutions, and of its citizens. When it comes to issues that are strictly concerned with women and their sexuality, there is little difference from the rest of Latin America. Even the priests who were the greatest promoters of social justice, who helped women organize to demand better conditions and were actively responsible for bringing down a repressive government, still accept no discussion of sexuality, contraception, or abortion. Women can demand better salaries for their husbands and better schooling for their children, but companies still demand letters of resignation to keep in their files in case a woman employee gets pregnant. Some offer safe abortions, others demand a certificate of sterilization. Anything in order not to have to comply with the law and pay four months of maternity leave. Brazil might have better gender laws and more government funding, but millions of women, women like Josefa, are as marginalized as they are in my backward Barranquilla, which has no Amelinha, no Pitanguy, and no pretense of being open. Women are just as much at risk of contracting AIDS in Brazil, of being victims of domestic violence, or of having to resort to dangerous abortions as they are elsewhere in Latin America. This is not what I expected from a country that has seen the strongest women's movement on the continent and a culture distinguished by the image of its openness toward sexuality.

One of the first efforts of the new federal agency, the CNDM, was to launch a national campaign against domestic violence. Pitanguy ordered a study that found that more than seventy percent of violence against women is carried out by husbands and boyfriends. It also established that crimes of passion are regular and go unpunished. About 150 women were killed the previous year by their partners in a rage of jealousy; only one man was convicted. The agency created the famous *delegacias de mulheres*—police stations mostly run by women for women to report cases of violence. For the first time, women were being told what constituted abuse while being provided a place where they could denounce it. The number of complaints went from zero to the many thousands. But although the CNDM was able to create national consciousness, few of these accusations resulted in convictions. The issue was brought to the forefront, and women now know that they have a place they can go to lodge a complaint if they are abused. But the situation becomes less ideal when one reads a Human Rights Watch report that shows that eighty percent of the judges in the countryside still believe that crimes of passion are pardonable, that a man has to defend his honor, and that hitting and raping a wife is a man's conjugal right. These judges also believe women who are not virgin may be raped, a father may throw a daughter out on the street if he learns she has been deflowered, and a new husband can return his bride to her family for the same reason. "Even women judges don't convict," said the report. "They are trained to think like men." I bring this up not to take away the credit for the immense work that the women's movement in Brazil has accomplished.

It feels heavy to see how ingrained these thoughts, these traditions still are today, how strongly they are still being propagated. My vision of what life for a woman in Latin America can be becomes bleak when I see how slow and tedious the changing of laws is, and I realize that all the work that Amelinha and Pitanguy have done up to now may be a fruitless undertaking.

In Brazil one sees rivers of cheeky information concerning AIDS. Teenage girls holding condoms, famous movie stars posing with them as earrings or hairbands. Street vendors sell T-shirts that read AVOID AIDS HAVE SEX WITH ME. Married women are invited to private parties to talk about protection. They are given educational literature and condoms. But if even women judges think like men, and the women at state-funded family-planning clinics also do, then that first impression one has of Brazil, that there is space available, that there is a possibility for things to open up for women, is what makes the country so blurry.

Most other countries in Latin America are clearer. They are straightforward: Sex is forbidden here. One will never find Brazilian-type prevention campaigns in Colombia, or in Chile, where the church was able to prevent AIDS TV spots from being aired on national television. No one in Guatemala's congress has proposed to decriminalize abortion. Instead, the equivalent of the CNDM is a fervent advocate of the Vatican's position.

During the presidential campaign of 1994, the two candidates were asked about their positions on abortion. Both Luis Ignacio da Silva—Lula, the candidate for the PT, probably the most progressive presidential candidate in Latin America in the past twenty years—and Fernando Henrique Cardoso, a former Marxist economic professor who in the past had declared he was an atheist, played it safe. They were clever enough to say that they were personally against abortion. So in Brazil there is room to talk about sex, about AIDS, about women's rights, but little room for changes. Women's issues are a tool for political leverage, a way to get votes, but the position of presidential candidates is a stark reminder of how hard it will be to change the minds of our leaders.

As a result, young women like Mariana become unskilled labor-
ers and young mothers who have dangerous abortions and unprotected sex.

After I left Mariana's home I decided to find out for myself
what would be available to me if I were pregnant, desperate, and
poor in Brazil. I enlisted my friend Matt—an American journalist
living in Rio de Janeiro—to accompany me to every drugstore we
could find in one evening and ask for Cytotec, which was by then
already illegal.

We went to more than a dozen places and found out that the
availability of Cytotec is directly related to where you live. Just as
safe illegal abortions are available to the daughters of the rich,
Cytotec provides the equivalent of flying to Miami to a middle- to
lower-middle-class urban woman, but it is not so available to girls
like Mariana. She was lucky it had been given to her by her friend
at the beauty pageant. She would never have been able to afford
it. In 1995, in Rio de Janeiro, four pills ran between forty and
eighty dollars.

In the poorer areas, the favelas, the Rio equivalent of Mariana's
neighborhood, Matt and I were not successful in finding any. We
were told it was available in the drugstores *do sul*, the ones in the
affluent neighborhoods. We drove south on the wide boulevard
of the Avenida Atlântica, past the famous Copacabana Palace.
On one side, the avenue is lined with the well-guarded luxurious
high-rises, the five-star hotels, the outdoor cafes where pimps,
prostitutes, street children, transvestites, and tourists, mostly single men from Germany, Italy, and the United States, sip coffee,
champagne, and guarana, and talk and sell and buy sex. Anything
is available to a pregnant girl living on this side of the avenue. On
the other side is the ocean and the Pão de Açúcar and, way in the
back, close to the horizon, where one sees in the distance a flurry
of flashing lights, flickering pink and blue and green, the favelas
glow like an intermittent Christmas tree. Each dot is not holiday
lights, but a house built with scant resources on an illegal piece of
land. Each light is a crowded house with no sewage system but
with a color TV, an abusive husband, a frigid wife, and a desperate daughter like Mariana, who wishes she could swim across to

the other side where the rich women wear thongs, live in condominiums with smoky mirrors, and where Cytotec is available.

In Botofogo, a middle-class neighborhood of high buildings with less marble than in the affluent areas, I was told, politely, that Cytotec was controlled and that I could find it, but not there. "It is used for abortions," the pharmacist said, staring at me with disapproval. "It is illegal to sell it without a prescription."

At another pharmacy down the road, I had not finished asking for it when the lady behind the counter snapped, "Abortion is a crime."

"Let's get out of my neighborhood," said Matt, worried about his reputation among the local pharmacists. "I'm going to need to come back and buy aspirin here one day."

We decided to go downtown, to the business center of Rio where everything and anything is for sale. We took a taxi to the rua Rodrigo da Silva, a busy avenue filled with street vendors, coffee shops, fruit stands, shops selling cheap clothes, funny slippers, video tapes of pirated movies, and smuggled sound systems. We detected a few *drogarias*. But we got severe shakes of the head at two and were kicked out of another.

"Get out, we don't have that here." I started feeling the desperation and the humiliation that most women who want to find it must feel.

Finally, a young pharmacist in a white coat signaled us to follow him outside.

"I have someone who can get it, but it cannot be done here," he said looking only at Matt and speaking like a drug dealer. "Meet me in an hour at the place where they sell the *pão de queijo* down the street. Do you know how to use it?"

I was the one who had made the request. I was the one who was supposedly in need of the drug. But he would only look at Matt.

"Quanto tempo está atrasada?" he asked Matt: How late is she?

"Dois meses," said Matt, being a good sport.

"Tonight she takes three orally, one vaginally. She'll start hemorrhaging before morning comes. It will be seventy-five reais for the four. See you there."

The next day, with the same question in mind—what are the alternatives for a pregnant and poor nineteen-year-old?—I called

BEMFAM, the largest family-planning government agency with more than two thousand posts nationwide. I called a doctor who was often quoted in the press, talking about BEMFAM's work. I told her that I was interested in learning about the work they did in their family-planning clinics.

She interrupted to correct me. "You have to understand that in Latin America 'family planning' just means contraception. Family-planning clinics just hand out birth-control pills. We are different. We offer reproductive health assistance."

"What's the difference?" I asked, thinking about that certain Brazilianness.

"We offer gynecological assistance, Pap smears, prevention of sexually transmitted diseases and AIDS, sterilization referrals. We look at reproductive health in a comprehensive way." Her voice was educated, assertive, and pasteurized—the tone one hears from panelists and experts who spend too much time talking about their subject. The words sound good but they lack enthusiasm. All that was missing was for her to say "empowerment," a word I put in the same category as "gender": They are great-sounding, yet how do you make them stop being words in academic papers and allow them to weave into the flow of everyday life? How do you translate them to Josefa, to Mariana, to their husbands?

The doctor suggested that I visit one of their clinics before talking to her at length. She arranged for a van to pick me up at eight the next morning to take me to the Clínica Meier, the largest reproductive health clinic in Brazil. She was sure I would be impressed by the work they do.

June is the beginning of the winter in Brazil, and that morning the fog was dense. As we drove away from the beaches of Boto-fogo toward the north, we left behind a Christ covered in clouds. We passed the pink and blue Maracaná stadium and the Sam-bodromo and entered a Rio de Janeiro that stops being the magical Rio the world seeks. It became any other poor sprawling urban center. This could be Bogotá, Mexico City, or East L.A. The tanned bodies of Ipanema turned into tired bodies. The playful smiles turned into ashen faces that worry and work hard. The redeeming Christ was nowhere to be found for the thousands of wage earners who line up for the trains to go where He is, where they can make two or three times the minimum salary, about a hundred dollars a month, working in the stores and in the homes of the rich.

The van left the rua Vermelha, the highway built for the Eco-Summit so that the whole world would bypass the poverty of the favelas, and we entered the hustle and bustle of the rua Herme-nengande, where we stopped in front of royal blue gates. Behind them, a white villa stood surrounded by grounds of Brazilian green. This looked like the home of a wealthy Rio family, not a clinic that more than one hundred women of scant resources visited each day.

A young pregnant woman came out and, with that Brazilian warmth, took me over to hear the Wednesday workshop on AIDS prevention. There I saw Bettinha, a vibrant psychologist in a short, colorful dress, holding a black plastic penis in her hand and joking that it needed to be *durinho*, a little hard, before a condom could fit properly. She went on to explain that oral sex is the least risky of practices and anal sex is the most risky when it comes to contracting AIDS. She spoke with complicity and with comfort, stripping sex of any association of sin and instead filling it with the possibility of pure pleasure. The twenty women in the room giggled constantly, and the four teenagers—aged thirteen to seventeen—sitting in the back row were permanently blushing.

Bettinha handed out a green booklet as she explained that it was women, married women, women of one fixed partner who were getting infected. On the cover of the booklet a woman is looking at a man as if she has something she wants to talk to him about. He looks annoyed. *Conversando e que a gente se entende* is the title—talking is the way to understanding. Bettinha reads the title out loud, and opens the booklet to the first page.

" 'You know, Neuza, I just heard a strange conversation,' " Bettinha read from the booklet, which shows two friends meeting on the street. " 'Ilma is ill. It seems like she is never feeling right. They say it's AIDS! But isn't that a homosexual illness?' "

Bettinha stared at the class and asked two of the women, a manicurist and a telephone operator, to read the rest of the booklet out loud. She asked the only adult male present to read the part of the man. He was there because his wife had forced him to come, and he looked as uncomfortable as the man on the booklet's cover.

Antonia, the manicurist, read. " 'That is one of the reason for our meeting. The question is: We can all guarantee that we only have sex with our partners, *nao é?* But who here can guarantee that her husband, partner, or boyfriend doesn't have another woman outside?' "

"Guarantee," Bettinha interrupted, "listen careful, *e gente,* who here can guarantee that?"

The women in the class shook their heads.

The operator took her turn. " 'From the doors out, I don't put my hand in the fire for any man. Not even for mine!' " she read. " 'I already tried asking him to use condoms, telling him it is dangerous not to, but he says it's just *bobagem,* foolishness, and there is no way he will use them! I am scared, but what can I do?' "

Bettinha took her cue again. *"Medo, gente?"* she asked the group. *"Medo, resolve?* Is fear a solution?"

" 'I know now,' " the man read the end of the story, in which Ilma's HIV-positive husband speaks to a group of men, " 'that everything could have been avoided.' " He does not know how he was infected or by whom and that if he would have used a *camisinha,* a condom, he would not have infected Ilma. " 'But I didn't think about those thing. I would just go, *tranquilo. . . .*' "

The women were completely immersed in Ilma's story. I could almost hear their hearts and read their minds—they could identify with Ilma, with Neuza, with the fact that they know their husbands are unfaithful, that they are even aware of AIDS and how they are helpless when it comes to asking their partners to wear a condom.

"Has anyone here asked her husband to use condoms?" Bettinha asked the class.

The manicurist raised her hand. *"Meu Dios,* it is so difficult. Macho, macho, macho," she says, twirling the bag filled with nail files, scissors, and polishes. "He says he is a man. He is a macho, and a macho does not accept condoms. Last time I got pregnant, I was panicked."

"Does panic bring solutions?" Bettinha tried again, but the manicurist gave her no time. She had already started to defend her husband.

"He suffered with me. He is a dignified man. He felt my panic but he still doesn't wear them with me—he says it's like eating a candy with its wrapper on—but he assures me that he does . . . you know. I find it's okay if he doesn't like them. I know there is nothing I can do. If he doesn't like them, he won't wear them. Of course, if it was up to me, *I* would."

"I spoke with my husband already," said one of the women in the back of the room, kind of proudly. "This is the second time I've come to the workshop."

"Did you use the condoms I gave you?" Bettinha asked.

"No, no. I'm still not using condoms." Her pride became an embarrassed giggle. "Ooohhh, what's the difficulty? He says for him is not necessary. He trusts me. I am his woman, I trust him. He trusts me."

After the workshop was over, Bettinha invited me for a *cafe-zinho*. "To talk to their husbands is to create confusion in the home. And they don't want to fight. Then once they talk, they think that the husband will change his behavior outside of the house. This is wishful thinking." Still, I was impressed to see the housewives and the young kids at the workshops, so I asked Bettinha, as we sat in the clinic's kitchen, where they came from. The women were patients at the clinic, and the kids came from a nearby school. A class assignment, she explained. The students had to choose a subject they were interested in learning more about. These four had inquired about AIDS, so the school had sent them over. This is a perfect example of that paradoxical Brazilian openness. Wherever you look in Latin America, Brazil, or Colombia, statistics show that teenage girls are having sex by the time they are fifteen to seventeen years old; boys start as early as thirteen. Yet I cannot conceive my friend Eugenia's daughter in Barranquilla, who just turned sixteen and has an official boyfriend, wanting to sit through this open discussion about sex. Nor do I see the possibility of the nuns at Marymount calling around to find out where girls could go listen to a psychologist holding a rubber penis explaining how to have safe sex.

Isto É, an important Brazilian weekly, had a cover story on teens and sex in June 1995. The first paragraph of the piece is radically different from what Eugenia or her daughter would read in a comparable magazine in Colombia:

> Sex is no longer a sin. Loss of Virginity is no longer a taboo but is now an option. Teenagers are freer to choose their sexual initiation. There is an exceptional bombardment of information and a favorable climate to talk about sex and to experiment with it. Sexuality is more openly discussed with parents and in schools.

As open as this writing is, it is just such paragraphs that make Brazil confusing for me. In 1991, a cover of *Carinho,* the Brazilian version of *Seventeen,* showed a teenage girl holding a condom. This is yet to be seen in the United States, let alone other Latin American countries. The comparable magazine in Colombia that year had an article about AIDS with a title that would scare anyone off: "He Brought Me Flowers, Chocolates, and AIDS."

What is curious, though, is that Brazil's apparent openness does not seem to translate into responsible actions. Like Mariana, many of these sexually active young women do not use condoms, or any form of birth control, for that matter. Most become mothers. As I stood outside the favela women's clinic where Mariana's sister works, I saw young mothers arriving for consultation, many with babies in their arms. They talk about their babies, and their men. The brashest of them gloated about how she had made her mother a grandmother at thirty-four.

"My mother was nineteen when she had me, and I was fifteen when I had my *bebê,*" she says proudly.

Maybe she had wanted to be a mother at fifteen, maybe she had planned her pregnancy. Latin women are rarely encouraged to plan anything, especially not sex. Men think less of women who take precautions, because that means they think about sex. And God forbid we do *that.* Our bodies need to be fortuitous, our ovaries left to the whims of God and Chango and the semen of our men.

Another possibility is that this girl had already been pregnant and, not wanting to have another scary and dangerous abortion, she decided to carry the pregnancy through. That was what happened to Mariana. She had an abortion she felt so guilty about that, when she got pregnant again, she had the baby, dropped out of high school, gained twenty pounds, and does not leave her house even to take him for a walk. She is afraid something might happen to him. Her life stopped. She now belongs to Michel. God punished her, she says, because she had that abortion, *ne?*

But if places run by BEMFAM offer birth control pills, IUDs, condoms, diaphragms and jellies for free and a consultation costs eight reais, about seven dollars, how come Mariana got pregnant again? All she had to do was walk down the street to the clinic where the German nurse would have given her any of these. But she didn't. Why?

"There is a lot of touching and very little talking," says Bettinha when I ask her why teenagers get pregnant, and why women are testing HIV-positive if the resources for protecting themselves are, to some extent, available. There is talk about sexuality and about women's issues on television and in the newspapers. There is talk among the politically active, the women's movements, the feminists, even the Catholic Church and the Congress about abortion and domestic violence. But there is little talking between man and woman.

Josefa does not talk to her husband. Mariana doesn't either. Culture is stronger than talking heads. Common law is fiercer than any group of people with political alternatives. That Brazil's political establishment allowed a strong feminist movement some entry into the political arena does not immediately translate into an actual change in behavior. That a national campaign denounced domestic violence does not immediately mean husbands or boyfriends are going to stop abusing their women, stepfathers raping their stepchildren.

I felt the fear in the faces of the women who listened to Bettinha. The threat is so real to them that most women skip work to attend the workshop. They come more than once. They leave every time convinced they need to demand condoms. They walk out holding those condoms, absolutely certain that they will have the courage next time to ask. But when they return, Bettinha hears the same story.

This is Bettinha's way of translating the textbook notions of gender inequality and empowerment, and making them recognizable and useful to the manicurist, the telephone operator, the unemployed housewives holding babies who are gathered to learn about AIDS prevention. Bettinha knows that this is a way to reach them about other things, she tells me after the workshop.

"Women need to learn how to negotiate condoms," she insists. "If you negotiate condoms, you can negotiate other things."

Jacqueline Pitanguy, Bettinha, and Amelinha are impressive, admirable women. Pitanguy represents change at the high level. She is an elegant woman of academia, funded by the MacArthur and Ford foundations, who attends the women's summits in Cairo and Beijing, who speaks about women's issues globally, who taught at Harvard, and whose essays appear in most anthologies about gender issues in Latin America. Bettinha and Amelinha are grassroots. Bettinha speaks to wives about condoms, and Amelinha speaks about women's rights in a language that is accessible to average women. But they all face the same problem. They get women to listen but few men.

Barbara, the clinic administrator who had first received me at the entrance, and Agraça, a BEMFAM social worker, join us at the kitchen table. Barbara and Agraça brought along the glossy literature they use to teach women about their bodies. They were going to explain to me what the doctor over the phone had said about overall public health and not just family planning. The books were large books with colorful illustrations. They looked like children's books, with the same type of illustrations as the book my mother read to me when she called me into her room to explain some things after I had started menstruating. I was fourteen and I remember leaving her room not knowing what she was talking about. I had seen pictures of flowers, puppies, cats, horses, one on top of the other, and naked people who looked like Barbie dolls holding hands and lying in bed with sheets over them. Not these ridiculous pictorial boards again, I thought. I blame those books for leaving me blind for many years about the wonders of procreation. They are using the same bland images to tell more than one hundred women a day how not to procreate!

I was getting impatient with the show-and-tell. Barbara's voice was irritating me as she went over the different methods they offered while holding the boards on her knee. It was too sweet, too girly. When she started talking about the mucus method—"You can tell if you're ovulating, depending on the type of mucus your vagina excretes"—I gripped my pencil hard, bit my tongue, and tried to keep my cool.

"And next you will show me how to use the *tabelinha*," I said sarcastically.

"Yes," she said cheerfully. "We teach that too."

"It is a very risky method," I said. "Many women get pregnant like that."

"I know," she said. "I am a *tabelinha* baby."

The morning was almost over; my head was twirling, and I wanted to get out of there while I still could thank them and say good-bye nicely. So with the same directness with which Bettinha had spoken in her workshop about anal sex, I asked my question: "What about abortions?"

Silence. The soft rumbling of the air-conditioner in the room became audible, and the welcoming warmth I had received from the staff of the clinic turned as cold as the air coming out of the ancient unit in the back of the room. Bettinha, without doubt the most outspoken of the three, blurted: "Why do you Americans so much like the question of abortion?"

Because, without the help of BEMFAM, women are having more abortions here than in the United States. Because here more pregnancies end up in abortions—1.7 million recorded and who knows how many not. All of them are illegal, clandestine; more than ninety percent are self-induced.

I ask Barbara if I can go over some of the charts that women fill out during their first visit to Clínica Meier. She is so polite it is somewhat irksome, especially now that I know how she feels about abortion. Having an abortion is like killing a baby, she has told me, adding, "I am Catholic."

She is married, and sitting there in front of Bettinha's free condoms and BEMFAM's literature on safe sex, she tells us she does not ask her husband to use condoms. She knows he wouldn't like it. This is the person running one of Brazil's largest family-planning clinics—no, sorry, running a "reproductive health clinic." What kind of empowered name is that? I decide not to call back the doctor who sent me on this tour. I don't want to sit through any more talk about how important the work they do for women is.

Barbara walks me over to a tall filing cabinet near the reception desk, opens the drawer where the questionnaires are kept, and leaves me there after offering me another smile. Thousands of files, of sad histories of women's sexual lives.

The question about abortion is asked indirectly: How many terminated pregnancies?

I go over many charts, only concentrating on the answers to that question. I shudder as I read. The women, on average, have had four or five terminated pregnancies Many women answer that they've had more than ten abortions.

I can see Barbara's pregnant silhoutte in the other room as I keep reading. I walk over to her and ask:

"What do you do if a pregnant woman comes into the clinic saying she wants an abortion? Would you tell her where to go and have a safe one?"

"No. We don't work with abortion. We are preventive," she says with that calm smile again.

Her angelic face, her sweet smile, and her protruding belly under her flowery cotton blouse and indigo jumper all feel sinister knowing that she too knew what was written in these files. Thirty to forty-five percent of all pregnancies in Brazil are terminated. Twenty to thirty percent of all Brazilian women have had abortions. According to the World Health Organization, the figure is about three million abortions each year in Brazil alone. As BEM-FAM has calculated, that comes out to 250,000 a month, 8,333 each day, 347 each hour, or almost 6 self-induced or dangerous abortions per minute.

Barbara has to know how most of these women have abortions, I thought. She knows that those unschooled numbers translate into pregnant women insert knitting needles, Coca-Cola bottles, tree branches, barbed wire, trying in desperation to touch and scrape their uterus clean. And she knows that these procedures are so dangerous that almost half of the women end up in hospitals and face doctors who are only hardhearted and judgmental when they have to treat complications of abortion.

"I stayed three days on a *maca* in the hallway," a black mother of eleven—another thirteen were born dead and four aborted—says about her visit to a hospital in São Paulo. For her first abortion she had gone to a *curandeira*, an unlicensed midwife, who inserted a *sonda*, a probe, that caused so much bleeding she went to a clinic. The doctor threatened to call the police, so she ran out and went to see another midwife, who finished the abortion without local anesthesia. Four years after that, she was pregnant again. She decided to terminate it herself. She used a *talo de couve*, then took some tea from abortive plants and some Cytotec. She bled for a week. Two years ago, she needed another one. This time, infection sent her to the hospital where she was left in the hall unattended for three days. Every time the nurses went by, they referred to her as the assassin.

A nurse who works in the maternity ward of the largest hospital in São Paulo, where most women go after they experience a ruptured uterus or nonstop hemorrhaging or dangerous infections from their bad abortions like the black woman, admits she insults women who she knows are there for such a reason. *Folha de São Paulo* interviewed this thirty-five-year-old nurse on condition that she not be identified. She acknowledges having mistreated women for eight years.

"Are women who provoke abortions mistreated here?" the reporter asked.

"Those women who take medicine, use tree branches, a *cutuca*, are careless. They come to the hospital to create scandals. And you know we professionals are not here for little games. We are here to care for the people who really need us, not for one who provoked an abortion. If she did that, she has to bear the consequences. She has no right to scream, no right to cry. She must suffer quietly."

"Do you do *curetagem* without anesthesia?"

"Yes. On purpose."

"Have you had cases of abortion in your family?"

"I do. My sister. It was a stupid abortion—she perforated her uterus and she had to have it removed. She almost died."

"Do you disapprove of your sister?"

"No. At first, I was shocked and distraught. But then I understood that she will always carry with her the consequences of her thoughtless and foolish behavior of being an assassin, and will have to live with her mutilated body."

Pope John Paul II says women like me want to impose a Western model of feminism on the rest of the world, that we are influenced by the developed world. Maybe the fact that I was educated in the United States makes me fall in the category of following an imperialist model. The Pope complains that we are not letting women outside of the United States be what they want to be, mainly mothers, virginal ones at that. But Josefa and Mariana and the women that Amelinha and Bettinha talk to want the same things I want. They want to talk openly about their sexuality, and they want to feel sexual pleasure, intimacy, love, and respect from their partners.

As Josefa told me her story, she offered me some of the feijoada she was making for her husband's dinner. She set out a green plastic plate for me on the kitchen table and maternally ordered me to finish everything.

"I'm the one that does everything that needs to be done. I'm an excellent wife, mother, good housekeeper, but I'm not good for *that*," Josefa tells me. "How do you think that makes me feel?"

During the time I was there, she spoke of her life, turning every so often to Mariana and warning her again and again to be careful not to end up like her. "Look at her, a girl, nineteen and already a baby in her arms," she says. "Her *marido* behaves now, when they've been together for one year only, but I tell her all the time: men, men, men."

The idea of what a marriage is seems to have changed little since 1914, when Ricardo Uribe Escobar, a young Colombian political science student who advocated women's work outside the home, wrote:

Colombian women have always been kidnapped inside the home. And don't tell us that because of that our families are ruled by calmness . . . this calmness is like the peace in cemeteries. . . . She has no rights to a life, her activity is reduced to keeping up the household and to rendering humble homage to her husband. The man commands, directs, represents his home; the woman suffers and resigns herself, not even complains, and naturally, the house is filled with peace.

Uribe Escobar was writing about Colombia more than eighty years ago, but it is that same false sense of peace that I have felt in Josefa's home as the sweet smell of the feijoada entered the bedroom, as Mariana fed her newborn, and as the giggles of the grandchildren mixed with Josefa's complaints. It is an appearance of peace that Josefa will guard ferociously. She will trade respect, communication, and sexual satisfaction for a figurehead husband. This, she feels, is all she can ask of him. It is a peace that needs to be shielded no matter what because the fear of surviving alone, without a man around, is so strong that she will bear anything rather than confront it and demand change or leave. It is a fear that allows Josefa to feel frustrated as a woman but safe as a mother and grandmother.

When it was time for me to leave Jose's impeccable, almost pretty, yet unhappy home, I felt she didn't want me to go. I remembered Amelinha's words. I remembered speaking to the educators in the *creche* a few blocks from this home, up the stream that serves as the sewage outlet for the entire favela. The educators, knowing that working women trust their children with them, have started giving three-day workshops on AIDS prevention, to which the mothers are invited. The first day, the women get to know each other. The second day, they talk about things that, most probably, they have never talked to anyone about: the first time they got their period, how they lost their virginity, what feels good about their sexual life with their partners, what feels bad. The third and last day they are introduced to the prevention of AIDS. The educators are always surprised at how eager the women are to continue talking. The mothers don't want the workshop to end and ask if they can meet for longer.

"This is apparently a normal life," says Josefa, standing at the front door of her home. "But it is not."

III.
The Man of My Dreams

*-But no, in this home we don't speak
about problems from the waist down.*

*-Pero no, en esta casa no se habla de
problemas de la cintura para abajo.*
    —Gabriel García Márquez
    *Diatriba de amor
    contra un hombre casado*

"Mami, a señora is looking for you," my brother shouted so that
our mother could hear him upstairs. She was in her bathroom
preparing herself for a party my father and she were attending
that evening. And he was in a hurry, running out the front door to
play *bola de trapo*, a kind of minisoccer played on the streets of
Barranquilla with a small ball made out of rags. My brother was
about eight and, like most boys his age, he would come home
from school and head out to the street, where he would shoot at
birds with the BB gun he had gotten from el Niño Dios for Christmas. He would set weedgrown empty lots on fire, and he would
play soccer with the other boys of the neighborhood and with the
gardeners, drivers, and security guards who took care of the homes
of Riomar, the new and elegant barrio where the city's up-and-
coming powers, men like my father, had built big Spanish-style
homes.

In a city where seventy percent of the 1.5 million residents
make less than a hundred and fifty dollars a month, owning a house
like ours and a couple of cars was reason enough to feel threatened by *los ladrones*, the thieves. I grew up waiting for them to
come into our home and ransack it in the middle of the night.

That's why José, our gardener, slept on a thin mattress in the back room next to the kitchen.

"Thieves" was just another word for the poor—*los pobres*—as we referred to anyone who did not live in a house like ours. As a child, I hardly ever saw the poverty that lay beyond our privileged borders. But I knew it existed because our old clothes and my old toys went to them: *"Eso ya está para dárselo a los pobres,"* my mother said about my white dress with the blue fish appliqués. She was saying it was time to give one of my favorite dresses to "the poor." I took the collectiveness of the term seriously. I could never imagine a particular *niña pobre* wearing my dress. Instead I would picture a thousand girls with my favorite dress. The poor were faceless.

Poverty became scarier when I saw a gardener lining the high wall that surrounded the patio of my grandparents' house with pointy pieces of glass. "It's to keep the *ladrones* out," he said, referring to the young men, poor, of course, who were constantly jumping the walls surrounding our homes. It was common to see, coming home from school in the middle of the day, men running fast through the streets of Riomar with the coconuts, the mangoes, guavas, *guanábanas*, limes, *ciruelas*, and *nísperos* that grew in our backyards. Someone would always be chasing them, screaming furiously: *"Estos pobres son todos unos ladrones."* But it was the same underclass that we mistrusted and feared that kept our families functioning as they had been for decades before I was born.

That afternoon my brother had just yelled his usual *"Me voy"*— "I'm leaving"—when he saw the person asking to see our mother and asked, "Who's looking for her?"

"Malena."

He was taken aback by the harshness of the voice. With her Farrah Fawcett hairdo, the person in front of him looked like someone whose voice would be as soft as the gauzy Indian tunic she was wearing. My brother looked down and saw a pair of delicate feet shod in high-heeled sandals of woven straw and toenails that were perfectly shaped and painted red. The feet were unnaturally long, about a size twelve.

"I'm here to fix her hair."

This was not the first time my brother had seen our mother's

hairdresser come to our home. Whenever Mami had a special occasion, like a last-minute plane to catch or a sudden death in the
community, she liked having her hair done at home, not at the
beauty parlor. But it was understandable that he did not recognize the person standing next to him. This was the first time that
Manlio, whom we had gotten used to having around, had come
to our house dressed as Malena.

Now that he was being sought after by all the high-society
señoras and the *reinas de belleza*, the beauty queens, he was confident enough to show his true—if not genetic—self. He could afford to stop hiding his enlarged breasts under a manly Hawaiian
shirt and keeping his hair pulled back and tied. That was how my
brother knew him. He was financially stable now—he could dare
tell a lady from the ritzy barrios that he was too tired to do her
hair—and finally he was showing off his cleavage. After all, he
had paid enough for the silicone implants, and the synthetic chest
measured up to any of the young *reinas*, many of whom had implants themselves.

Manlio, or Malena as he prefers to be called, is a transvestite.
He is a man with a penis and woman's breasts who dresses in
women's clothes and talks about himself in the feminine gender.
Transvestites feel "like a woman in spite of having a dick between
your legs," as a Puerto Rican transvestite in New York City explained to Dr. Alex Carballo-Diéguez, an Argentine-born psychologist researching sexual behavior among Latino men who have sex
with other men. Transvestites have sex and fall in love mostly
with men—with men who, if asked, most likely would not think
of themselves as homosexual. In Latin America, men who take
the active role in a sexual relationship, meaning that they are the
penetrators, will rarely think of themselves as homosexual.

I asked an epidemiologist in Bogotá if he had an explanation.
He answered by citing a popular phrase: *"Soy tan macho que me
cojo otro hombre."* I am such a macho, I even fuck another man.

Malena is a hairdresser because, apart from prostitution, it is
one of the few careers—cabaret acts being another—available to
men who decide to assume a lifestyle that can be labeled feminine. Malena, like most transvestites, is a man who wears bras
and makeup and who prefers thumbing through the latest fash-

ion magazines to reading about soccer scores and fast cars. Such men want to be courted by a man rather than to court a woman. And they want that man to act as men act—transvestites want macho men, men who think of themselves as heterosexual, men who act like their clients' husbands or suitors.

Transvestites like Malena represent the epitome of femininity, of beauty, of always being well turned out. They act the way my grandmother, my mother, my aunt, my religion teacher wanted me to act—meek, *indefensa*, virginal, and delicate. Madonna, born John Frey Rodríguez Vergara, a nineteen-year-old transvestite in Bogotá, told me of the personal struggle surrounding his decision to go into prostitution—at the age of fifteen. "I wanted to be a good girl. I wanted to wait for the man who would take care of me forever." For a while, Madonna would only service his clients with oral sex, refusing to be anally penetrated because "I was saving myself for the right man," for the man of my dreams.

Beauty is their primary attribute, as it is for women, the asset that will attract that man, a man who resembles the image of macho. Malena has always been as *bien arreglada*—as soignée—as my mother. Today, twenty years later, Malena and my mother both wear the same chignon, the one that rests low on the nape of the neck, favored by elegant Latin ladies when they reach their forties. In their search to become the perfect woman, as shown in the glossy women's magazines like *Vanidades* and *Buenhogar*, transvestites become the perfect connoisseurs of femininity. Transvestites like Malena know more about how to look like Christy Turlington, Princess Caroline of Monaco, and Salma Hayek than most of their clients, probably because they have to start from scratch. They have to turn strong features into soft ones, make beards disappear, create cleavage and shapely legs and swaying hips. The process is painful. A combination of surgery and hormones, either taken by pill or injected, makes body hair fall off, swells the breasts, creates high cheekbones and curves. But it is also unaffordable to most, and it makes them tired, irritable, and depressed. They are willing to compromise pleasure for appearance—often they complain that the hormones make them unable to ejaculate.

Many turn their skill at transformation into the basis for economic independence, knowing that, to survive as a transvestite, their only alternative is prostitution. Their constant studying turns transvestites into the best makeup artists and hairdressers. Transvestites are among the most exclusive and expensive hair stylists not only in Barranquilla but all over Latin America. It is common for women of privilege to have their hair done by them. They know what hair color and what hair style suits each client and, because they are interested in the same things as their clientele, they make the best confidants. This is acceptable to their clients' men as long as it is done outside the private space of family life.

My father did not allow Malena to come back to our house, but I could go to Malena's salon whenever I had an important party to attend, usually a *quinceañero* for which I had to wear a long dress. Feeling the importance of being beautiful—beautiful as seen by our class—I followed all the rules. To be beautiful was to have blue eyes and blond hair, or at least straight hair. Dark curls like mine are too much a sign of mixed breeding, so I dreamt of having hair as straight as spaghetti. "Please make it super-straight, *plánchamelo,*" I would ask Malena as the blow-dryer burnt my ears.

Malena treated me well, I think out of gratitude and respect for my mother, who had been one of his first clients when he had returned from Paris and didn't have steady work at a salon. Eager to build up an important clientele, he came to our home at all hours and on short notice. But as his roster of clients grew, he became less accommodating to my mother's requests, and she complained that now that everyone wanted Manlio—by now everyone called him Malena—to fix them up, he was not doing his job well. This only meant he was no longer available at her beck and call. In less than a year, Manlio was doing better than any of the other hairdressers in Barranquilla. But that was because he had an advantage after he came back from Paris: Paris.

Ladies from Barranquilla want to be as close to Paris as they can get. That Manlio had studied in Paris made them feel they were being coiffed with the celebrated French elegance. That Manlio had attended a third-rate *institut de beauté* while working as a prostitute in the Bois de Boulogne, where most of the working transvestites come from Latin America, was irrelevant. Manlio understood that serving upper-class women meant being their slave—and he understood that, in Barranquilla, Paris is automatically elegant.

While Malena flattened my hair straight and flipped the ends out, I overheard her conversations with the other hairdressers, most of whom were also transvestites or *locas*, men who do not inject hormones but whose manner is very effeminate. *Loca* literally means "crazy," but the colloquial meaning is "queen" or "queer." In Latin America the words for homosexuals—*locas*, *mariposas*, *patos*, or *maricones*—are applied, with disdain and mockery, only to those men who act very feminine. In Latin America none but the very effeminate men are considered homosexuals. In a continent where homophobia can turn into rabid violence, the *locas* do not deny their sexual orientation but wear their homosexuality openly. The word *gay* has just recently started to be incorporated into everyday language and is used by those who are active in gay liberation movements—mainly visible after the advent of AIDS. For the most part, gays are still *maricones*, faggots—and, like transvestites, outcasts.

Malena wore women's clothes and makeup. The *locas* wore androgynous clothing—tight pants, tight or see-through shirts. Their hair was never feminine looking. *Locas* kept their baptismal names and with them their male identities. The transvestites and the *locas* laughed, gossiped, and exchanged beauty secrets as they did our hair. Often they spoke about beauty pageants and passed around photographs. Sometimes I would snatch a glance at the snapshots, and through them I could enter a part of their lives: Malena, wearing a tiara and glittery gown, was carrying a sceptre and looking as regal as any Miss Colombia on the day of her crowning. She was surrounded by other men who, like her, wore fabulous women's evening clothes. In the beauty pageant organized every year by a popular transvestite bar, Malena had been chosen Barranquilla's most beautiful transvestite.

This was my first contact with the transvestite underworld. But as a teenager I was never curious to ask where these beauty competitions took place or who their audience was. Years later I would see them in Bogotá, Panama, Mexico, Rio de Janeiro, São Paulo, New York City. Very few of the women who come to have their hair done, who sit in the same chair as I did and see the photographs being passed around, are curious enough to want to know who transvestites really are, what makes them tick, what makes them want to be as beautiful and as feminine as they are.

If they did, they would discover that they and the transvestites are interested in exactly the same men—and that, in fact, some of the very men for whom they are getting their hair straightened and lightened are themselves interested in men like Malena who wear skirts and have cocks. If women in Barranquilla activated their sexual antennas, they would understand that they might very well be competing for the same men. Transvestites want to be as feminine as their clients. They want to be beauty queens and *señoras de sociedad*. The hands plucking their clients' eyebrows and dying their hair do it so well because the owners of those hands dream of having their clients' lives. They too want to be taken care of by a powerful and successful man. They want to spend their days like the señoras they beautify before sending them off to cocktails, weddings, husbands, and beautiful homes. For the live performances at the bar where Malena won the beauty title, transvestites take on the names of Mexican soap-opera actresses, million-dollar models, and Hollywood stars. And they also appear on the catwalk as their clients. Malena, for example, could have chosen to be Dionne Warwick or my mother.

As a joke or as an insult?

Gustavo Turizo, a conceptual artist in Barranquilla who has done a whole series of installations in celebration of transvestites and as a challenge to expose men's sexual interest in them, says that it is neither: "That's their dream. They act it out because they know that they will never be able to be like them. Their dream is to be a *niña bien*, an upper-class girl."

The day that Manlio showed up at our house as Malena, wearing a shirt that exposed his overgrown nipples, my father found it disrespectful and told my mother that he could return only if he dressed as a man. I don't remember if he came back, but for my brother that encounter became a favorite anecdote. When he tells the story, he imitates Malena's femininity. By mocking the moment, he makes Malena become faceless, and thus acceptable. We treat Malena the same way we treat *los pobres*. As a class, we assert our control and set limits on when, how much, and how often anything threatening—poverty or transvestite hairdressers—can be allowed inside our fragile Latin Camelot.

My father would allow Manlio in as long as he resembled a man. Being our mother's hairdresser, he was treated as one of the help. We, the owners of the houses, the rulers of the city, the keepers of the social mores, had the power to define their identities. Manlio is allowed in, Malena is not. Just as my mother changed the name of one of her servants because she didn't like it, my father could decide what shirt Malena could wear to fix my mother's hair.

Husband and wife both understand that transvestites—like the poor who work for us—are essential for traditional family life. Upper-class Latin women need servants to keep a home and need hairdressers to keep up their appearances. That the best hairdressers happen to be transvestites or *locas* is one of the few things men cannot control, as they cannot control poverty. They try hard, however, to control the level of interaction. Transvestites, like the poor, need to be kept out of the home. The men do not care who fixes their wives' hair as long as they don't have to bump into them inside their carefully decorated houses.

A few years ago, a lovers' quarrel between two *locas* left the ladies of Sincelejo, a small Colombian city, without their favorite hairdresser. Rafael Contreras, the hair doyenne of this provincial town, was accused of murdering his lover and assistant David Sierra. As David lay on the sidewalk dying, a pair of scissors stuck in his jugular, he screamed, "Rafael killed me, Rafael killed me." Contreras spent a week in the hospital; he too had been wounded in the fight. During his stay, his room overflowed with flower arrangements sent by all his clients—the ladies with influential husbands.

The hairdresser was convicted of murder and is serving a long prison sentence. But his clients can still have their hair fixed by their favorite hands. There was so much pressure from the local honchos, whose desperate wives needed to tend to their tresses, that the prison director had to allow for them to come to have their hair done inside the prison. From ten to six, Contreras's prison cell is a beauty salon complete with a wall-to-wall mirror, a washbasin, a purple and yellow beauty chair, and posters of women with elaborate hairdos on the grimy walls. His assistant, convicted of robbing a jewelry store, washes the ladies' hair, and Contreras keeps making them happy. "And they, the beautified ladies of Sincelejo," writes Colombian journalist Ernesto McCausland in *The Beauty Cell*, his chronicle of this case, "assure you that they feel no fear when Rafael Contreras slides his sharp hair-cutting scissors close to their necks."

McCausland's story makes my point. To them, Contreras is not seen as a murderer, because they have never seen him as an individual. He is staff. Cooks cook, maids clean, *nanas* take care of their children, and transvestites or *locas* fix their hair. The help are just that, help, people devoid of any complexity of personality. Contreras will only be seen as the faithful and indispensable servant.

To the wealthy *patronas*, the servants, especially maids and homosexual hairdressers, are also eunuchs. Malena and Contreras are sexless—just like Elda, Ludis, María, or any of our maids who slept in a room lined with single cots, as in a convent. The señoras always say how they prefer hiring spinsters. They make the best maids: They concentrate on their work and are not always asking for permission to go out after work like the young ones. It is different for the male servants. José, the gardener, was never around after seven. His job ended the minute he opened the garage door for my father coming home from work. It resumed the next morning at dawn when he had to get up to turn on the water heater so that we would have hot water for our showers before school. This way, the *patrón* would keep the sexuality of the servants outside the home. But in this tacit agreement, menservants were given the space they needed to have a sexual life, and women were denied it. The gender rules of the rich are applied to the poor, at least in appearance. Much was spoken about José's many girlfriends, who included a number of the maids on the block. In fact, my mother had to finally fire him after a second maid in the barrio claimed she was also pregnant by him.

When Manlio comes in as sultry Malena, the traditional gender roles, the foundation on which Latin America's society stands, tremble. Husbands understand that women have their beauty needs and that they go and have their hair done by transvestites or *locas*, even in prison cells. But their acceptance of them stops there. If the women were never curious about the sexual lives of their hairdressers, for men it just might be too much of an open parading of a hidden sexual behavior that is accepted only outside the home. As hairdressers they are helpers, as transvestites inside one's home they are transgressors. Like the poor who are viewed with mistrust when they walk the streets of the rich barrios, and the *roba cocos* who get chased down for taking the coconuts we will never eat, transvestites are kept outside the bougainvilleaed and sharded high walls.

Whether as confidants to society ladies who rely on their talents as beauticians or as important figures in the fantasia of the festivities of Carnival, transvestites are as ubiquitous, and as integral to our lives, as the poor. In Barranquilla, in Rio de Janeiro, or in any place that celebrates Carnival, transvestites and men in drag dance every year in all their regalia in front of the city's mayor, the governor, the bishop, the business elite and their families. As faceless Carnivalesque creatures, they are amusing and somewhat accepted. Still, like the poor and the homosexual hairdressers, they are assigned their place: They can drink and dance and exhibit their breasts and muscular legs like everybody else, but until 1998, they were not officially accepted in the institutionalized festivities. It was stipulated in the decree of Barranquilla's Carnival that homosexuals were not allowed to participate in the grand Batalla de Flores, the official parade that opens the three days of uninterrupted and uninhibited celebration. They danced around anyway, but outside.

In 1995 a group of gays, in one of their first forays into political activism, asked to be recognized and included in the Flower Parade. This past Marteo de Carnaval, the first *gay* float paraded behind the long line of *carrozas*. But in an almost uncannily perfect metaphor, it stalled, breaking down before parading up the main avenue. Their effort is commendable and the openmindedness of the Comité del Carnaval is surprising, but the straight men who label themselves defenders of gay rights do so in ways that are as discriminatory as when politicians claim they have nothing against women in government because it is so nice to be entertained by their beauty during their boring meetings. "One needs to understand their weaknesses," says City Council member Orlando Rodríguez, explaining why he favors gay participation in the parade. "After all, it is by wearing costumes that they can exteriorize their aberration." Archbishop Félix María Torres says that "we have to respect them, but without giving social importance to an abnormal situation."

Knowing that this is how they are treated, I was surprised to see a transvestite at Barranquilla's inauguration of its first art-film house. The city's establishment, *la sociedad,* was present in all its splendor. Speeches were given by the ministers of communications and education. The important men of the city, sweating under their long-sleeved shirts, shaking their glasses with the iced *whiskicito,* their wives dressed in starched linen and stiff hairdos, toasted the pioneering efforts to introduce a film culture to the city. Mingling in with impudence was an unusual-looking couple, so unusual that it was hard to miss them. Towering over the man, in a tuxedo, was a platinum-haired woman at least six feet tall.

The couple walked over to say hello to the friend I was talking to, and they both kissed her cheek. Like me, the statuesque woman was dressed in white silk, except her dress showed a deeper décolleté smothered in silvery threads. Her eyes and lips were heavily delineated with shiny makeup. Up close, her gender was obvious. I shook a glittery glove that went up to the elbow. The handshake was that of a stevedore.

"John Pantoja," she said.

"Nice to meet you," I responded.

She remarked on the similarity of our dresses, describing me as a nymph, which flattered me, but then her teasing wordplay turned nymph into nymphomaniac. I was amused by her antics, by her need to shock.

When the couple moved on to mingle with as many of the

guests in the open courtyard as possible, my friend explained to me that the "couple" was part of Gustavo Turizo's installation on transvestites. He had been showing up at social events accompanied by transvestites. John Pantoja, the most masculine-looking Marilyn Monroe I have ever encountered, took his part seriously, prancing around introducing himself with the airs of a leading lady on premiere night. Some of the guests smiled with the lofty tolerance displayed when seeing something amusing yet a little vulgar or ridiculous. But mostly *la sociedad* smirked with disapproval. The consensus was that Gustavo Turizo had gone a bit too far with this transvestite folly.

After all, this was not the first time he had tried to shock traditional society. That had started at the opening of his show "The Most Beautiful Women in the World Are Men." The show included life-size paintings of transvestites, some almost seven feet tall. "I wanted to make sure people did not confuse them with anything other than what they were, men dressed in women's clothes. I made sure I gave them huge muscles, big wigs, the highest heels, a big thing between their legs. I didn't want anyone coming in saying they were just big women, or *marimachas*, tomboys. No one could fail to see that it was the painting of a transvestite."

To the opening of the exhibition he invited his muses and his models. John Pantoja was the most important of them. Inviting them to an art gallery was acceptable. Art galleries are neutral spaces where a certain amount of stretching of the rules is allowed. Turizo then decided to take Pantoja to impersonate Grace Jones at the inauguration cocktail party of Comfamiliar, the city's main lending institution. Even that had been considered amusing. Important men have always been entertained by buffoons. But who ever thought of allowing jesters to assume equal footing with the kings as John Pantoja was doing that night? Who would dream of inviting a man with a tall platinum wig and exposed breasts into the same room as ministers and important members of the community? Pantoja could be a performer, not a guest. What was he doing acting as if he was part of *la buena sociedad*? Offended, society labeled Turizo's act an *atrevimiento*: How dare he. Most agreed it was *una falta de respeto*.

"I wanted to demystify the image these people have of trans-vestites," says Turizo. "I wanted to give them a place, especially a place in society, to have them stop being dolls in the shows of their underworld where few outsiders know who they really are—those few who go to the clubs and maybe two or three of the clients they coif, but only those who they feel they can invite, that would dare go to the clubs."

Turizo inadvertently ended his career as a sexual integrationist when he organized an event for the inauguration of the new home of the Alliance Française. It was a typical drag show, per-formers dressed as divas lip-synching to music. John Pantoja did Edith Piaf and a duo of mulattos sang the sexy Caribbean music of Azúcar Morena. The surprise was reserved for the end. Turizo had brought the biggest, burliest transvestite he could find, not sophisticated like Malena or John Pantoja but "a member of the underworld of the underworld," a transvestite hired from the low-rent clubs of downtown Barranquilla who did an amazing version of "Don't Cry for Me, Argentina." The audience's heavy clapping overexcited the performer. To him, it was already the most im-portant day of his life as a transvestite—to be performing for such powerful people, to be dancing in front of the rulers of the city. In an effort to give more to his audience, to the people whose recognition he valued so much, he began peeling the blue chiffon skirt of its many layers. One by one, each of the scarves came off, and his dancing became more erotic, his pelvic thrusts more ex-aggerated as he stripped to a bare G-string. The applause turned into a horrified silence as the performer began making signals of proposition to the men in the audience. That was the end of Turizo's work. He had dared bring the enemy into space reserved only for the respectables.

But that was exactly what he had intended. He wanted to take them to places where people would never expect to see them. He wanted to take them first into the halls of power and then to the movie theaters, the supermarkets, the open markets, and the business sector—"to the common world where they are used to people making fun of them, or screaming at them that they are the scum of the earth." Turizo hoped to break down some of the latent and virulent homophobia of our city. But the task was beyond his pioneering efforts.

Excluding transvestites from officialdom is common throughout Latin America. When President Guillermo Endara of Panamá learned that his culture minister was planning a Festival de Travestis at the pristine National Theater, the pride and joy of Panama's cultural elite, he was incensed. "How dare he think that he would be able to have an act of this nature in the same place where I gave decorations to the magistrates of the Electoral Tribunal? I will send in the National Police. I will not permit the theatre to be converted into a pigsty of homosexuals."

As with the poor, transvestites are good when they work for us, when we have the control and the power, dangerous when not. As individuals they are invisible, scorned and segregated. As hairdressers, Carnival curiosities, subjects of an artist's work, they are accepted as long as they can be contained, as long as they play by the unspoken rules. As anything else, as streetwalkers, as intruders in traditional places, as individuals, they are harassed, mocked, and often beaten—sometimes to death.

If having a transvestite fix my hair was as much a part of my teenage years as listening to Barry White's sexual moanings while being told that sex was not for a girl like me, transvestites were also a part of teenage boys' outings. To them, they were the men in dresses and heels who stood a few steps away from their favorite hangout, and whom they had to be careful not to mistake for the female prostitutes they would sometimes pay for sex.

"You could get confused and instead of stopping for a *puta*, you could be in for a big surprise," my longtime friend Beto from Barranquilla admitted to me in a long conversation we recently had about sex as teenagers.

We had been on the phone—he in California, and I in New York—for more than an hour. I had called to ask if he would be willing to explain to me what his sexual initiation had been like. Beto and I knew each other well in Barranquilla. He was a classmate, a soccer teammate, and a nighttime buddy of my boyfriend at the time. I hadn't seen him, or spoken to him, since then. Like me, he had come to college in America and stayed on. He is a successful architect, with an American wife and two sons, ten and six.

I thought that because he has been living in the United States as long as I have, it would be easy for him to talk to me about the rites of passage of a Latin American boy. Beto, I thought, would be the voice of all the boys I knew then. I called him at his office and explained.

"Hold on, let me close the door," he said.

He was willing to participate. These are issues, he told me, that he himself confronts every day. "The last thing I want," he tells me, "is for my boys' first sexual experience to be with a prostitute. Like mine was."

He was thirteen, the youngest member of the school's tennis team. On a tournament trip, his host, an older boy, announced that the team would be going to a brothel that Friday night. Beto was petrified, he tells me, but he also knew that a real man, a macho, never says no to going to the prostitutes. From that day on, he returned often.

"What about the money?" I asked. "How did you pay for it?"

"Like we all did," he says. "Papi."

"Would you ask him directly? My God, weren't you embarrassed?"

He laughs. "I remember one Friday night, we were all finishing dinner—my mother, my sister, my brothers, my father, and myself. I was about fifteen and I put on my most grown-up, manly voice and asked my dad if I could see him alone after dinner. I needed to talk to him about something important, I said."

Beto didn't have to explain any further. His father knew exactly what his son wanted. With pride, he walked Beto to the door and handed him a huge bill.

"Easier than to ask him for money to take your girlfriend on a date," I joked.

Beto's laugh signaled his agreement.

"So until when did you have paid sex? Did you have sex with your girlfriend of those days?"

"No way," he shrieked.

"Why?" I asked.

"Oh, come on, you know why. You guys were the good girls,

the virgins we were supposed to marry." I could sense he was feeling comfortable talking about this, and I was appreciating his candor. I also noticed that, like me, Beto was speaking in English. It felt easier to talk about sex in our new language, the language that has given us education, adulthood, and different social mores.

"But did you want to?"

"No, not really."

"Really?" I asked, although I believed him.

"Now that you ask, I don't think it ever even crossed my mind. It was just something that was not possible."

"And it wasn't possible because we wouldn't let it happen?"

"No," he said. "We wouldn't want it to happen either."

Plus, it was not as if they were not having sex. As a matter of fact, they were having lots of it. They were having it with the prostitutes over at Estela Reyes's, where it was common for them to see their fathers, their uncles, and their classmates. As I heard someone refer to the madam, she did away with the virginity of a whole generation. They were having it with the *numeritos*, the little numbers they called them, those girls who, while not prostitutes, did not go to our schools or belong to the club or have a good last name, but did go to discotheques and danced with them tight in the darkness of El Gusano. It was okay to have sex with the little numbers—"That's what they were for," Beto confesses. They were not *niñas bien* like us, their girlfriends. The boys would never marry them, so there was no virginity for them to protect.

I was enjoying having my first conversation about sex with a boy from Barranquilla, but I also had an agenda. I needed to know what role transvestites played in Beto's life. "You also picked up prostitutes on the street?" I asked. "You know, like the *putas de la setenta y dos*."

My question was a bit dishonest. I wanted to understand how close transvestites were to their sex lives. I knew Seventy-second was the street corner prostitutes and transvestites shared.

"Sure," he said, reminding me that by the time they were sixteen, he and his friends had cars and a prostitute allowance.

"Did you ever run across any transvestites?" I asked, getting a little nervous.

"Oh sure," he said with a boisterous laugh. "Yeah, once, we stopped—I was with your boyfriend—and we stopped to pick up some girls and this big red dress and big blond wig walked over to the car window and then in the hoarsest voice said: 'And what can I do for you boys today?' God, we got so scared, we just took off."

Beto had just confirmed how present transvestites were in his and his friends' sexual initiation; he had also confirmed my suspicion that my boyfriend who told me that touching my breasts was "for when we are married" had sex with prostitutes. But a question remained: If prostitutes and transvestites hang out on the same corner, is it because they share the same clients? I couldn't muster the courage to ask it. I hung up telling him that I would call him back, but realized that it was not fair to put him on the spot. He had opened up as far as he could have, and that was much more than I could ask a man who was raised to believe that to turn a boy into a macho meant taking him to a brothel.

In Panama, where I spent time in my early twenties, I heard my friends tell stories much like the ones Beto had just told me. They would speak openly about their good times at Maxim's and Le Palace, the striptease joints, really brothels, smack in the middle of our conservative and fancy neighborhoods. Although my friend Jaime had a steady girlfriend, he was unfaithful and frequently picked up prostitutes. He told me of one night when he and a friend picked up two prostitutes on the street, nothing uncommon, and took them back to Jaime's house. Only the maids were there. His parents were traveling—his father held a ministerial post and they were always away. Jaime swiped two bottles of Dom Pérignon from his father's private stock and offered one to his friend. He lent him one of the many bedrooms in the house and disappeared with his "date" into his room.

On his bed with the striped sheets that his mother had bought in Miami, he caressed the prostitutes' nipples and noticed the hardness of her breasts. They felt like baseballs. Fake, he thought, moving his hands away, exploring lower. The abdomen was unusually tight and the legs spread out on his bed, once revealed, seemed stronger than his own. His hand kept descending until it felt the bulge he was, by now, almost expecting. Furious and humiliated, and probably very scared, Jaime jumped.

His gold and enamel Cartier alarm clock reminded him it was already dawn. This meant that the armed vigilante outside in the front yard would still be keeping guard. He yelled out the man's name. The watchman came running in. Together they kicked the transvestite out. The guard used his wooden stick. Jaime threatened him with the .38 Magnum he kept in his walk-in closet, underneath a pile of about ten pairs of unworn Fiorucci jeans.

Jaime told me this story shortly after it happened, but I was not shocked by it. Picking up a prostitute was acceptable not only to him but to me. That this time he had run into a transvestite just added a piquant twist to the ordinary story of boys going to brothels.

It was also with him and with his friend Raul that I would drive around Panama City on Fridays and Saturdays. One of our favorite pastimes was to pile into Raul's tiny sportscar. Raul would sometimes announce that we were going to "pay a visit to the mamis" and would head, with four or five of us squashed in the back, to the Avenida de los Mártires, the four-lane highway that divided the Panama Canal Zone from the rest of the city. To the Panamians, it is the Avenida de los Mártires; to the Americans, it is known as the Fourth of July. On the Panamanian side, the avenue gave access to the city's red-light district, strategically positioned across the street from United States territory. American military personnel stationed in Panama and seamen in transit just needed to stroll over to the other side. The army barracks, the manicured green lawns, the Officers' Club gave way to the seedy underworld of Panama's strip joints.

The Ancón Inn, Raul would tell us, was the most popular with the gringos. "They love to come here. The girls here are definitely the prettiest, but then the gringos end up falling in love and marry them. They even take them back to the States with them," he would say, mystified. He and his friends had been going to prostitutes since they started wearing a jacket and tie to attend *quinceañeros*, and none, none of them, would ever consider marrying a girl from the brothel.

But his dismayed interest in gringos marrying low-class strippers was not as strong as his fascination with the transvestites who stood on every corner of the highway that divided the sex zone from the Canal Zone. As we approached the handful of men dressed in extravagant clothes, Raul would slow his car, honk the horn, and blink the lights.

"Pssst, hey *mami, ven acá,*" he would say, sticking his head out the window. But as soon as one of them made any move toward the car, Raul would yell out, *"Maricón!"* and accelerate the car so fast that the screech of tires drowned our roaring laughter. We thought it was hilarious. It was so much fun to make fun of transvestites. It never crossed my mind that our idle game had left a human being with feelings, humiliated and angry. As we saw it, it was our right as the children of those with power to have fun at the expense of whomever we chose.

Raul chose the transvestites. Today, I wonder what his fascination—and the latent violence—with the transvestites was all about. For me, they were like the *putas* that my boyfriend was having sex with but whom I never connected with sex, perhaps because, although I had a boyfriend, I never connected him with sex either. Transvestites to me, the ones on the street or the ones blow-drying my hair, were curiosities, like the *zeburro*, the cross between the zebra and the donkey at Barranquilla's zoo.

Now I see a different picture. When I see John Pantoja dressed as Marilyn Monroe, I see him as someone who is brave not to hide who he has chosen to be regardless of the discrimination, the humiliation, and the danger brought by displaying his chosen identity. He has assumed his fantasy and he lives it openly.

In the catalogue for "The Most Beautiful Women in the World Are Men" Turizo writes: "Transvestitism is not a trend. It is a form of life. I do not promote it, I only discover it. It is gallantry and style, survival and self-confirmation. It is dreams of fame, success, and beauty. It is a fantasy lived in ferocious splendor. Transvestites don't have blue blood or crowns but they are as pretentious as those who do. They are the New Queens," he says, alluding in double entendre to the obsessive importance our society gives to beauty queens. "That's why everyone, even the most muscular man, after seeing them, wants to be like them."

They are more honest with themselves than the society that shuns them. They are, after all, just one part of the equation. If one looked for the other side of the coin, what would one find? Who is attracted to John Pantoja dressed as Marilyn Monroe? Who wants to feel Pantoja's manly body disguised as female? Transvestites are not isolated individuals, as they are presented, who like to inject themselves with feminine hormones and change their names to Lucía Mendez, Madonna, or Tyra Banks. Somewhere out there, there is a segment of the population that searches for the man with a penis, enlarged breasts, and a man's ass. During my teens and twenties it never crossed my mind to ask who they were. Like most Latin women, I would probably have spent the rest of my life without seeing them as individuals, without realizing who it is they dress for, and without asking who appreciates the cock and the ass of the man under the skirt.

The first thing I noticed when I started asking myself the question was how obvious and ubiquitous transvestites are in Latin American everyday life. And they are not there to fulfill the sexual fantasies of eccentrics, weirdos, as society—especially women—suppose. The fact is that they are there to service "normal" men: the man who works at a factory; the man who attends business meetings and church; the man with wife and kids. "I have a client who comes around on Sundays pushing a stroller," a teenage male prostitute tells me in Bogotá, "usually around lunchtime. He leaves the baby and his wife at the restaurant and comes to me while they eat."

Are there more transvestites working as prostitutes in the streets of Quito than in Chicago, more in Rio de Janeiro than in New York City? I have been unable to find any statistics. I doubt they exist. Can I say that transvestites are more present in the everyday life of Latin America than in the United States, or that most transvestites come from Latin America? According to the *New York Times*, most of the transvestites in Rome come from South America. The Brazilian transvestites in the Bois de Boulogne in Paris—regarded as the most beautiful in the world—are legendary.

All of a sudden, they were easy to spot. I saw a pack of them in Quito, Ecuador, as I drove back from my sister's wedding dinner at two in the morning on a Saturday. Six men in Lycra miniskirts paraded down the Avenida 6 de Diciembre, one of the city's main streets, the equivalent of New York's Fifth Avenue around Rockefeller Center and St. Patrick's and Saks. I also drove past them as I went down the narrow roads of Bogotá's downtown on a Sunday morning, on my way to the flea market held next to the bullring—young men, mostly teenagers, wearing skirts, with their hair disheveled and their makeup smeared, walking back to the seven-dollar-a-day rooms they call home after a night of work. In São Paulo, tabloids display the picture of Roberta Close, Brazil's most famous transvestite, linking her with former president Fernando Collor de Mello. I saw transvestites on street corners in a Latin neighborhood in Jackson Heights, Queens, and in clandestine cabaret shows in Havana, Cuba. In rural Mexico, even the small towns have a bar where a transvestite will serve both drinks and sex to the macho ranchers who stop by. Today, when I am driving back to my parents' house in Bogotá after a night out with friends, I pass them at 82nd Street and 15th Avenue, and then on the Pepe Sierra, and then again on 115th. And I immediately wonder who will stop to buy pleasure from them. Anyone I know?

I now know that the paying customer is *un macho*, a straight man, a man-man, a married man, an old man, a young man—a man who would never admit to it. I asked men surreptitiously and they all answered obliquely, making references to jokes or to passages in literature. No one has admitted to me that he has had sex with a transvestite. The closest I got was listening to stories like Jaime's or Beto's—of touching one by mistake, of being tricked into thinking he was fondling a woman.

My question—why are there so many transvestites working in prostitution if no man seems to want to pay to have sex with them—remained unanswered. I needed not only to explore the idea that a man who fucks another man is more of a macho, but to confirm that it is widely held. The answer became integral for understanding my sexual culture and the added risk that this unspoken behavior brought to women. On the psychological and emotional level, it meant that relations between men and women were laced with a new element of deceptive behavior. If a husband told his wife that he was out drinking, he could also be having sex with a prostitute—female or male. The wife might suspect infidelity with a woman but never with a man. On the physiological level, this left many wives at high risk of contracting the HIV virus.

As I was not getting answers from the men, I went and asked the transvestites themselves: Who stops when you are standing so openly on these corners?

Claudia was the first transvestite I met in Brazil. She—I will refer to Claudia in the feminine because that's how Claudia refers to herself—was standing under a bright streetlamp on the main avenue of Lapa, a working-class neighborhood on the fringes of downtown Rio de Janeiro. I could have chosen to go to Copacabana, where transvestites are as beautiful and glamorous as James Bond's escorts and as uncensored as the tourist industry expects them to be. Instead I decided to talk to the transvestites who serve, not the foreign tourists who pay in dollars or the rich Brazilians, but the men of the middle and of the urban lower class—men who seem to be more attached to traditional gender norms and yet are consumers of the same underworld of sex.

It was a rainy Saturday night, two-thirty in the morning. With the American photographer who was working with me, I walked up to her. Brian and I were both nervous. He thought the transvestites would get violent if he tried to photograph them. "They might throw rocks, take away my camera," he told me when I explained what I wanted to do. Brian is a robust man with the arms and pecs of an ex-Marine. He fought in Vietnam, and as a photojournalist in Brazil he has covered riots in shantytowns, police violence toward street children, the struggles of human rights workers with cattle ranchers in the Amazon. Yet he felt that to talk to the transvestites of Lapa it was prudent to hire a bodyguard. For twenty dollars, we hired Bruno, a cop on his day off, to protect us.

I was nervous for different reasons. I knew I wanted to ask questions that would be difficult to articulate. I was going to ask very intrusive questions, questions about sex—who pays you, what do your clients want, do they just want to penetrate you, do you wear condoms, do you think of yourself as a man or as a woman? My

Portuguese is limited. Brian's is perfect. I asked him if he would serve as my translator whenever I got stuck. Brian was not enjoying this assignment; if it weren't for the money he would have bailed out. He might even have felt a little tricked. I had told him I was working on a story about AIDS. He probably thought it only meant photographing people dying in hospitals.

The taxi drove around the boulevard a few times and I saw transvestites standing on almost every corner. I was excited: "Look, there's one—oh my God, look at that one—Brian, check that one out, can you photograph her?"

I noticed I was the only one excited in the car. The taxi driver and Bruno, our bodyguard, were confused. Brian had to assure them that I really was a journalist, that this was strictly work.

We stepped out of the car a few blocks away from the streetwalkers. Brian decided it was best to leave the cameras in the car and instructed the car to wait for us at a discreet corner.

As we approached Claudia, her interest was definitely on Brian. I knew my chances of getting an interview were better if I let him explain.

"We are journalists," he said in Portuguese. "I am a photographer and she would like to ask you some questions. Is it okay, will you talk to her?" he said, pointing at me.

"Will she pay?"

I shook my head no.

"Questions about what?"

"About your life?"

"Okay," she said, smiling at me for the first time. "It's a slow night. The last Saturday of the month, clients are out of money. But if they are coming, they will start arriving soon and I will have to go." She tapped her wristwatch. "By now, clients are drunk enough to stop their cars."

"Who stops?" I ventured.

"Oh, *homems casados*," she said without giving it a thought. "Mostly married men who don't think they are gay," continued Claudia. Her real name was Claudio. She was eighteen and started working the streets two years before. She didn't hesitate for a second. This seemed too easy. I joked with Brian, telling him he must have coached her on what to say in order to get the interview over with.

"What do they look like, these men?"

"Como homems, como homems normales."

"Really, like normal men? Why do they come to you?" I asked. I noticed how beautiful she was. She had black curls that came down to her exposed midriff, and her black Lycra miniskirt and her knee-high black suede boots showed off taut and long legs that I envied.

"We are better than the wife." Claudia then boasted that most of her clients—an average of ten a night—are regulars. "I give them what they want."

"What is it that they want?" I asked Brian to ask her. "Ask him if they mostly want to be active."

"What do you need to know that for?"

"Just ask."

"Fuck."

"Come on, man, it's an interview."

"Que querem os clientes?" Brian mumbled, looking down at his black hi-top Nikes. Never, not in a million years, he later told me, did he think he would ever be asking this question.

"What do you mean what do they want?" asked Claudia, flirting with it.

I needed to know if most clients preferred being passive or being active—the passive clients wanting to be penetrated, the active ones wanting to penetrate. According to my research, most men want to be penetrators. I elbowed Brian, pleading. "Please?"

"Ativos?" Brian asked.

Claudia flashed a coy smile. *"Ativos, sim."*

"Thank you, Brian. The rest is easy. Ask her if would she tell us about her life?"

She works Tuesday through Saturday. Sundays and Mondays she goes to the beach and rests. She enjoys her work and she is able to make more money than her father, who works as a mechanic. She lives with her parents. Her life is fun, she said.

"Do they know what you do?"

"A-ha," she said, tilting her head and resting her hand on her right hip. "I help them out."

"Are you always in women's clothes?"

"A-ha." The head tilted the other way. She has breakfast with her parents in a negligee every morning, she said. As a matter of fact, she only wears men's clothes on two occasions: To go to an aunt's who refuses to let Claudio visit in women's clothes, and to vote. Claudia opened a small leather bag and handed me an ID card. In the photo, Claudia has short hair, a two-day stubble, and delicate features.

"Are you this man?"

"No. *Sou Claudia.*"

"When did you know you were Claudia?" I asked, feeling like Oprah.

He told us that when he was twelve, his fourteen-year old cousin "seduced" him. His mother found them.

"Is your cousin a transvestite?" I asked.

Claudia laughed.

"Is he gay?"

"He's married."

With her seductive and studied smile, Claudia begged me to ask. It felt as if one of my closest girlfriends were teasing, ready to blurt out the confession that would make us both hold our stomachs from laughing. I took the cue.

"Do you still see him?"

"Claro."

"Do you still fuck?" I asked, surprised at how blunt I could be, how easy and how relieving it was to leave behind the language of the good girl forbidden to talk about sex. As a journalist talking to transvestites and prostitutes, taking notes, I can ask anything.

"Claro."

Of course.

"Obrigada," I said and walked away with a sure smile. I thought it would be more difficult than that.

Feeling a little triumphant and a little distrustful of Claudia's answer—I cannot argue my case with one testimony and the boulevard is packed with possible interviewees—I tell Brian we should go talk to others.

He tries to back out by telling me he is nervous about leaving his camera behind with those guys. "They might just take off," he says, hoping his tactic will persuade me to stop. "Anyway, I think their time is up. They're going to start charging us extra."

"We'll pay them extra," I say, completely mesmerized by the sight at the next corner.

A tall silhouette is opening a white see-through chemise, exposing perfectly round breasts and a bulge in a black G-string. I notice the same suede boots Claudia wears, except hers have fringe. In spite of the heat, knee-length black boots seem to be the preferred footwear among transvestites of the tropics.

"Wasn't that enough?" he asks.

"No."

Marcela Playboy is as loud as her outfit. As soon as she sees us, she starts dancing vigorously. She is thrilled when I open my notepad. Marcela is twenty-seven. She has worked the street for ten years, starting when she first moved to Rio from Minas Gerais, where it was too hard to be herself. Prostitution is the only type of work she has ever done. Marcela is seasoned and it shows. As she talks to me, she also keeps her eye on the cars going by. Her body language never stops inviting customers to stop. I notice a red Fiat go by for the second time.

"Client?" I ask.

"He'll stop eventually, but he'll drive by at least two more times." Marcela is sure about her speculation.

I ask about prices and about condoms—this time with little help from Brian. Marcela understands my Portugnol, which is mostly Spanish words spoken with what I think Portuguese sounds like. She also knows basic English, especially when talking about negotiating prices. Marcela works many nights in the streets of Copacabana. She can also say how much a blow job costs in German, French, and Italian.

"Fifteen dollars for oral, thirty if it's complete. But if I'm in Copa it's at least double." She says she uses condoms, talks about the need to protect herself from AIDS and about how she will get mad and leave if a client refuses to use them. When I ask her if she has condoms with her, she says, "Sure," but refuses to show them to me. I doubt she has any.

The red Fiat stops. A man with a beard, a man probably in his early forties, a man wearing a white button-down shirt, a man who I would guess is a government bureaucrat or a midlevel executive, a man who I would assume has a wife and at least two children. The man offers her a ride home.

"He's too embarrassed to accept that what he really wants is to *transar* with me," says Marcela as she waves and blows us a kiss good-bye. *Transar* means to fuck.

I am not ready to call it a night, so I walk over to the transvestite with long blond hair and cowboy boots. With her red miniskirt and the white leather bustier under the open blue-jean jacket, Beth looks more like a Dallas Cowboys cheerleader than the Brazilian male he is. I start with the same question I posed to Claudia and to Marcela. Beth's answer is more elaborate.

"My clients," she says, "are not only married but the majority are fathers." Beth has a certain sophistication that the other two didn't. The voice is elegant, the language more educated.

"Do they tell you they are?"

"They don't have to. The wedding ring says everything. They also tend to be very nervous. They're afraid someone will see them."

"Why do you think they come to see you?"

"Because they are missing something at home. I am a complete woman," she says as she grabs her hair, twists it, and puts it up, securing it in place with a makeup pencil.

Beth talks about how she has a boyfriend, someone who was a regular client, a married man who broke up with his wife and is now asking her to live with him. He even wants her to have a sex change operation. As she says this, I realize that there are many types of relationships between transvestites and their partners. Not all clients want to be active. Marcela Playboy told me that many start by saying they only want to fuck her, but that sometimes the tables are turned. And Beth now tells me that she met a client, a man that loves her, a man that makes her happy, a man that wants her to be more of a woman. Sex, passion, love is a tree of many colors, of many branches; a tree that gives many shades. Transvestites bring out the most recondite shades—the good, the bad, the perverse, the tender—of men one would never suspect, of men who are described by one transvestite as "not fat, not old—middle-aged, good-looking guys, just like doctors and things like that."

Male prostitution in Latin America is of a different kind from that of Christopher Street, the Castro, or any of the other U.S. gay districts. One does not see macho-looking men working Latin American street corners. No Chippendale-like dancers, no men in leather and chains, no men who spend hours working out in gyms. Instead, one sees transvestites, or very young and very effeminate teenagers. These are boys who have been on the streets from an early age, as soon as they were abandoned, kicked out, or simply found no other escape from abuse than the street. These are boys who survived by sniffing glue, eating scraps from garbage cans, sleeping on benches, on steps, in corners, under a light so as not to be stepped on. The lives of these boys is short. They die early from drugs or disease, or from violence. Surely, some simply die of sadness from being abandoned—as a pigeon would without its mother nestling it until it can fly. Those who make it to be teenagers know that they can always resort to prostitution to survive. There will always be a man proposing to buy them a hot meal, to give them the equivalent of five dollars or ten dollars or twenty dollars in exchange for sex. But as I would discover later, being eight or nine does not keep these boys from being asked by the same men for sex either. As it turns out, they are as coveted as the teen-age effeminate boys at the Terrazas Pasteur, or as Marcela Playboy. Furthermore, they are bought for less and, being the defenseless creatures they are, they are less likely to rob their clients of their wallets or scream loud if something goes wrong. They are dazed from the fumes of glue; they are hungry; they are tiny.

AIDS has exposed this behavior—men having paid sex with children. Organizations have been formed to work with street children who are greatly exposed to AIDS. I attended the Second Conference on Street Children and the Prevention of STD/AIDS in Rio de Janeiro in 1991. There I met a Dutchman running an AIDS-prevention organization that teaches street children how to negotiate safe sex. When I visited his office, he was proudly wearing a T-shirt showing a street kid masturbating on a park bench with a condom on. He was getting ready to go with his assistant, a former prostitute and now social worker and student of psychology, to hand out condoms to the homeless boys who often exchange sex in back alleys, cars, and motel rooms for food, a shower, or the equivalent of a few dollars.

In Colombia the experience of AIDS-prevention outreach is similar and has allowed me to ask the question: "Who goes to male prostitutes?" I asked Augusto Pérez, a sociologist in his forties who runs Casa Vida, a halfway house for teenage male prostitutes who have tested positive for HIV. Pérez spends his time talking about sex to adolescents in public schools and universities.

"Who goes to male prostitutes?" Pérez responds by asking back the question I just posed to him. "You want to know, ha. Well, men." He is so ready to rock the system that he takes my question a step further than any other expert and answers it straight forwardly. "Men, usually my age, mostly married, looking for a sexual adventure."

"Do their wives know?"

"Wives and mothers are my public enemy number one," he says. "When I talk about sex among teenagers they tell me that I am promoting prostitution and promiscuity. Studies show that boy and girls here are sexually active by the time they are fifteen, and that means they are more than just kissing, but mothers refuse to accept that their daughters are sexual beings. They think girls play with Barbies until the day they get married. If they don't believe their daughters are having sex even when they come home pregnant, you can imagine whether they are going to accept that *this* is going on."

This is the denial that I wish to shatter.

Transvestites and prostitutes, male and female, are a part of the sexual space of some Latin men. In part because macho culture is so homophobic, men with homosexual desires tend to prefer to suppress their desire for men and assume the role of husband. They know that once they are married, if the desire remains, anonymous sex with another man is readily available. But that is not the main reason. Machismo is about power. The man who is most macho fights harder, drinks harder, fathers more children, fucks anything—the laws, the women, the street children, the donkeys. In a culture that sees men as superior beings, fucking a man is the ultimate proof. Having sex with a woman is not at all impressive. Having sex with many women is somewhat better, but having sex with a man is the uttermost expression of manhood.

My intention is not to incriminate anybody or to talk about a sexual behavior in a way that portrays Latin American men as freakish or deviant.

I am interested in exposing the behavior of married men in Latin America because it is this secrecy, this sense that men have a right to everything and women have a right to much less, that is putting women at risk of contracting HIV. A study conducted in São Paulo in 1992 revealed that an alarming number of transvestites were HIV-positive and that they continued working in prostitution after having been diagnosed. Of 112 transvestites surveyed, 60 percent tested positive for HIV, 56 percent for syphillis. The average number of clients per week was 44. If, as my interviews have shown, most of these clients are married, there are a lot of married men having sex with HIV-positive sex workers. If the married men go home and have sex with their wives, and neither they nor their wives think of using condoms, it stops being a mystery why in Latin America so many married, monogamous mothers and their newborns are HIV-positive.

But during my research, I have also come to sympathize with transvestites. Women, gays, and transvestites have more in common than they would ever think they have. All three groups share the consequences of an unequal hierarchical system that sees men as being at the top. Transvestites are shunned by those who are privately glad they are around. "It is that part of society that is the most discriminatory that uses us the most," says Priscilla, a Brazilian transvestite who has been working as a prostitute in the streets of Curitiba, one of Brazil's more conservative cities. She claims her clients are engineers, merchants, men in *cargos fortes*, in important positions. "It's all the high society, and they think that people will think it's a woman who is getting in his car, but really he's going to *transar*, to fuck, with a man."

It is the same men who are paying the transvestites and the male prostitutes for sex who are violent to them—to the extreme of ordering or colluding in their killings. Many of the transvestites I talked to emphasized that they are more afraid of death from police brutality than they are of dying of AIDS. Is it because the men who use them are threatened by the straightforward, candid, and honest way in which they parade their fantasies in their faces? Transvestites are exterminated in social-cleansing-type operations in Brazil, in Colombia, in Mexico. Do the men in *cargos fortes*, as Priscilla describes them, think that if they don't acknowledge them as individuals, they can negate their sexual relations with transvestites and street boys? As the men who make up the rules, they have the power to order or instigate the killings.

"Infidelity here is acceptable," Dr. Bernardo Camacho, a Colombian epidemiologist working with AIDS patients told me as we sat in the cafeteria of the Hospital Simón Bolívar, "but what happens is, women think their husband's infidelity is only heterosexual, not homosexual. And those with bisexual behavior operate with a hermetism that the best unfaithful heterosexual would envy." Dr. Camacho, an epidemiologist running the infectious disease department at Bogotá's largest public hospital, is talking about the forty married women he has treated in the past six months—eighty percent of whom were infected because of the bisexual behavior of their husbands. He knows this because the men, usually on their deathbeds, confess to him or to the nurses on condition that they don't tell their wives.

"The behavior is very hermetic, very hidden, very clandestine," says Dr. Camacho. "Plus, they carry on a sexual relationship with the wives so there is no reason for suspicion." Fabiola Chinchilla, a committed nurse who works closely with the patients and who spends her free time and thirty-eight dollars a month of her own money—a big chunk of her two-hundred-dollar salary—to talk to married women about the dangers of AIDS, also sees how the men, the husbands, do everything to prevent their wives from knowing they are HIV-positive. "Women can't explore on their own," says Chinchilla, a stout woman in her late thirties with a warm smile and arms so round that the short sleeves of her white coat leave a red mark on her copper skin. "I see how they are manipulated into not allowing themselves to think for themselves, to think about how he might have gotten infected." She has seen how wives get pregnant even though their husbands know they carry the virus. She has heard husbands prohibit their wives from talking to Chinchilla or Dr. Camacho on their own. She has felt her stomach burn every time she hears the husbands tell the wives it is no use looking back and she sees the wives simply nodding and saying yes, yes, yes. She knows about a husband who misled his wife by telling her that his constant diarrhea was due to sadness over his mother's recent death, not that he had AIDS.

Men usually don't bother themselves with providing explanations. They neither accept nor deny. But what Chinchilla finds most disturbing is the acceptance by the wives once they do find out. "Women are so understanding," she says, wishing it weren't so. "They immediately adopt an understanding behavior, a passive acceptance, they don't recriminate a thing, they don't reproach or question. They even want to ignore what the source of transmission was. It's all part of the reigning machismo, this submission of women. She doesn't feel she has a right to think for herself, and he closes her in."

Dr. Camacho and Chinchilla have introduced me to Luz, a widow and mother of two, HIV-positive with no health benefits and no job prospects at the age of twenty-eight. Her three-year-old son also carries the virus.

Luz was infected by her husband, a taxi driver, the only man she ever had sex with. Both the doctor and the nurse know that her husband was infected by a lover, another married man who in turn was having sex with another married man who was HIV-positive. They are pretty certain, they tell me, that Luz does not know about her husband's sexual escapades. When she found out her husband had AIDS, she didn't really know what AIDS was. She had heard the commercials on TV, but she says she never paid attention to them.

"I was in my home, doing my chores, I never thought AIDS had anything to do with me," she tells me when I ask how she feels about being HIV-positive. "But it wasn't such a shock when

I found out. Fabiola told me that with AIDS I would lose my defenses. I realized that it was bad and I started to cry, but I was crying because he had it. I thought about him, about how I had little time with him. I was a little angry but it was not worth it."

I have come to pick her up at her home, an upstairs apartment in a two-story building on an unpaved street in the south of Bogotá. I arranged to take her in a taxi to the office of a doctor, an AIDS activist who had promised to get her AZT for free. I knew my offer meant a four-hour drive in Bogotá's merciless traffic of horns, insults, big buses, and narrow streets. But when she agreed to talk to me, I felt I wanted to do something for her.

Normally, she takes four different buses to get to the doctor's office. The trip takes up her whole day, and sometimes she waits there for hours and leaves without even getting to see the doctor, much less with medicine. But she tries week after week. If she doesn't get it from the doctor, she goes without. A twenty-day supply of AZT, the medicine she needs to keep her immune system running, costs the equivalent of $130, the average monthly salary in Colombia if she were to work. But Luz has never worked a day in her life.

"My husband never allowed me to work," she says with pride, as if that made her husband into a caring protector. "I dedicated my life to my children." She was taught by her mother that women stay home with the children. Her mother took care of eight; her husband's mother took care of ten.

She tells me that her life was "a fantasy." As she describes her life, I realize that there is no reason for her to have suspected her husband's sexual behavior. For eight years she stayed happily at home with the children. While he drove a taxi, she cooked him his favorite dishes—pork chops and fried plantains or ribs and beans—for lunch. The evenings were spent watching television.

"He was the most well-behaved man," she tells me as she sits next to me in the backseat of a rattling Renault. "He never made me suffer because of other women, like most men do. He never spent a night out of the home. I married a marvelous man." She smiles mistily as she remembers her late husband. "He was the man of my dreams."

What strikes me most about Luz is her ordinariness. She could be any woman in her late twenties born to uneducated, urban poor parents on the outskirts of Bogotá. There are millions and millions of Luzes among the seven million inhabitants of this chilly metropolis more than three thousand feet above sea level: her short, plump body; her jet-black, straight and thick Andean hair; her white skin with rosy spots; her reserved manners, *muy cachaca*; her shyness bordering on meekness; her short skirt paired with a shiny fuchsia blouse, black pantyhose, and worn black leather pumps; the small crucifix around her neck. I notice all the makeup she is wearing, the heavy black eyeliner, the fuchsia lips that match her shirt and her nails, and I kick myself for expecting Luz to look jaundiced and disheveled because she carries the HIV virus. It is the fact that I know she is HIV-positive that makes her ordinariness absurd. Luz is the traditional Colombian housewife, and the irony is that it is the women who look like Luz—women who are reserved and shy because that's how women should be; women who have sex but are uncomfortable talking about sex; women who think AIDS is something that only "the women of the street" get, not those who stay home like she did with the children; women whose language and views about love and romance and sex, like Luz's, are faithful to those of soap-opera heroines—who are today greatly exposed to AIDS.

I notice her hands. On her left hand she wears a wedding band attached to a ring with a minuscule diamond. On her right pinkie she wears a ring that belonged to him. I remember Chinchilla's words: "They will defend their husbands. They will stand by their man. They feel that is their obligation. There is no room for them to be angry, only to take care of him and then honor his memory."

She met Humberto, a taxi driver, when she was eighteen. He made an impact on her the first time she saw him.

"What did you like?" I ask her.

"He was tender and thoughtful."

For her, it was love at first sight. She was attracted to his beard, his big build. "So manly," she says, "such a gentleman."

He courted her the old-fashioned way, the way her father had told her a man should behave with her if he valued her. On dates, they would go to family gatherings where he would dance only with her. On her birthday, he serenaded her with mariachis. Never during their two-year courtship did he ask to have sex with her. That proved to her that he was the perfect man.

Luz's parents are poor, but her father bought her the fanciest, fluffiest, whitest wedding gown. She wore it with pride. She admits she was nervous about having to be with Humberto alone the night after the wedding. She was a virgin and she had never spoken to anyone about sex. When she asked her mother about it, all she would hear was, "Wait till the day you marry." When she did, she didn't dare talk to Humberto—"What would he think of me?"

Sitting in the courtyard outside the doctor's office, I ask her if she enjoyed sex with her husband. She blushes, smiles, rolls the magazine she is holding into a tube, and nods yes. "But I never asked him for anything. I would only do what he liked. I only wanted to make him happy. You know how it is in sex when you get married. Men have more experience, so we mold ourselves to them. If he liked to be hugged in a certain way, I would hug him that way. If he wanted to be kissed this way or that, I would, but I don't ask for myself."

She learned about birth control from the family-planning clinic in her neighborhood. In Colombia, Pro-Familia has done an incredible job lowering birth rates. Ten years ago, the average number of children for a Colombian family was six. Today it is three, and according to the latest studies it is still on the decline. Regardless of Catholic imposition, more than seventy percent of Colombian women use birth control. The family-planning clinic provided Luz with vaginal suppositories at first. After her two children were born, she started using an IUD. But she was never told about AIDS or about condom use. As a matter of fact, she confesses, she has never seen one. She still thinks no married man she knows will use one.

"Why?" I ask.

"They say that the relationship is not the same, they ask you why you would need a barrier between you and them," she says. "I think they would rather not have sex with their wives than use them. So the wives hope they are being careful outside the home. It's all because of machismo."

I cannot believe my ears. Luz used the word "machismo." HIV has made her aware. What a price! She tells me that she goes to a support group for people with AIDS, mostly gays. It's the first time that she has done something on her own. She likes helping out, handing out AIDS literature in shopping malls even if people don't take them. And she really looks forward to the social outings they organize, like the picnics in El Norte. The organizers have taught her many things, she tells me. She has learned that "gay" is a better word than "maricón," so she now uses the word "gay" when referring to someone who is a homosexual. "The gays tell me that they are alone but that I have to fight for my children, that's why I take the AZT, that's why I take many buses in one day to come here."

Although Luz has had her consciousness raised, she quickly reverts to being docile, and it is clear she leans heavily on her romantic memories. "I married a marvelous man. The man of my dreams. We never had a fight. My life was a fantasy, a model. He was always telling me how happy I made him." When he serenaded her, the mariachis would always play her a song called "Dulce Hogar." I ask her if she remembers the words, and she tells me it went something like "Thanks for the pretty and sweet home that God has given me."

But during eight years of blissful marriage, Humberto was also having sexual relationships with other men. He confessed his bisexuality to the doctor who tended him in his last days. To his wife, it seems, he never said a word. If he did, Luz has blocked it out.

"How do you think he was infected?" I try to bring up the possibility of his bisexuality, but Luz refuses to let me take her there.

"I think and think and I cannot come to a conclusion. Maybe another woman."

But she immediately discards that option. "He never spent the night outside of the home," she says nervously. "I never suffered because of other women. *No era un hombre tremendo, era un hombre sano.* He didn't drink. He didn't smoke. Life is cruel."

When she awakes in the middle of the night, the images are always the same—the family vacations to Melgar, where she felt hot weather for the first time; the day of her wedding, her fluffy dress. "I have friends that are wild. My marriage is blessed by the Church. I wore white. He was my first man. What can I attribute this to?"

I try again.

"What do you think, Luz?"

This time I notice her hands are grabbing on tight to the magazine to quell the shaking. I look for her eyes and she hides them from me. "He had a toenail operation once, maybe it was that. I've actually been meaning to ask his mother, because I think he had a blood transfusion a long, long time ago, before he met me."

But despite her efforts to dodge the issue, she admits that being infected forces her into a position where she has to hear about the unfaithfulness of married men. She knows that the women in her family use her as an example to get their husbands to be faithful. It humiliates her.

"I hear people talk and I hear what they say and I really don't think a completely faithful, faithful husband exists. I don't know. There are faithful wives, dedicated to their homes, but men, because of machismo, very few are dedicated."

"Luz," I say as gently as I possibly can, "it is possible that married men are unfaithful to their wives with other men."

She recoils as she pulls down her miniskirt and straightens the neck of her shiny polyester blouse and looks at me straight in the eye for the first time. "Do you really think that's possible?"

The contradictions of sexual life in Latin America—where sex for women has always been silent, secret, and laced with feelings of sin, while male bisexuality, prostitution, transvestitism, and other high-risk practices are accepted, even routine, parts of men's lives at all levels of society—are today exposing women, especially monogamous married women, to AIDS. To be a man means to experience sex with multiple partners, to never have to control sexual urges. But above all to be penetrators. To be female means to be submissive, to be shy, to want protection from a man. Sexually, women are expected to be naive, inexperienced, and penetrable. Before AIDS that meant, at the most, that as women we would be sexually unsatisfied. Today it means women are running a high

risk of becoming HIV-positive, of being young widows with children, of being desolate and in economic distress. Luz followed
the rules, and that's exactly what happened. As she was never
expected to work, she has no skills that she could fall back on
to find employment. She relies on relatives and on the grace of
strangers like the doctor we are visiting to support her and her
two children.

But if in Colombia, as Dr. Camacho asserts, bisexual behavior
is common, the word "bisexuality" is not. Dr. Camacho is using
the word as a medical doctor, as an educated professional. He is
recognizing what most Latin men will not. He, like any social
worker, epidemiologist, or public health official in Latin America,
is being confronted every day with the tragic evidence of a hidden
reality. "Married women are not afraid of AIDS," says a gynecologist for the rich in São Paulo. "It's part of the culture to have
other women. Women know about men having other women. They
fight but they stay married. Women accept small affairs. They are
afraid of women, not of men." But when I ask him if he talks to
them about the risk of AIDS, he answers by telling me that he has
had patients for twenty years and has never discussed sex with
them. His patients, especially the married ones, would find it inappropriate. But he does have patients who have already lost their
husbands to AIDS.

Throughout Latin American, AIDS is exposing the bisexuality
and homosexuality that has been kept a secret. A study in Medellín, Colombia, in 1993 concluded there were "large numbers of
cases of bisexual men, many of whom are married or have a stable heterosexual partner," testing HIV-positive. In Rio de Janeiro
a study concluded that "male bisexual behavior is an important
factor in understanding the increasing evidence of HIV infection
among Brazilian women." In Chile, a study of the rates of transmission from 1984 to 1992 concluded that "bisexual patterns
also stand out. It is possible that the stigmatization of homosexuality leads individuals to develop bisexual patterns of behavior." A study done by the U.S. Centers for Disease Control and
Prevention about bisexual men with AIDS concluded that bisexual Latin American men, regardless of birthplace, were more
likely to be currently married than all other bisexual men. In

Colombia, researchers at the Ministry of Health say they were startled when tabulating a survey of heterosexual men to discover that many had sex with other men. When I asked the vice-minister of health, he told me that the study provided persuasive evidence that bisexual behavior is "an important trend among males." Joseph Carrier, an American anthropologist who has been studying homosexuality in Mexico for the past twenty-five years, writes that "perhaps a larger percentage of Mexican males have at some time been involved in homosexual behavior than have Anglo-Americans."

Reinaldo Arenas, Cuba's Paul Monette, tells in *Before Night Falls* about his coming of age as a homosexual in Fidel Castro's Cuba, about how he was censored, persecuted, and jailed for being gay and being critical of Castro's revolution. "Being a 'faggot' in Cuba," he writes, "was one of the worst disasters that could ever happen to anyone." In his matter-of-fact way, Arenas writes that he thinks that in the Cuban countryside "it is rare [to find] a man who has not had sexual relations with another man."

Psychologists and anthropologists trying to explain this behavior argue that sexual orientation in Latin America is defined not just by having a same-sex partner but by the role played in a homosexual act. "Active macho men who have sex with men are just men," Richard Parker, an American anthropologist and author of *Bodies, Pleasure and Passion: Sexual Culture in Contemporary Brazil*, a comprehensive study of Brazilian sexual culture, told me as we shared a coffee in one of the many cafés of the avenida Atlântica. "In all of Latin America we can expect the epidemic to become even more heterosexual," says Parker, who is very active in the gay AIDS activist movement in Brazil. "One of the reasons is the double standard that men can have sex with other people, so there are more connections for HIV to work with." Parker, an expert, was confirming what my anecdotal evidence already suggested. As long as a man is the active partner in a homosexual relationship, he will not be considered a homosexual, only more of a man.

Every time I explain this behavior in New York where I live, American men smirk or are appalled or amused. Their eyes widen. They say that they have "never heard of anything like that," or that such a statement is "too weird." But when I talk about this behavior to other Latins, many have a story, a comment, a joke that shows that they too have heard about it. A Brazilian woman, well traveled and sophisticated, a member of the upper class, told me about the night she went out to dinner with a group of friends. They were at one of São Paulo's finest restaurants—great food and much liquor. The check was paid by one of the men at the table who was there with his wife, and who murmured in his drunkenness that all he needed before falling asleep was "a man's ass."

A Cuban friend called me from Miami once just to tell me the following joke:

"What's the difference between a straight Latin and a gay Latin?"

"What?" I asked.

"Two drinks."

While Anglo-Americans classify a homosexual encounter by the gender of those involved, in Latin America it is the role one plays, the position in that encounter, that will define a man either as a *maricón*—a faggot, a butterfly, a *loca*—or as a straight macho. A man may be having sex with another man, but he will deny it is a homosexual act. In this macho world, where active men are macho men and only faggots and women are passive and penetrable and therefore weak, penetration takes on a cultural meaning beyond the sexual one. If one thinks of how men, and the Church and the state, see women, it is easier to understand why this is so. If machos are the highest form of being, if not allowing anyone to penetrate you is a sign of virility, then those who are able to penetrate become Herculean. And those who are penetrated are inferior, degraded beings—usually compared to women.

The distinctions made between who "gives" and who "receives" form an entire language and posturing that is, in fact, everyday parlance. Common comments one hears among Latin men, usually said in jest and mostly in times of heavy drinking, are: "I am such a man, I've even had sex with another man" and *"hoyo hasta de pollo"* and *"cualquier hueco es trinchera"*—any hole is a trench. As it is in war, the more trenches you win, the more powerful you become; the more holes you penetrate, the more macho you are.

Men in New York are perplexed when I explain. But George Chauncey, in his book *Gay New York*, suggests that this was the case in turn-of-the-century New York. The book, an examination of New York City homosexuals from the 1890s to the 1930s, explains how "fairies" and "queers" were only labeled as such if they "assumed the sexual and cultural roles ascribed to women." Homosexuals, then, did not seek or desire sex with each other but with those who termed themselves "normal" men. Their ideal partner was a "real man," ideally a sailor or a soldier, or some other embodiment of the aggressive masculine ideal: someone who was not effeminate but who would accept the sexual advances of a queer.

Chauncey quotes a young gay man in the 1930s who wanted to have sex with a straight man. "There was something very hot about a married man! And a lot of straight boys let us have sex with them. People don't believe it now. People say now that they must have been gay. But they weren't. They wouldn't look for it or suck a guy's thing, but they'd let you suck." Chauncey points out that especially among young working-class straights there appears to have been little or no stigma attached to such activity, as long as you remained sexually disinterested in your "fairy" partner and were never penetrated. This all sounds straight out of what I had been hearing about men who had sex with other men in Latin America.

Chauncey believes that the Stonewall riots in 1967 and the rise of the gay movement made away with these definitions. But Latin America is only slowly opening up to gay rights, and activism there was born out of the need to face the AIDS epidemic. Today in most Latin capitals there is a significantly large agency working against AIDS, run by gay men who are out. In Bogotá, Manuel Velandia runs La Liga Gay Contra Sida; in Brazil, Walter Gallegos founded Luta pela Vida, or Struggle for Life. Velandia and Gallegos, as pioneers and activists, often appear on national television and are quoted by the press.

Latin America is starting to raise the heavy curtain that has hidden homosexuality. In the past ten years, important anthropological works have been published about these issues. Roger Lancaster has worked in Nicaragua, Joseph Carrier in Mexico,

Ian Lumsden in Cuba, Richard Parker in Brazil, Alex Carballo-Diéguez in New York City. But for all the merit and the importance of these works, they have something else in common. They are all published in English. Sadly, the chances of them being translated and displayed in Latin American bookstores is rather slim. These works will probably go unnoticed and their value to create consciousness and awareness that would help organize an active gay movement will be limited. As Chauncey points out, the insertive-receptive versatility only happened in New York in the '60s and '70s as modern gay sexual culture began to consider this role separation a form of self-oppression. As of today, the gay movement in Latin America is still incipient. Maybe with its growth, the same positive changes will start making their appearance. Bogotá already has its first glossy gay magazine.

This definition of homosexuality by sexual position crosses all Latin borders. It is the same in Mexico City, in Managua, in Montevideo, and in Castro's Cuba, the land that would produce the *hombre nuevo*, the "new man" that Che Guevara wrote about, and a whole generation believed would be the place where every man and every woman would be emancipated. Castro has said that Cuba "needed strong men to fight wars, sportsmen, men who had no psychological weaknesses." Read, heterosexuals.

Reinaldo Arenas recounts that it was exactly this active/passive distinction that finally got him out of Cuba, thrown out with the criminals and the mentally insane on one of the Mariel boats. He knew precisely what to say to get on that boat. "At the police station they asked me if I was a homosexual and I said yes," he writes in *Before Night Falls*. "Then they asked me if I was active or passive and I took the precaution of saying that I was passive. A friend of mine who said he played the active role was not allowed to leave; he had told the truth, but the Cuban government did not look upon those who took the active male role as real homosexuals."

"In male-male social relations any number of pecadillos—heavy drinking, promiscuity, the active role in same-sex intercourse—become a status marker of male honor," writes Roger Lancaster in *Life Is Hard: Machismo, Danger and the Intimacy of Power in Nicaragua*. "A man gains sexual status and honor among other men through his active role in sexual intercourse (either with women or with other men.)" In neighboring Honduras, a man is a real man only after having had sex with at least two women and with a *culero*, a man he can penetrate. *Culo* in Spanish means "ass"; *culero* is someone who allows himself to be butt-fucked.

But what does this intimacy among men imply for women? If the most manly thing a man can do is have sex with another man, what does this say about how men view women?

It is humiliating. The fact that a man has sex with other men because that makes him macho implies that a woman can never make him feel that good. The whole business about being active or being passive is all related to the issue of power and how it is manifested not only in sexual acts but in the day-to-day communication between men and women, lovers or not.

Why should I or any woman care that men are having sex with other men, that some prefer to be taken and that others will only do the taking? Why do I care to broadcast the fact that men pay to have sex with transvestites, that they go out with their buddies on what in Barranquilla they call a *viernes cultural*, a "cultural Friday," and return to their homes drunk after, possibly, having had sex with another man or having had paid sex with a prostitute, a transvestite, or a fourteen-year-old boy? Apart from the implications of degradation to women that I oppose. Because it is through this underworld of male sexual encounters that the women of Latin America are being infected with the HIV virus. That men come home and have sex with their female partners happens more often than is acknowledged. Men know it's common, and yet a grown woman with a normal conjugal sex life like Luz would not have an inkling of this possibility. During the AIDS conference in Berlin in 1994, I attended a presentation by a Peruvian epidemiologist who said that about seventy percent of the women in his sample of 350 were not aware that men who defined themselves as heterosexual had sex with other men. Dr. Carlos Cáceres suggested that the men who engaged in such behavior were usually the most homophobic and were prone to having multiple female partners. It was not surprising that he reported little condom use.

Outreach programs targeting these men in an effort to increase awareness of the need for condom use have been established in

New York, Mexico, and Brazil, where AIDS prevention campaigns are active, and relatively well funded and organized. In Mexico CONASIDA, the branch of the Ministry of Health in charge of the HIV prevention campaign, has prepared a video to address the issue. According to CONASIDA's data, approximately two-thirds of the men who frequent gay bars and nightclubs have had sex with women. One-half report having had sex with a woman in the last year.

A Little Bit of This and a Little Bit of That is a forty-five-minute video that shows two men dancing in an apartment, neither of them fitting the stereotype of the effeminate homosexual. They both look macho by Mexican standards. As they start unbuttoning their shirts, one of them says, "I like women better. This is an occasional desire."

The video shows men enacting off-camera interviews talking about their bisexual behavior. One married man confesses to having sex with another man once a month and using no condoms with his female partners. "Few women use them," he explains. Another man says that he will engage in sex with other men while single. "This doesn't mean I don't like women," he says. "I feel it's a bit more sticky to have sex with women. It's easier to have relations with a man." Another man faults his girlfriend: "After I take my girlfriend home because she doesn't want to do it, I come here to enjoy." All the three bachelors believe they will stop once they get married. "Making a home with a woman is important," says the first one.

But of the men who think that once they get married they will stop having sex with other men, few follow through. The video shows a middle-aged, balding man, married for eleven years and the father of two, who confesses to having had homosexual relations since the age of fourteen. Years ago he stopped having sex with his wife. Today she still does not know why.

Luis Nieves, the program director of Entre Hombres at the Hispanic AIDS Forum in Jackson Heights, Queens, regularly makes the rounds of gay bars inviting men to come to support meetings where they can find a place to talk about their behavior. He is certain, however, that despite his weekly visits no married man who has sex with men has ever been to the support groups he organizes. "I've maybe given him a condom at a bar. That's about it."

More than ten years into the AIDS epidemic, there are small signs of increased awareness. A headline in the November 1995 issue of the Latin edition of *Cosmopolitan* magazine caught my eye: "You don't demand that he wear condoms?" I read the brief item, sandwiched between an article about money and another one about how high heels flatter the figure: "Whenever you feel tempted to run that risk, think about this: A major study (U.S. National Health and Social Life Survey) revealed that more than half of the men that have sex with other men do not consider themselves homosexuals or bisexuals. And they are not going to take care of you. . . . You take care!"

Surprising, but I know these few lines of text do not a revolution make. For all the good intentions, I am afraid that the way it was worded and the way it was presented—an extra tip next to how heels flatter behinds—will have made its urgency go unnoticed. I would be surprised if any woman was as alarmed as she needs to be. As AIDS activists have recognized, condom campaigns are ineffective if these behaviors are not demystified—especially if women are not even aware that their partners may be clandestinely engaged in such behavior.

One next wonders whether men who have sex with men and yet will not consider themselves bisexual are especially discriminatory to women. Alex Carballo-Diéguez, an Argentinian psychologist in New York City who has studied the behavior of Puerto Rican MSMs, finds that it is just such men who are the most homophobic and who most strongly see women as inferior to men.

Carballo has defined four categories of men who have sex with men: straight men, gay men, bisexuals, and drag queens.

The first group, the straight men, are those who take the active role, those who penetrate orally and anally. They are called *bujarrones* in Cuba and Spain, *cacorros* in Colombia, *mayates* in Mexico. They are referred to as macho, as normal, as *varón* or male, or simply as *hombre*. Most of their experiences with other men are through commercial sex.

The second group, the "gays," are men who are both active and passive, men who are *entendidos*, meaning that they are out of the closet, up front about their sexuality. They are the *locas*, the *mariposas*, the *patos*, the *maricones*, the ones who are mocked, the ones who are beaten.

Then there are the bisexual men who have regular or occasional sex with other men and also have regular or occasional sex with women. They are seen as open-minded, and bisexuality is less stigmatizing than being gay or queer.

Lastly, there are the drag queens, the men who have breasts and assume feminine identities, the ones who call themselves Verouschka or Claudia, Diva, or until her death, Lady Di. Sexually they play the receptive partner in both anal and oral sex. They are considered neither male nor gay, but closer to women. They are the ones who are the most discriminated against and the most attacked—often beaten, sometimes to death.

Out of the 182 men of Puerto Rican descent that Carballo-Diéguez interviewed, about ten percent described themselves as heterosexual or straight and considered that their having sex with another man did not make them any different from men who had heterosexual sex. When asked to define a gay man, a straight man who had engaged in sex with other men responded: "A gay man is someone who likes to get it up his ass. Someone effeminate. A queer. A person who feels good imitating a female." The implication was that wanting to do something considered female makes a person inferior. *Locas* are constantly beaten up because sexually they like to do things that only the lowest sort of women would do.

The study quotes a man who tells the interviewer that when he is having sex with another man, he always feels even more of a man. Asked to explain, he says:

"I feel like a man, *hombre,* you know, I don't feel low, I feel good."

"And how do you see the one who is having sex with you?"

"That depends on how he acts. Some act like women, in the way they dress and talk. I see them like women."

"And if they act like men?"

"I try to see them like women as well."

"Has any man ever asked you to do oral sex to him?"

"Yes, but I never did. I wouldn't like it. If I did it, I would see myself the way I see them. As a homosexual. I would feel very low."

"And when a woman does it to you, do you see her as very low?"

"No. Because she is already a woman. But if the man does it, he wants to do what women do. Why would a man do that when there are women to do it?"

These "straight" men have macho-sex rules. Apart from being the penetrators in anal sex, it is also macho to have oral sex done to them without reciprocating it. "I do whatever I have to do *to* the person, but I don't let nothing be done to me," said one man. Another: "As long as I don't get fucked, I'm not a faggot. So the faggot is the one that gets fucked, and the one who fucks is the man, you know. I don't give blow jobs. So I always play the man's part."

Once again, HIV has thrown the paradoxes of sexual culture into stark relief. Up until ten years ago, there was virtually no field research about homosexual behavior in Latin America. The AIDS epidemic has triggered these recent studies and shown that homosexual sex among straight Latin men is more frequent than suspected. Carrier's study about Mexico, *De Los Otros: Intimacy and Homosexuality among Mexican Men,* provides a clear indication of how frequent the liaisons between straight men and openly homosexual men are. For example: Arturo, a gay man from Guadalajara, would go into bars in order to have sex with men. He estimates that in one year he had sex with thirty to forty partners who were "regular masculine" middle-class men from twenty-two to forty-five years old, and who usually picked up the tab and knew where to go to have sex.

Arturo recounts one steady relationship with a married man. At first, they met in the private steam rooms of public bathhouses to have sex. Soon after, Arturo moved into the married man's house. The man told his wife that he was renting the room for extra money. Arturo remembers that his partner was very relaxed about and was willing to do anything with Arturo that "he would do to a woman." There was plenty of foreplay—hugging and kissing—followed by good anal sex. Arturo was always the receptor. And he had to be very careful. He could never touch the married man's rear end. "It was the only thing that would make him angry."

This rule is so strict that those who break it have paid with their lives. A young male prostitute in a small town in Mexico who penetrated his client, a straight man who had become very drunk, was found dead the next morning, shot in the head.

Men who spend time both in the United States and in Latin America play by the local rules. While in the United States they feel free to be both active and passive, to be *internacional*, as Mexican gay men refer to men who take it both ways. But in Latin America they are very careful not to put their hands where they are not supposed to. They play only the passive role. Not doing so could be fatal.

The irony of the situation is that, although studies show that bisexuality is higher than one suspects, the violence against the men they are having sex with—the transvestites, the young male prostitutes, the ones they consider *maricones*—is pervasive and brutal. In Brazil, Renildo José dos Santos, a member of the city council of Coqueiros in the state of Alagoas, announced his bisexuality in public and was found dead the next day—shot by policemen.

In Nicaragua, Chile, Peru, and Ecuador, homosexuality is a crime as stipulated in the constitution.

In Colombia students have been denied entrance to universities because they appeared "effeminate." Men have lost their jobs just because they were getting phone calls from other men.

In Chile discotheques frequented by gays have been bombed. A clandestine antigay group operating since 1993 attacks and harasses members of the country's gay community. The group calls itself Grupo Carlos Ibáñez del Campo after a dictator in the 1920s who allegedly arrested homosexuals and ordered them to be thrown into the sea. Five years ago, a gay discotheque in Valparaiso, a coastal resort city, burned down. Nineteen homosexuals died in the conflagration. A few days after the fire, the Carlos

Ibáñez group claimed responsibility. Gay support groups campaigned for an investigation. They are still waiting.

In Brazil more than 1,300 gay men have been murdered in the past fifteen years.

In Mexico, according to the International Lesbian and Gay Association, between 1992 and 1994 about thirty gay men and transvestites were murdered. Many were leaders in the gay movement working with AIDS prevention. In Mexico City, on July 13, 1992, Dr. Francisco Estrada, a gay physician and founder of a group working with gays and AIDS prevention, was killed along with two gay friends. "To date," the report states, "none of the cases have been solved by the local police, who consider these murders to be crimes of passion or vengeance within the gay community, despite clear signs of professional marksmanship and a striking similarity among many of the cases."

In Colombia the figures are even more grim. Going through the roster of alleged murders reported by a human rights organization becomes a window on the dark and lurid world of social cleansing. In February of 1992, thirty-eight homosexuals were murdered and six were wounded. In March it was thirty-nine killed, two wounded. In June, forty-four more homosexuals were murdered, and fourteen wounded. Among the reported incidents was a rampage that took place in a bar outside Medellín, the city known more for the violence of drug cartels than for the violence of individuals, organized or not, toward men who are openly homosexual. A group of men fired 9-mm. Uzis inside the Taverna El Carriel, killing Hector Mario Nárvaez, Carlos Arturo López, Luis Javier Hurtado, Oscar Monroy, and Alberto Valencia—all listed as "homosexual" in the police report. A few days later, the report states that on the Atlantic coast "Alberto de Jesús Barrera, a.k.a. Catherine, homosexual" was murdered. On September 19, in Cali, "John Emilio Pacheco, a.k.a. Wendy, homosexual" was also murdered. In Barranquilla, the body of an unnamed homosexual had been tortured; part of his right index finger was missing. A man was murdered in Montería; he was identified as "a.k.a. Monica, homosexual."

Under Colombian law, only those corpses that go into the morgue wearing women's clothes are labeled homosexual. "Homosexual" is considered a gender, and one associated with the female gender. As a woman, it is frightening to think that men feel the urge to kill another man who would prefer to dress in women's clothes. It reminds me of the insult I heard boys scream at boys when they really wanted to insult them—"*Ay niña, niñita,* tell your mommy to dress you in girl's clothes." Or understanding that *"ven, chúpame la pinga, maricón"* was perversely linked with a nonviolent act that I or any woman could enjoy and desire.

In 1993 the average number of murders of homosexuals significantly decreased, but there were still some horrific examples of violence. In the month of August in Bogotá, obituary announcements appeared in local papers. The announcements, paid for by the merchants, entrepreneurs, owners of industries, and *hombres de bien*—gentlemen, "decent men"—extended invitations to the upcoming funerals of prostitutes, thieves, and criminals. The announcements also assured that violence against *los marginados de la sociedad*—"society's marginalized," meaning those sectors that remind us of the poverty and the hidden sexual behavior of the country—would resume. In the neighborhood of Los Mártires, residents claimed that the campaign involved, in addition to groups of business owners, military and Security Forces personnel.

As if to prove it, a month after the threat, two police officers picked up and beat eight homeless men under the Puente de las Américas. A week later "Miguel the Poet" died as a result of the beating. In November the number of dead had risen. And by February of 1994 it had jumped to twenty-six. On February 27, two unidentified transvestites were killed on the same corner, the murders a half hour apart. When friends of the first victim gathered around his corpse, several individuals "accompanied by members of the Police" drove by, shooting and killing one of the transvestite mourners.

A few months later in Medellín, the body of a man was found, killed by a bullet to his head. He was wearing an auburn wig, a black leotard with long sleeves, a black miniskirt, one black shoe, and a black brassiere. Less than two weeks later, an eleven-year-old street boy was killed in Tuluá by several unidentified individuals while he slept on the street next to a ten-year-old who was severely wounded. Sources stated that seven children had been assassinated in this relatively calm city shortly after these murders.

This is only a partial list of murders over a two-year period in Colombia. Most of them are unsolved, most of the corpses remain unidentified. They are all murders attributed to operations of "social cleansing." Individuals are being killed because certain sectors of Colombia's society consider them *desechables*—disposable, like dirty diapers or used needles. Many Colombians believe that eliminating such "elements" benefits society as a whole. To many—especially members of the middle and upper class—beggars, street children, the poor who are presumed criminals, the poor with mental problems, the poor who are sex workers, transvestites, drug addicts, scavengers who live on the street, openly homosexual people are all seen as disposables. Although statistics show that an average of 1.8 of them are murdered every day, human rights groups believe the number is much higher, as the majority of the murders go unreported.

Most murders of *desechables* are attributed to groups like Mano Negra—Black Hand—a death squad operating in Barranquilla in the 1970s. The group proclaimed that by picking up suspected criminals and murdering them, they would stop crime in the city. To make their statement clear, Mano Negra left small cardboard boxes around the city, in places they believed were visible to criminals. The boxes contained the hands of alleged criminals. By "disappearing" them and exhibiting the hands, Black Hand claimed they were cleaning the streets of crime, providing a public service.

Black Hand has disappeared, but hundreds of death squads operate in Colombia today. The Anonymous Avenger, Black Flag, the Cobras, Committee for the Cleansing of Magdalena Medio, Death to Car Thieves, Death to Homosexuals, Green Commandos, and the Relentless Imparter of Justice are some. Their target: individuals or groups who are homeless or live in destitute conditions. What in my neighborhood of Riomar we called *los pobres* these groups call "disposables." Since living in poverty is reason enough for someone to be blown away, there are more than eight such killings every day. After all, there are a lot of people that meet the requirement. In this country of mine, a third of the thirty-six million people who inhabit it live in conditions of critical poverty. In Riomar, we dealt with poverty by erecting high walls, by making our gardener guard the first floor of our home with a machete. My father kept a small Smith and Wesson in the closet a few steps from his bed. For Mano Negra, our *paredillas*, the high walls covered with ivy and glass, the dark-tinted windows of our cars that kept poverty out of our sight, were not enough. They were attacking the problem at the root: Let's get rid of poverty by getting rid of the poor. For them, being poor made you a potential criminal. Their goal—kill you before you became one.

Transvestites are the number one target for these groups, especially the poor transvestites who work in prostitution. According to a report published jointly by three human rights organizations in Colombia in 1997, transvestites are being killed by the local business people, the authorities, the paramilitaries, the death squads, skinhead nationalist groups that beat them up before they kill them. This is not solely a Colombian phenomenon. Human rights groups have also denounced the murders of transvestites by both the police and death squads in Argentina, Mexico, and many Brazilian cities.

Most of the murdered transvestites wind up listed as homosexual men, since Colombian morgues identify bodies as either female, male, or, if the cadaver is a male wearing women's clothes, "homosexual." Thus the statistics not only fail to include the murders of many homosexuals—those not wearing female attire—but misrepresent the highly specific violence against transvestites. Each one of these men was murdered because he was a transvestite—not an inconspicuous if successful hairdresser but a visible, poor streetwalker. The high-class transvestites, the ones on the Boulevard del Prado, are mocked, insulted, and humiliated, and hairdressers like Malena or Gustavo Turizo's muses are not invited into fancy homes, but they are rarely in physical danger. Outside of the nice neighborhoods, other rules apply. The business owners "dispose" of transvestites. To have them hanging around their establishments is bad for business.

Transvestites are *escoria*, scum—to the traditional lifestyle imposed by our country's Catholic vision of family. But there is a sinister hypocrisy. It is exactly those members of society who have sex with transvestites who also insult them, who consider them scum, who execute them. Transvestites talk about being raped by the same policemen who beat them. They tell me their clients are the same men who make the laws, the merchants who think that having them parading in front of their shops is bad for business. Jovana Baby, a Brazilian transvestite, the head of a national network of transvestites fighting for their rights as citizens, refers to law-makers and to the police who beat them up as *falsos moralistas*— fake moralists.

Is it because it is too threatening for men to be reminded of their secretive behavior that transvestites are targeted for violence and death? Do such men kill them because they don't want to be reminded that it is often they who pay the poor transvestites and the young male prostitutes for sex?

The end of communism and the globalization of market forces has forced Latin American governments to address and to be more accountable for human rights abuses. It is a step in the right direction to see the peace processes of El Salvador and Guate-mala, the campaigns to eradicate judicial impunity and corruption. As they did in the 1970s when the democratic processes demanded a space for women and governments began creating their Min-istries of Women's Affairs, today they are opening offices to moni-tor human rights abuses. Barranquilla, like most Colombian cities, has a human rights ombudsman—a *defensor del pueblo*, a defender of the people. These *defensores* denounce the violence of the army against peasants, against union organizers. Yet no local ombuds-man has denounced antigay violence.

Furthermore, when human rights activist Juan Pablo Ordóñez interviewed Barranquilla's ombudsman Oswaldo Henríquez Linero about his views on gay rights, his answer was a dark reminder of how far Latin America has yet to go.

"Two faggots can be married for one hundred years but they'll never have a child," he said. "From that standpoint they'll never guarantee the survival of the species. Their rights as persons should be respected; they should be tolerated within the proper realm of tolerance for human beings. But they are abnormal."

"So they should keep a distance from society?" Ordóñez asked.

"Not distance, but social control should be exercised over them to ensure that they don't become harmful. It would not be good for others to follow their example. As I see it, they are not an example of anything."

"You were saying that they should keep their distance from your home?"

"Ah, yes! As far as possible. Because the moment a faggot starts hanging around my house, human rights are over. I won't accept that. No way. I radically oppose that sort of thing. Woman was made for man and man for woman. That is, I'd rather have a daughter who is a whore than a son who is a faggot."

"What would happen if one of your children were homosexual?"

"He should get out of my sight. I would treat him as if he were sick. I would treat him like the family dog. I would treat him like another case in the office. I believe I love my dog more than I'd love a faggot."

I was caught in the hustle and bustle of Rio de Janeiro's Avenida Presidente Vargas on a Friday at six. I joined the swarm of men in business suits, men in short sleeves, men in cheap clothes rushing home after a week of work. I passed the cafés overflowing with people having a *cafezinho* and a *pão de queijo* and those in the luncheonettes where people stop for a *prato da verão*—a summer feast of slices of mango, papaya, melon, oranges, and white cheese. I was attracted by the many kiosks with the postcard stands, the candy, and the newspapers. I walked along, watching the street vendors selling both sweet and salty popcorn and peanuts, or offering the winning number of the *jogo da bicha*, Brazil's favorite lottery game, or a pirate video of a Steven Seagal movie or any number of cheap Chinese toys and Mickey Mouse slippers.

I was looking for the address of the Guanabara Palace Hotel at the end of Rio Branco, and every time I asked I was told, with a smile, to keep walking down the avenue until I was across from the Igreja da Candelária. I was late for the opening ceremony of the Third Congress of Liberated Tranvestites, and I thought I was in the wrong place when I faced the rundown yet stately building opposite the church. An American friend who has lived in Rio for more than ten years and really knows his way around, told me he had never heard of the Guanabara when I asked him for directions. "It must be a really seedy place," he told me over the phone. "Transvestites hang out in seedy places."

A doorman in a maroon uniform opens the heavy doors and I walk into a pleasant lobby. The Guanabara, built for the World Cup soccer games of 1962, has seen better days but is still elegant. To my left, worn brown leather sofas and big armchairs look comfortable and tasteful. Free copies of *O Globo*, Brazil's leading newspaper, on lacquered coffee tables give the room an air of understated dignity. I walk over to the board announcing the day's events. In the Salon Barcelona, Unibanco, an important local bank, is running a conference. Salon Madrid 1 is reserved by Vilha, Mazzoni, a law firm. Salon Madrid 2 simply announces a health meeting.

My friend was probably right, I say to myself. There must be another Guanabara. I walk to the desk and ask the concierge to verify the meeting location.

"You're looking for the health conference," he says politely, and arranges his burgundy tie. "Second floor."

As I am about to take the elevator, I hear a voice next to me asking to check in for the ASTRAL conference. What I was looking for! ASTRAL is the acronym for Associação de Travestie Liberados, the Association of Transvestites and Liberated Ones.

"Of course," says the same man behind the desk. This time, he buttons his blue blazer.

Standing beside me are two transvestites. One is skinny with frizzy shoulder-length hair, wearing blue-jean cutoffs and a latex bustier of the same yellow as her dyed hair. The other one is stockier and black-haired, wearing shorts and black clogs.

"We just arrived from São Paulo, dead tired and dirty after that long bus ride," the skinny one tells the concierge, who smiles courteously and hands them check-in cards to fill out. "Do we have time to change? Are we late for the inauguration?"

We are, he says. The three of us walk fast toward the elevator. I get off on the second floor alone and they go to their rooms to shower and change. The conference room is in happy disarray—more than a hundred transvestites saying hello, kissing each other's cheeks. The first one I meet is Simone Françoise, the transvestite we all imagine, the one we see in the shows, the one depicted in the movies. Dressed in a strapless dress and high heels, she has a certain resemblance to Tina Turner. She apologizes for the black-and-blue marks, explaining that she just had a face-lift but did not want to miss the *encontro*, the meeting. She leaves red lipstick marks on her long, thin cigarettes, the kind that are supposed to be smoked by women.

As soon as she finds out I'm a journalist, she takes a newspaper from her handbag. "I'm an internationally recognized performer," she says, pointing to a color photograph. "This was taken in Spain." She is lying on a bed naked except for a feather boa around her neck. "Do you want to hear about my sex change?"

"I have to register," I say, sneaking away. I want to hear about transvestites demanding rights.

Behind the registration desk is Beatriz, black and six foot three, the manliest feet in women's gold sandals and the warmest, most welcoming smile I've ever gotten from anyone handing out press passes at a conference. She hands me mine and calls me *menina*, girl. I stare at a large laminated cartoon of a transvestite wearing a miniskirt and red heels standing on a street corner smoking a cigarette. In bold red-faced letters it reads: LA CIDADANIA NÃO TEM ROUPA CERTA—Citizenship doesn't have a type of dress. "We are saying that society cannot discriminate against a man because he is dressed as a woman," Dr. Celia Szterenfeld, social worker and organizer, tells me. "We are demanding their rights as citizens."

I thank Beatriz, pass the pink string around my neck, and ask her about the opening act. She tells me I missed history in the making. It had been great. Many important public health officials had shown up. Even Congressman Fernando Gabeira made a brief appearance. Marta Suplicy, the popular sexologist and congresswoman, sent a letter of support. But the applause and the admiration went to Jovana Baby, the leader of the transvestites' movement.

In 1994, at the First Brazilian Conference of Gays and Lesbians Who Work with AIDS, the group decided to include transvestites and to fight for their rights. A motion was passed and the group became the Brazilian Conference of Gays, Lesbians, and

Transvestites: "The plenary reached consensus with regard to the joining of forces between gay and lesbian groups and groups of transvestites, principally in light of the violence and lack of respect for diversity."

Two years later, the transvestites want their own organization. "There are many differences between gays and transvestites," says Toni Reiss, president of the gay movement, and the person whose idea it was to mobilize transvestites. Reiss understood why they would want to branch out. "They are much more discriminated against than us. They are doubly shunned, and not only by the Church but by all segments of society. They are discriminated against because they are homosexuals and they are discriminated against because they work in prostitution." For Reiss, it is almost a relief to have them form their own group. The transvestites do not identify themselves as gay. They see themselves as women, and this Reiss says is sometimes frustrating. "I want to find the first feminist transvestite, but they all feel like they are princesses. They just act like spoiled brats, you know, like a *mulher perua*. They say they never have a problem. They are concerned only about their beauty and they're afraid of aging. Their dream is to find a very macho guy who will protect them even if they are slapped," says Reiss.

That might be the reality, but the fact that they have managed to organize into a national network with fifty-two chapters suggests to Reiss that he could be about to see the burgeoning of a feminist transvestite movement. He traveled from Curitiba to support them.

"To be a transvestite is in our blood." Jovana Baby is addressing about a dozen transvestites sitting in a circle at the panel the next day. Jovana Baby defies the stereotype of transvestites wearing too much makeup and uncomfortable heels. Instead of gold lamé, cleavage, and rhinestones, she wears a simple tunic and comfortable shoes. She looks matronly—the Betty Friedan of transvestites. She is the spokesperson for the 130 transvestites present at the event—three days of meetings and panels discussing topics ranging from AIDS prevention to sexual fantasies to police brutality. Demonstrating once again the admirable openmindedness of many Brazilians, the conference is funded by the Ministry of

Health and the secretary of health of the state of Rio de Janeiro. Representatives from various states' public health offices instructed the transvestite groups on how to apply for state funding in order to be able to continue their work. Journalists covered the event as an important health meeting, not just as a Carnivalesque event. Jovana Baby's goal is to mobilize transvestites as a political force, to demand that they be recognized as citizens and not just as ridiculous creatures. She aspires to raise public consciousness of the fact that some of them actually do not want to be prostitutes or kept women. "We have demands to make to the government. We demand that those of us who work as entertainers be accepted by the artists' unions. We want our shows to be unionized, and the artists' union has never invited us to join. We want recognition for our work. What we do should not be a crime. We are part of the market. We are sex professionals. We want our jobs to be legalized."

Adriana, rail thin and blond, and Naja are also at the meeting. Adriana explains that it is imperative that transvestites have their own voice and explains how working for Reiss's group was frustrating. "I call the Associação Brasileira de Gays, Lésbicas e Travestis and the secretary general tells me they have no money for any of the programs that have to do with transvestites," she says with conviction. Her mother has had to lend her the money every time she needs to send letters denouncing police violence toward transvestites. "There are different dynamics inside the group. The transvestites feel marginalized by the gays. Gays and transvestites are not really fighting for the same political things."

Jovana raises her hand. Naja, who is serving as moderator, calls on her and Jovana repeats herself to strengthen the point. "That's why we are here. We want to create a national network so we can communicate among ourselves and have a national outreach. I would personally like to see some kind of union." There is vigorous applause and the air fills with the same energy of political activism one could feel at a meeting of mine workers. Instead these are men in women's clothes who demand to vote as women, to get jobs as women, to have conjugal rights as women.

"But how are we going to work together?" asks Paola. She is the transvestite I met at the reception desk, the stocky one. Now wearing a bandanna that makes her look like Bruce Springsteen, she looks less like a woman and more like a man wearing a wig and women's clothes. Her arms are muscular and tattooed. "Many transvestites don't want to be part of this. They only think about fun and makeup and working the street."

"Don't generalize," Naja admonishes her in a tone that speaks of experience in organized movements. Naja is more feminine-looking than Paola. She wears her long black hair in a headband, little makeup, a white T-shirt, purple leggings, and running shoes. She reminds me of a woman activist I might have encountered at the human rights conference in Vienna or at the AIDS conferences in Berlin or Amsterdam. But on Naja's arms I notice scars that run from her wrist to her elbow, and I wonder whether they are reminders of police brutality or self-inflicted. "Don't speak for them," she says. "They are not here."

Jovana continues speaking. "We are tired of cleaning houses or being prostitutes. We want regular jobs. We are afraid of violence. We make reports. But we know the police don't do a thing. We need to join forces and demand our rights from the *falsos moralistas* who call themselves *senhores* and *doutores*, and come to us for sex."

"That's right." Naja backs Jovana. They are the experts. "We need to focus on health issues and not get sidetracked. They are not up to speed on much, they only care about beauty, okay, but coming here they will learn a lot. Transvestites think it's a waste of time to be *conscientizada*, but through AIDS we must get the transvestites to think of themselves as citizens. Transvestites don't read much, so we need to use every second that we have them here. AIDS is a damnable virus, but it can help us build our citizenship. Condoms can protect us from AIDS, but what is going to protect us from the police?"

"What goes on in the mind of the police who beat us?" asks Paola, who removes the bandanna she is wearing to reveal the spot where a policeman hit her with his wooden baton the week before. "Is it that we make more money than them? Is that what makes them angry? I would leave the streets tomorrow if I could."

Paola says she makes good money working as a prostitute. Charging fifteen reais for a blow job, thirty reais for a "complete job," she can average about seventy-five dollars a day. What a policeman makes in one month, Paola makes in two days of "complete jobs." But Paola says she wants "what anyone wants—a home with a man who loves me. I want to own a small business. I am a licensed nutritionist."

After the panel, Paola and I go sit on the comfortable chairs down in the lobby. She smokes cigarette after cigarette and tells me about her life. At twenty-four she has worked in prostitution for three years. The man who was keeping her, a successful business owner who had left his wife for her, left Paola in turn. This is nothing but the same old story of a Latin man and his two women, I think to myself, like the common stories of infidelity that crowd the annals of our families' lore. It is what Colombian novelist Lola Salcedo refers to as *la trilogía del macho*, macho's triad—the wife, the mistress, and the *loca*; the queer.

"I now have to work as a prostitute because no one will hire me," she says, adding that she checks the classifieds every week. When something sounds interesting, she sends out a resume. But the resume is in the name of Luis, Paola's legal name, and it is hard to hide the waxed eyebrows, the six pounds of silicone on the chest, and the exaggerated cheekbones when Luis shows up for an interview. The moment Luis walks in, the job is out of reach. "No company hires a transvestite," says Paola, "so to survive I have to do prostitution, exposed to STDs and AIDS and police beatings. One day soon I will die, killed by AIDS, by death squads, or by the police."

Naja is right about giving transvestites a chance to learn more about their rights. It is true that many might care only about issues of silicone and facial hair and that many are uneducated, even illiterate, but they still crave recognition and respect. Isabelita Kennedy, as beautiful and elegant as Audrey Hepburn, traveled more than ten hours by bus to attend the conference. "I want to be recognized," she tells me, adding that this felt like the most important thing she had ever done. She reminds me of the women invited to the AIDS workshop, showing up because they felt for once recognized and once there not wanting to leave.

Curious about her name and knowing she gave it to herself, I ask her what it means. "Two women I admire very much," she says. I assume she is referring to Isabelita Perón, the second wife of Argentina's populist president Juan Domingo Perón, and to Jackie Kennedy. I think she got Isabelita confused with Evita.

"How do you spell Kennedy?" I ask her, making sure I have the correct spelling.

She shrugs her shoulders. "Buh."

For three days, the hundred-odd participants asked questions, vented their anger, consoled and supported each other. A plastic surgeon explained the risks and benefits of silicone, a psychologist talked to them about sexual fantasies, about religion, about how to deal with transphobia—hatred toward transvestites. At panels, the transvestites were open to learning and eager to talk. Naja, Adriana, and Jovana were patient, teaching them the rules of participating in a conference—things like raising your hand to speak—and explaining what it meant to be an activist. They took notes. They browsed the books being sold outside the main room—books about AIDS and about human rights along with *King Lear*, the Kama Sutra, a biography of Marilyn Monroe, a book of prayers, or a book on how to eliminate cellulite.

They felt, for once, important and part of something. They could have been men in suits discussing trade negotiations or women meeting about reproductive rights. In the hallways after the panels, they continued the discussions intently. They made plans for the future. They chatted with each other. They laughed, they flirted, they smoked cigarettes and drank coffee.

I am invited to join them at the Starr Club, a dark cave with strobe lights and disco music. The organizers are throwing a party for all the participants. I arrive in the same clothes I have worn all day to the conference—jeans, boots, and a T-shirt. I feel bad for being underdressed, for not taking their celebration seriously. Isabelita looks beautiful in a cat suit with a leopard print collar, curls streaming down to the crack of her behind. Beatriz comes to me with her arms outstretched and kisses me on the cheek. Her beard pricks me but she looks lovely and feminine in a gold tunic. Paola applies red lipstick, which she keeps in a tiny silver handbag. Her blond friend is wearing a black lamé dress and freshly shined white pumps. Adriana is wearing a shirt that exposes her skinny midriff as she proudly keeps her arm around an elderly-looking woman, a matronly countrywoman with white hair and glasses attached to a string dangling on her chest, a woman who I never expected to see at a transvestites' bash. "My mother," Adriana introduces her to everyone. The woman says she is there to support "my daughter."

The dance floor overflows as the samba and Donna Summers oldies keep playing. Everyone is enjoying themselves, caipirinha in hand. Everyone is dancing with everyone: public health officials, AIDS workers, gays, transvestites. A circle of transvestites dance around Toni Reiss—they are grateful. Everyone has brought their inexpensive little cameras and they all want a picture with Jovana Baby. When she takes the stage to announce the cabaret-type show they have planned, they give her a standing ovation. An overweight transvestite dressed in feathers and black gloves lip-synchs to "Don't Cry for Me, Argentina." A tribute to Evita, she says: "I admire her for going from prostitute to First Lady." Everyone applauds. "But also because she asked her husband to free all the imprisoned homosexuals." More applause.

Jovana Baby announces a surprise. Elke Maravilha has arrived. Not knowing who she is, I turn to Priscilla, who is standing next to me. "The most famous and beautiful transvestite," she says. Elke Maravilha walks onstage. She looks like a cross between Brigitte Bardot and la Cicciolina, and everyone's excitement is so overwhelming that I realize she is an important idol. She says she is there to support them and goes off to sign autographs, which she stamps with her lips. I feel so unfeminine, so unwomanly, that it is hard for me to stay there and enjoy myself. They ask me to join in the dancing, but I feel so drab and unkempt that I prefer sneaking out.

The second day, the mood of the conference is more serious, there's the sense that something needs to be accomplished, that there's no time to waste. Everyone awaits the two o'clock meeting. A sign outside the reserved room announces that it is Only For Transvestites. I ask Naja if I can sit and listen, and she allows me in. Seasoned activist she is, she knows the importance of being "covered" by journalists.

At two sharp, eight transvestites sit in a circle of chairs. The veterans are all there—Jovana, Adriana, Naja—welcoming the newcomers. Isabelita and Paola are nervous. It is their first political meeting. Beatriz will take the minutes.

"Our agenda," says Jovana, "is to organize a national union of transvestites, but I am aware the word 'union' might not be right. It smells of government. Maybe 'network' is a better word. What we are asking for is to be respected."

"We are just figureheads inside the gay and lesbian group," says Adriana.

"The important thing is that we try to form something for tomorrow," Naja reminds them. "We need to form a group and create a directorate."

The circle that started with eight participants has now expanded to twenty-four. Everyone is attentive and anxious to participate. At times, they all start speaking at the same time.

"You need to raise your hand and wait to be called on," Naja reminds them.

I now understand what Naja meant when she said the day before that AIDS is a damnable virus but it can help build citizenship. At this meeting, she keeps repeating it. To assume, as is commonly done, that all transvestites want to be prostitutes or hairdressers is to not recognize them as individuals. When they demand to be legally recognized as citizens, when they ask that the name on their identification cards be the name that they live with and identify with, not the name given to them by their parents at baptismal or registration time, they are asking to be free members of a society. They are not just Carnival creatures, lip-synchers at cabarets, or *coisas,* "things," as the Brazilian police call them. They are demanding to be seen as individuals and as citizens with rights and duties. They want control of their lives, not to be controlled by others, they want equal opportunities. The irony, of course, is that they are being discriminated against, their rights trampled on, by the same men who have sex with them. Not very different from what happens to women. I would like to go to Jovana, to Naja and Adriana and tell them they should invite housewives to their next conference. To see a list of the things that gays, lesbians, and transvestites are fighting for is enlightening. At a panel about citizenship, the list of problems that, for them, interfere with citizenship includes: the nonrecognition of their sexuality, the loss of right to inherit, and persecution. They are demanding the same things women also lack.

During the afternoon break, as coffee and pastries are being served, *cantos de louvança* and hallelujahs seep through the walls. Everyone runs to the windows. It is the celebration of Corpus Christi, and on this day a full-size image of Christ is carried from the Igreja da Candelária, facing the hotel, to the cathedral, as has been the tradition for more than one hundred years. Escorted by military police, the archbishop heads the convoy in his white car with the open back, similar to the famed Popemobile, which turns left at the main boulevard. Many transvestites rush downstairs to join the procession.

Dom Eugênio Sales, archbishop of Rio, is followed by thousands of parishioners, devotees, nuns dressed in powder-blue habits, priests wearing cardinal-red hats, street vendors, and children as he makes his way to the cathedral to conduct the Mass in celebration of the body of Christ as it is represented in the Eucharist.

The multitude walks slowly, singing as the body of Christ is transferred from one church to the next. More people join in from the side street of Rio Branco. From the third floor of our stately hotel, the streets become a cross made up of people.

"Muito bonito," says the young *bicha* next to me as he crosses himself. *Bicha* literally means "insect" in Portuguese. But in this case, it is the Brazilian term for a very effeminate gay man. It is derogatory if spoken by straights and empowering if used by them, like Queer in Queer Nation.

"Where is the body of Christ?" asks his friend, who is gay but not a *bicha.*

"His body goes in there," the *bicha* says, pointing to the archbishop's vehicle.

Curious about how excited they are, I ask them if they are practicing Catholics.

"I was a Catholic," the *bicha* tells me. "I had this idea of purity. Today, I still continue to have faith in God but not in the Church."

"He tells us we are not Catholics," says his friend, pointing at the archbishop, whose back is to us. "He is not kind to us. If he discriminates against us, we'll discriminate against him too."

Still, their faith is important to them. Later that afternoon, when all who spontaneously joined the procession of Corpus Christi have returned, the plenary session resumes. Adriana begins by asking for a minute of silence on this, the day of the body of Christ, to pray for the transvestite victims of police brutality, and makes special mention of her close friend and colleague Gisele Gaga killed by the police. Gisele or Gastão Luis Pereira Sobrino served as vice president of the Grupo Esperança, the Hope Group, working to build citizenship for transvestites. Gisele was shot point-blank by a military police officer on the final night of the conference of Gays, Lesbians, and Transvestites on January 31, 1995. Adriana also wants to remember another friend killed just months ago, also by military police.

Everyone in the room bows their head, some hold hands, others cry softly, their eyes shut. What would Archbishop Sales say at the sight? Or the military escort that marches next to the body of Christ as it is taken to the cathedral aboard the archbishop's car?

The next morning Naja chairs the closing session, and as always she speaks eloquently. Any women's group would be lucky to have such a committed leader. "We have to give the proposal a direction. We have to decriminalize the sex profession of the transvestite. We need to be recognized as sex professionals and say no to the violence. We need to begin with AIDS, but we are looking for human rights and citizenship."

By the end of the meeting, they have achieved their goal. A public health official from the state of São Paulo has offered to support the transvestites in getting the state to fund workshops to talk to police about sexuality. Toni Reiss has instructed them on how to apply for federal grants, how to tap money available to fund groups like theirs.

Jovana looks committed on the dais as she reads the proposal stating that the transvestites want to separate themselves from the gay movement and join forces with the transsexuals. She proposes that the new group be called RENATA, a woman's name and a word that conveys rebirth, the acronym for Rede Nacional de Travestis e Transsexuales, the National Network of Transvestites and Transsexuals. They take a vote.

RENATA is born.

"Where should we have next year's meeting?" she then asks.

The participants yell out their home towns: "São Paulo." "Curitiba." "Santo André."

"I propose Brasilia," a hoarse voice says from the back of the room. "It's where the power is."

Everyone turns their heads and finds the voice.

"My name is Lorena Gruber. I'm the president of the Grupo Estruturado in Brasilia. We have three hundred transvestites in Brasilia, and it is where all the men of government are. I have pull there."

I walk over to the large man in the black pageboy wig. He is built like a rugby player and wears a loud Hawaiian shirt and a red lycra miniskirt that comes to about a centimeter beneath his protuberant gluteus.

"What do you do that you have so much pull in Brasilia?" I ask.

"I am a housewife," said Lorena, whose real name is Jorge. "I am the mistress of a sergeant in the army."

While transvestites are making some progress in getting their human rights recognized in Latin America, street children remain helpless. For many, the justification of killing them is simple. Crime in Colombia is rampant. More than any other nationality, Colombians have the highest statistical likelihood of being murdered. It is a country where ninety-seven percent of crimes go unpunished. Feeling the police force offers no protection, merchants, business owners, and *padres de familia* take security into their own hands. Today the houses of the rich are protected by professionally trained, heavily armed security guards who sit outside awake all night. Private guards patrol the glitzy American-style shopping malls and the luxury hotels affordable only to foreigners from countries with strong currencies.

It was from one of these guards that I first heard people referred to as *desechables*, disposables. I saw two huge rottweiler dogs guarding the entrance to one of the city's few five-star hotels in the trendy Zona Rosa in Bogotá. Surprised to see such ferocious dogs in the heart of the chic neighborhood, I asked the young uniformed guard standing in front of the Hotel La Boheme what these dogs were doing there.

"To get rid of the *desechables*." He was dressed in black from his beret to his army boots and held a semiautomatic rifle in his left hand. He was no older than twenty-one, my younger brother's age.

"What do you mean by *desechables*?" I asked.

"Them," he said, pointing at two boys, under five feet tall, dressed in rags and torn shoes, who had obviously not bathed in days. The boys walked arm in arm. One of them held, close to his chest, a can of Boxer, the glue that street children inhale as a substitute for food and family warmth. The guard, to show he did his job, shooed them away, but the boys were too high to notice the dogs. Giggling, thinking they had gotten away with mischief, they continued their stroll toward the Centro Andino where Bogotá's young and privileged queue up to see the latest Hollywood blockbusters screened at the mall's movie complex. But the *desechables* will never get to see the movies. The armed guards at the mall have orders not to allow them inside. They will also be kicked away from the restaurants where they try to beg as customers go in. Rich Colombians don't like to encounter them when they venture out to eat at the many restaurants of the Zona Rosa where everything—their decor, their menus, and their prices—has been imported from SoHo.

I grew up seeing street urchins. My parents called them *gamines*, never disposables. Whenever my brother returned from playing *bola de trapo* my father would send him off to shower, telling him he looked as dirty as a *gamín*. And the word, a borrowing from the French, always evoked mischief and homelessness, never violence or danger. *Gamines* were boys and girls who weren't as lucky as me. They had no mothers, no fathers, and no big house to sleep in. According to the latest statistics, Bogotá has approximately 800,000 of them. Rio de Janiero has more than a million, Guatemala City about half that. In recent years, I've noticed more children living in the streets of Panama City, Managua, and Mexico City.

When I was about seven years old, my father was appointed director of planning for government expenses and had to spend Monday through Friday in Bogotá. Often we would fly to Bogotá to spend the weekend with him. While he was whisked away by a black government car driven by a man with a severe smile "to go work with the president," my mother would dress us up in our wool clothes and take us to the museums, to the movies, and to the park that faced the Hotel Tequendama, where my father occupied a two-bedroom suite.

Like the poor, *gamines* had no faces. They were a glob of dirty boys—I rarely saw a *gamín* girl—with little hands that stretched out and asked for things. Outside the ticket stand at the Museo Nacional, the hands of homeless children would reach out to my mom and ask for *una monedita*, a coin. Outside the movie theatres, as she bought us grape Charms lollipops and mint sticks so my sister and I could pretend they were cigarettes and smoke like sophisticated ladies, the *gamines* pulled on my skirt. *"Deme unita, no sea mala,"* they would ask, begging me to share my sweets with them. Mami would always jump in, telling them that that was my candy. Then she would go back to the stand and get some for them.

Coming out from Mass at the Iglesia San Diego next to our hotel, where we would go as a family Sundays at eleven, I saw for the first time the face of a street boy. A round face with puffy cheeks and slanted dark eyes, an Andean face the color of copper and strawberry with small brown islands of dirt splattered over it. His straight black hair stood up without moving when he shook his head. He was smaller than me and had stubs instead of hands.

He walked right up to us and stood facing my mother, who was holding my hand.

"Señora bonita," he said. "Can you be my mother? I don't have one."

My mother let go of my hand and leaned down to his level. "I can't," she said sweetly. "I already have three of my own."

She explained that she couldn't bring him home but promised that we could play with him every day in the park. That afternoon we looked for him, but he failed to show up for our play date. *Gamines*, to me, were unprotected kids who lived in parks outside churches looking for mothers. From that day to this, every time I see a street child, I want to give him a mother, a home. I want to see hands that do, not hands that beg.

I am not particularly proud of this, nor am I saying it to sound compassionate and caring. It is actually common for us, the privileged, especially for women, to feel an obligation to help, not to turn a blind eye to a begging, homeless child. I know many Colombians who will never deny a meal or a small amount of money to a homeless child. It must be a remnant of the legacy of Christian noblesse oblige that surrounded me as a child. After all, my grandmothers, my aunts, my mother fed the many children of their maids, most of whom were single mothers who had never been exposed to birth control.

Millions of dollars are spent by the international community to help the street children of Latin America. Throughout the region, I have found exceptional and admirable people who help street children survive. In Uruguay, Macarena Duarte receives them in a damp basement that a church organization lets her borrow and gives them a meal and a chance to get off the street. In São Paulo, Benedetto dos Santos created the Movimento de Meninos e Meninas da Rua, in which he mobilized hundreds of thousands of street children and consulted with them before drafting a bill of rights that is today included in the Brazilian constitution. In Bogotá, Father Javier Nicoló and Jaime Restrepo are as heroic as Robin Hood.

Over more than thirty years, Father Nicoló has rescued hundreds of thousands of *gamines* from the cold. Every night this Italian-born priest, a follower of Don Juan Bosco, drives a white van, stopping wherever he sees the bands of street children sleeping on the street, holding on to cans of glue and to each other. Padre Nicoló offers them a place to shower, a meal, a bed. In one of his houses, I saw a ten-year-old boy leave his *navaja*, his switchblade, and his can of Boxer, as the rules require. A social worker took his name and handed him a towel. After he showered, he sat on a bench in the courtyard under a basketball hoop and gobbled down the food inside a styrofoam box. I noticed on the box the

logo of Avianca, Colombia's major airline. The social worker explained that they received leftovers every day. Without talking to
anyone, the boy ate his food and walked out, picking up the blade
and the glue. Eventually, if the boy wants to leave the street,
the priest has a huge finca where more than five hundred boys
now live.

Jaime Restrepo, a wealthy chemical engineer during the day,
does the same work as the white-haired padre at night. He does
not ride the streets but goes under them. Dressed in rubber clothes,
like a fireman, Restrepo opens the sewers and climbs underground
where hundreds of kids hide from the cold, from street violence,
and from the police. He has the same offer for these kids. First, a
meal, a shower, a warm bed. If they follow the rules, the possibility
of a new life off the streets.

But most *gamines* never find mothers. If they are lucky, they
can find a bed in a state or privately run institution. Those who
stay on the street soon realize that to survive they have to do more
than beg for candy and for small change. Many try to earn some
coins by washing car windows and selling candy, newspapers, fruit,
loose cigarettes, flowers, and stamps of the Divino Niño. They are
known to steal hubcaps and windshield wipers, pick pockets, and
snatch the ever-present gold chains. Still, it is hard to see anything
other than hunger and desolation in the two urchins who would
be devoured by rottweilers if ordered.

Street children are a stark reminder of the inadequacies of our
system, our power structure, our institutions, our religion, and
our income distribution. Street children are, obviously, a result
of our economic disparity. But machismo also takes a large part
of the blame. The work of Padre Nicoló and Papá Jaime is
commendable. Yet these programs are Band-Aids for a gushing
wound. Unfortunately, they will not be able to prevent other
street children from running away, or from being born to poverty,
to abusive fathers and stepfathers, to submissive and uneducated
mothers. Housing them is necessary, but the problem lies much
deeper.

Street kids are the offspring of the poverty we refuse to address. They are the products of our laws, of our culture, and of
our Catholic rules. Fewer children would be homeless if women

became mothers only by intention, if they had access to education, to decent and dignified jobs, to a life that taught them how to say no to abusive partners and a public health system that taught them how to take care of their bodies. A woman who is financially independent, who understands how and when to plan a pregnancy, who is not afraid to enjoy her sexuality, who knows how to protect herself, who does not feel devalued or dirty if she demands condoms for sex, is the ideal to strive for. If the Church stopped proclaiming that the role of woman is to procreate, that sex is a sin, there would be fewer unloved, unfed children running away from home or being kicked out. There would be fewer children having to sell their bodies for sex because their mothers were unable to provide for them or to stand up and protect them when a new male partner moved in and refused to feed them.

Child prostitution is increasing around the world, experts concluded after a UNESCO conference in Brussels in April of 1992 on the sex trade and human rights. Reports point out that child prostitution, not surprisingly, is rampant in Brazil and Colombia, where the numbers of street children are the highest in the region. The correlation is evident. Street children, who resort to begging or stealing for food and lodging, are easy targets for adults searching to pay for sex.

Like poor transvestites who never make it as hairdressers, many *gamines*, especially those who are able to survive the street after a certain age, turn to prostitution for survival. And like transvestites, they are also being killed by the business owners' hired guards, by the police, by death squads. There is one in Bogotá that proudly calls itself Death to Gamines. Statistics show that eight *gamines* die in Colombia every day.

According to the Pan-American Health Organization (PAHO), two to ten percent of street children are HIV-positive. If there are thirty million street children in the world, as Lydia Bond, the regional adviser for PAHO, suggested during the Second Conference on Street Children and the Prevention of STD/AIDS held in Rio de Janeiro in 1991, there can be up to three million street children carrying the virus. I attended the meeting and again was surprised by the doors that AIDS has been able to open. Paulo

Longo, a handsome twenty-seven-year-old former prostitute, is now finishing a psychology degree at the University of Rio de Janeiro while he spends three nights a week cruising the places he used to work as a teenager—Cinelandia and Teatro Alaska, which he describes as "very hot despite its name." These days he goes with condoms and pamphlets.

What magazine in the United States has not published a photo of the lost gaze of a boy holding a can of glue in his dirty hands? We've all *done* the street children story, exposing the violence of the police, the harshness of their lives. This time, I want to know about their sex lives. I want to know why they are testing HIV-positive and whether it is true that "street boys prefer buying glue to buying condoms," as Lydia Bond stated at one of the panels.

I ask Anderson Oliveira Lima, also a former prostitute with a black ponytail, if he will take me along during one of his prevention runs. He is wearing the same T-shirt that Nando van Buren sported in his office with the cartoon of the street boy masturbating on a park bench. From behind a policeman is ready to beat him with a big bat. "That's what their life is like, so we need to reach them through things they know." He tells me he is trying to get donor organizations to send strawberry condoms because that is what the boys like, but mostly what gets delivered are expired condoms that tear easily. Anderson gives me the names of the places where he works, but prefers that I go on my own. Taking me with him could damage the trust the boys have in him.

I go looking for the *meninos da rua*, the Brazilian version of *gamines*. I show up at the train station at about ten o'clock on a Sunday night. As I leave the Avenida Atlântica, the one of the outdoor cafés and the famous beaches, I again notice how it doesn't take long to drive out of the Brazil of travel literature. I enter a road that shows an altogether different Brazil. I pass the Maracaná, the soccer stadium that gives Brazilians so much joy and pride, and the hangars where the Carnival floats are stored. I feel I'm driving through Rio's backstage. The cab stops and I see only skinny dogs, skinny adults, and malnourished children. Of course, this is how it would be. The rich and the foreigners travel by plane, not by train. Neither see the squalid reality that lies behind the famous beaches and the promontory with the statue of the blessing Christ.

Robson is wearing dirty red shorts and a blue T-shirt that was most likely given to him—a handout from a Brazilian or one of the hundred agencies that work with street children. It is way too big for him. He is barefoot and a plastic lucky charm held by a red thread hangs around his neck. He is sitting on the dirtiest blanket I've ever seen.

He says he will talk to me if I buy him a meat-filled turnover, which he himself goes to fetch. With food in hand, he sits with his back straight to the wall and stares ahead at nothing in particular. He nibbles on the empanada as he answers my questions. I can tell he has done this—talk to journalists—before. He says he is twelve, and that he has been on the street three years. He lived with his father and his stepmother, but his father would beat him up and so he left. Since then, he has lived on the streets. Sometimes he goes to the *creche*, the day-care center, where he can get a nap and a *cafezinho*, but he is not allowed to stay there. "It's good to go there," he says. "It feels secure."

Robson is so high on glue that his story is fragmented and his speech slurs. I ask him if he has heard of men that ask boys like him to have sex with them. His little head starts to nod. *"Acontece de madrugada,"* he answers. "It happens at dawn. At four, at five, at six." He speaks softly and incoherently about a guy who drives by in a white car with no license plates at about four in the morning. "He drove by the day before yesterday. He gave a mask to a *menino*, one of the boys, so that the other boys don't know which kid it is, so that the boy won't feel nervous when he gets in the car."

I ask him to describe the mask for me. He puts the empanada on the ground and covers his face with his little hands and makes holes with his fingers and places them around his eyes.

"Why?" I ask him. "Why do boys get in the car with that man?"

"They get *qualquer dinhiero*," he whispers. Some money.

I ask Robson if he has ever been inside this car. He shakes his head no. I ask him if he knows what the boys do inside the car and he nods yes. "They come back and they talk about what happens. They say it's something bad. They say they feel *dor*, pain."

Robson rambles about a man with white hair; "a policeman" who runs after minors and when he grabs them he "does thing to us"; about the men *que pagam a gente para comer suas bundas*; about the money *"we"* get to use our hands "like this," he says, gesturing with his hand rubbing an imaginary penis. He talks about the hotels around the train station that the men take them to and about the *calcinhas*, the panties that the men sometimes make them wear once they are in the room. The story is confusing because by talking about *a gente*, which means "us," he is including himself in the description.

"Robson, do you know what a condom is?" I ask him.

"It's a plastic thing you put on your thing to not get AIDS," he says. "AIDS *mata*, AIDS kills."

"How do you know that, Robson?"

"The guy that comes with condoms told me," he says. "*É legal*—he's OK. He is not afraid of us. He hugs us and doesn't mind that we are dirty. He treats us well."

While I am impressed by the broad outreach capabilities of Brazilian AIDS prevention campaigns, I can't help but reflect on what Paulo Longo said to me: "We must ask who are the high-risk groups: kids or men? Wouldn't we be better off trying to talk to the men as well and not just the kids?"

I leave the train station, take Paulo's lead and go to Cinelandia, so called because it is a row of old movie houses from the thirties. The Pathé and the Odeon were the grand movie houses of that time, but as Rio has grown and the rich people go to the movies inside malls, these beautiful Art Deco buildings are now closed and dilapidated. For years they showed XXX-rated films, and now they serve as the cruising place for prostitutes, especially young and male. It must be midnight by now, and the boulevard is wide and well lit but also quiet and deserted. Only a few policemen parade up and down. The place feels immense and I feel as if I am walking into a movie set. Everyone is at the Maracaná: one of Rio's favorite teams is playing, and when there is a soccer match all of Rio converges at the largest stadium in the world.

My new friends have, in fact, just come from there. They tell me how they get in without paying. I have bumped into them, six street boys sitting together on the steps of the city hall a few blocks away from the movie theatres, barely noticeable at first, swallowed by the immensity of the place. As I have come to expect, they too are passing around a can of glue. As with Robson, it requires patience to make sense of their stories, but like Robson they all have learned that a journalist will buy them a meal for their story. The boys say that they will talk to me if I take them out for pizza, pointing to the establishment with a yellow awning at the nearest corner of the wide boulevard.

I am in trouble. I know the Bar Restaurante Amarelinho would be expensive. Pizza for six is a price I cannot pay. We negotiate. Three slices of pizza, soft drinks, and all of my cigarettes, and we will stay and talk under the big wooden doors of the Câmara Municipal.

"Do you know boys that go with older men?" I ask.

"To earn money," replies André Luigi, fifteen years old. "They call us to their cars, buy us some food, take us to a hotel, tell us to take a bath, to lie down, and then they just do it."

The other boys nod in agreement as André Luigi explains this to me. They compare prices, which according to them range between 100,000 and 500,000 cruzeiros—between three and fifteen dollars. They name the different hotels in the area that they've been to. I ask them if they've all been to one. All except the tiniest say yes. He is nine.

"Do these men use condoms?" I ask.

"Oh, no," they respond in chorus. "No, no. No."

"But we insist," says Renato, who is fourteen and has been on the streets since age ten. "They tell us that if they are going to pay, they won't use anything. It's like blackmail. But we tell them that if we are going to work, then they will have to."

Again I see the contradiction between the efficacy of the outreach programs in raising these boys' consciousness and the practical consequences: I find it hard to believe that a boy this young, this hungry, and this drugged will have the negotiating skills to force his client, a man in the land of men, to use a condom. I ask them if they are carrying condoms, but like Marcela Playboy, they have none to show me.

I ask them to describe their clients.

"Strong men," says André Luigi. "Macho men. Timid men." There is longing in his voice when he tells me of a client who told him that he would have liked to take him home but he already had a family.

As I sit on the steps, I see more boys coming out of the woodwork. Many are returning from the stadium. A boy and a girl sleep curled up on the main steps. They all hold the expected can of glue, and they all ask for food. Those still finishing their pizza share it. Others walk away from the conversation and then reenter it after tagging and chasing other boys as if they were fifth-graders during recess—as indeed they should be.

Street youth have an early and active sexual life. It is one of the few ways they have to express themselves, experts have concluded. These boys have sex with adults for money, sex with each other, and sex with street girls their age. Renato, for example, gives me a full description of how he was seduced by a man for the first time. A few months ago a foreigner told Renato that he could have anything he wanted at the Bar Restaurante Amarelinho— the one they wanted me to take them to—and he would pay for it. Renato ordered pizza and orange juice, a barbecue, and ice cream. But two days ago, he tells me, he stopped selling sex because his *enamorada*, his girlfriend, found out he was in prostitution. He has promised her he will never do it again. But he boasts of the many other girls he also has. As Longo has explained, many boys prostitute themselves in order to be able to take their girlfriends to a movie or to a discothèque. And studies show that the boys definitely don't use condoms with the girlfriends.

Childhope and three local agencies conducted a study of the sex life of street children in Bogotá. After reading it, I realize that street boys are as much *machistas* as the *niños de papi* I grew up with. Reportedly, they gang-rape the girls both as a form of initiation and of punishment. They call it the *redoblón*, as in rat-a-tat. As one of the boys explains it, "the point is to take a woman of the gang or of the barrio, if she agrees or not, and pass her around sexually among all of us." At the same time, the boys claim to "protect" these girls.

When it comes to relationships among couples, the study concluded that attitudes toward sex and condoms among street girls in stable relationships resemble those of wives, like Luz, who are bunkered in their homes. Most girls feel *pena*—embarrassment— to talk about sex with their *"esposo."* Several of the street girls interviewed said that sex was not something that should be talked about. Few even acknowledge knowing about condoms. And as in most homes, girls are expected to do the wash and boys are expected to take care of them.

Javier Villada, a social worker from Casa Eudes, a foundation that shelters people with AIDS, took me to the Terrazas Pasteur, a middle-class shopping mall in the center of Bogotá, a block away from the square where I saw the face of a five-year-old street boy for the first time. Javier was trying to recruit a handful of homeless teenagers who had tested positive. The Ministry of Health had done some studies showing that the seroprevalence among young male prostitutes was higher than that among female prostitutes: while 2 to 6 percent of females tested positive, the rate for boys was between 12 and 15 percent. For the studies, funded by PAHO, the ministry had haphazardly tested forty-two of the young male prostitutes that work mostly in the redbrick shopping center, more frequented for these boys than for shopping. Of the forty-two boys, eight had tested HIV-positive, seventeen had hepatitis A or B, and seventeen had either syphilis or gonorrhea.

The government had given these boys their results and sent them back to the street armed only with a handful of condoms. Javier, a soft-spoken student of psychology who worked closely with Padre Vergara, the priest who started the first shelters for AIDS patients in Colombia, wanted to tell the boys that the doors were open at Casa Eudes. The house offers AIDS patients a compassionate end to their days, yet every time a house like Casa Eudes opens up, the neighborhood embarks on a campaign to close it down. One of the homes was set on fire.

Javier had gotten a few of the boys to move into a home where four other AIDS patients lived. But the boys ran away after a few days. They found the rules of the house too severe. They preferred being on the streets, even if it meant working as prostitutes, to living with no music and no freedom to come and go as they pleased. Plus, they didn't want to live so close to the specter of death. "I don't want to be surrounded by death," one of the boys who had spent fifteen days at the home told me. "One died last night and I couldn't take it anymore. I'm seventeen. I want to live intensely. I've never been to the ocean. Before I die I want to see it. I want to dance to Madonna and to house music. I don't want to go back there."

Javier was not going to give up. Every afternoon after five o'clock he would go to the Terrazas to try to convince them to come back. "They don't care about dying," Javier told me on our way there. "They've been close to dying too many times. What do they care about AIDS?" Javier goes at five because that is when the boys start arriving—it is after working hours that the men start flooding the atrium of the mall. Amidst the coffee bars and the clothing and music stores, men in business suits, in jeans and T-shirts, or in uniforms walk around, usually alone. If Javier had not explained to me how it worked, I would have thought they were there to shop, or to meet a friend for a coffee or a beer. But at second glance, it is quite clear that few come here to buy the latest CD or a new shirt. Instead, men ride the electric escalators up and down, down and up, looking for the teenage boys that Javier and I are also looking for.

We find a group of about half a dozen at a video-game parlor on the second floor. They say hello to Javier and continue their game of Space Invaders. They kid around, tease each other, once in a while check the door to see who walks in. After all, they need to start worrying about tonight's rent money. This batch lives at the Pensión Luis XV, one of the many one-room hotels where thirteen-year-old boy prostitutes live together with thieves and transvestites. Their smiles and their clothes—blue jeans, sneakers, and Mickey Mouse or Bugs Bunny T-shirts—make them look more like high school kids skipping classes than young prostitutes waiting for johns. "The only thing that scares them," Javier tells me, "is not getting the money to pay for the room. They are afraid of being out on the streets, not of death."

The game ends. They turn to Javier for coins to continue feeding the machines. When Javier says no, they ask to be fed instead. Javier introduces me as a journalist from New York, and they all smile at me and tell me their names—not their baptismal names but the names they acquire on the street, names that are usually very telling. Three introduce themselves as La William, Spray, and La Negra. The other three give no names.

They want to know about Batman's city and want to smoke my American Marlboros. We make a pact. I take them out to eat and tell them about New York if they tell me about their lives. *"Venga, hermana,"* Spray says, grabbing me by the arm.

We run down the stairs and they all know to go to the seedy Chinese restaurant around the corner. We crowd around a small white formica table and without asking for my approval they go right ahead and order full meals. Among themselves, they speak in their own dialect—a version of pig Latin mixed with gender-bending. *La mesa* becomes *el mesa*, or, more advanced, *el sa-me; el condón* is *la condón* or *la don-con*; *el SIDA* is simply *la SIDA*. The boys are all *ellas*—shes. That's why William is called *La* William and El Negro is *La* Negra.

As I buy them wonton soup, *bistec a caballo*—steak and eggs—and cherry cola, they tell me about their biggest fear—*la vuelta a Choachí,* the trip to Choachí, a dark winding road up the cordillera, the hills, where the police take them to beat them up and leave them there—often for dead. William, Spray and La Negra speak. The other three giggle and eat. They tell me where they come from and when they left home. They think they are all around thirteen; they're not sure. William is lanky and has rosy cheeks. La Negra and Spray look like what their names imply. La Negra is dark-skinned and Spray has big, stiff hair. William says his mother kicked him out when she found out that, instead of selling candy and begging as she wanted him to do during the day, he was turning tricks. La Negra and Spray say less—they simply ran away. But I know the chances are that they were driven out by an abusive stepfather or a weak mother whose new husband declared he was not a *maricón* to feed the mouths of her past sins. Machos only take care of *their* sons.

The gang eat with spoons and with their hands, stuffing their mouths so full that it is hard to find space to start chewing. Their eyes look straight at the plate, and after each mouthful they reach for the soft drink to wash down the food.

"Is it good?" I ask.

All of them slide their plates toward me. *"Coma,"* they say. "Have some."

I decline and La Negra, the cheekiest of the six, definitely the leaders, pulls his plate back. "This is not food for someone like her," he says, reprimanding the others. He turns to me. "But for us it's a banquet." I sense the irony and I don't blame him. "We haven't eaten in three days," he says, putting his hands in his jacket and producing, like rabbits out of a magician's hat, a family-size bottle of strawberry-scented shampoo and a huge stick of deodorant for men.

"Cheap," he says, placing them on the table. "Wanna buy them? A client paid me last night with them."

Their clients, they say, are all types of men: men in fancy cars, men on foot, soldiers, faggots, married men. As they recall some of their experiences, they make funny faces, mocking some of the requests they get from their clients. The one that likes to wear women's lingerie, the fat guy who likes to be flagellated, the *hijos de putas* who don't pay them and beat them up.

The mall is less than ten years old. But the practice of men meeting young boys for sex after work in this area is much, much older. Where the redbrick building now stands used to be an open parking lot used by a movie complex around the block and a hardware store specializing in toilets. The boys joke and tell me that the mall is also known as El Palacio del Culo, the Ass Palace.

"Condoms?" I ask. Those who are HIV-positive look at me with contempt. "I want to induct as many members as I can into the AIDS club," says the most aggressive one. Those who are not HIV-infected also see no point in protecting themselves. "If it is not AIDS," says one who shows me the burns and the scars left by the police, "it will be a bullet, so I'll die soon anyway."

A few transvestites walk by and everyone smirks at everyone. La Negra explains that there is a rivalry between the *pirobos*, as they call themselves, young boys who act very effeminate but dress as boys, and the transvestites, who dress like Barbies and have breasts. "They make more money than we do, but lately they see us as competition. They want us off their turf." The boys think this is because many of the transvestites are testing positive and the clients are starting to suspect it and they are scared. "It's good for our business," says Spray, who is himself positive.

For days, I have not been able to stop thinking of these three boys. I decide to go back to the Terrazas without Javier. I run up the stairs expecting to find them at Los Marcianitos, the video arcade. But they are not there. Maybe it's already too late, I say to myself, looking at my watch; they must be "working." It is past seven o'clock and I know these are busy hours. I take the escalator down and notice a good-looking boy wearing extremely tight jeans and black hi-tops sashaying across the atrium. I walk straight to him and ask him if he knows where I can find William.

"What do you want from him?" His smile implies that he too is for sale.

"To talk," I say.

"I can do that too." He introduces himself as Alberto Mario Caicedo and stretches his hand out to me. "But everyone calls me Corre, as in Correcaminos, you know, Roadrunner, beep, beep. They say it's because of the way I walk."

He takes my hand and leads me across the floor to one of the side entrances. I sit on a ledge and he stands in front of me. I tell him I want to talk to William about AIDS and he takes me by surprise.

"It's so important to be careful," he says. "I tell you, if my clients don't want to use condoms, I just won't work." His voice sounds strong, informed, and mature. "And on top of that, I go and have a test done every three months."

I am not prepared to meet such responsible behavior in a boy who was born and has lived all of his fifteen years by chance. His mother didn't want him. His father beat him up. "He mistreated me. He humiliated me. I think he hated me because he could tell I was a homosexual. He would beat me up. He didn't like having me around."

At eight, his parents sent him onto the streets to sell Frunas, small blue packages containing six individually wrapped fruity pieces of taffy. Seeing an eight-year-old selling Frunas is like seeing the blind man who sells pencils outside Saks Fifth Avenue in New York. No one expected him to make a living from it. "Maybe a box of Frunas—twenty-four packages—would be enough to buy me some soup."

When he turned twelve, he would stay out entire nights. He preferred a cold bench in a park sniffing glue, stealing, smoking *bazuco*, crack, with boys his age all night to spending a night near his father. He started staying away for weeks at a time. When he returned, he would be beaten even harder, one more smack for each day he had been gone.

The last straw came when his father broke his arm. "I hated him so much, and I helped my mother cook, so I took some rat poison and stirred it in his food. I wanted to kill him but he just got bad diarrhea. He asked me to leave and I did."

From then on, instead of Frunas, Alberto has been selling his body. A more experienced *gamín* introduced him to a man who took him to a hotel. When there were no clients, there was stealing, and there was always Pinocho and Enrique and La Chiquita, his new friends. The four of them began their *parche*, the patch, a tight-knit family of the street. "We learned how to steal. We shared everything. We protected one another. It's very dangerous. We have to protect ourselves from the police, from *la delincuencia*, muggers, and from the cold." Sometimes, to escape Bogotá's inclement chills, they took bus trips to Medellín, Bucaramanga, or Popayán. They sold their bodies to pay for their fares. When they settled as a group at the Terrazas, they added members to the *parche* and became Las Catorce Locas, the Fourteen Faggots—Corre, Pinocho, La Relajosa, La Boquinche, La Pastusa, La Pelos, La Sebastian, Jimmy, La Alex, La Mauricio, La Fabian, La Mery, La Milena, La Madonna.

My hands shake while I take notes. There is something about Correcaminos that seems different from the boys I met a few nights before. While they joked and boasted that they were ready to infect people randomly, this one speaks ceremoniously about safe sex. With the other boys I was acutely aware that they were answering my questions primarily because I was buying them lunch. To them, it was another transaction just like the ones they have with their clients.

But this boy meets my gaze steadily. He speaks softly and in full sentences, no street language. He tells me that he is on his way home, to the Pensión Luis XV where he rents a room; that he is glad he won't have to work anymore. He has just made ten dollars—enough for dinner and rent—from a fat middle-aged man who wanted to be flagellated with his own belt. "Before, I would stay up all night, have many clients, do a lot of drugs, get in trouble with the police. Now it's different, all I want is the money for the room. With AIDS now it's not worth it."

Suddenly his eyes leave mine. He runs his fingers through his thick black hair with desperation. "I think I'm going to faint. I feel very, very dizzy."

I sit him down on the glossy steps and I put his head between his legs. "Have you eaten today?" I ask.

He raises his head. His face is flushed. His upper lip is dotted with sweat.

"I'm going to tell you the truth." His eyes again focus on my face. "I'm HIV-positive."

Four years have passed since the day I encountered the boys of the Terrazas Pasteur. I never saw William or Spray or La Negra again. But every time I go to Bogotá, I go back to see Correcaminos. La Corre is now nineteen, he sports a scar down his left cheek, and he still looks for his night's rent at "the Ass Palace." But nowadays his "office"—as he refers to the shopping center—is losing its competitive edge. Clients know that many of the *pirobos* are HIV-positive, and many people now call the Ass Palace the AIDS Palace.

It's also been four years since "that lady from the government" invited them out for lunch and asked the boys from the Terrazas Pasteur if they would mind being given a blood test. A month later they were told, one by one, that they had tested positive. "Everyone cried when we got the results," Corre told me in one of our last conversations. "Now it's not such a big thing, it's not out of this world. You die the day you've got to die."

Of the Catorce Locas, seven have died, three from AIDS and four from police violence. The remaining members are closer than ever. The bonds between them have increased with each loss and trauma they have suffered. Mutual support is even more important now that they are between seventeen and twenty and work is harder to come by. As the *pirobos* get older, they must compete with the transvestites and the *gomelos*, the young boys who act manly who also work the Terrazas. "Now, we know how to live to help each other," he adds. "When you are between eight and fifteen, you work well *puteando*. It's easy then. Men look for you when you are a young boy. But when you become older, it gets harder. We have to find new ways to survive. In addition to rent and food, we need to pay for better clothes, because when you are older, your clients care about how you look. We might need to steal some more."

They could go work *en El Norte*, in the rich northern section, where they could charge more to the *gente cachezuda*, the refined people. But they prefer not to. They don't have the appropriate clothing and it is more dangerous. "You need expensive clothes to go work for the rich," he tells me. "We could go to the corner of Eighty-second and Fifteenth and you see all this *gente bien* in their big cars, their jewelry, their revolvers, their fancy clothes. They are *gente bien* and they have their wives. I've had all types of propositions from these people," he gloats. "But I don't like going over there anymore. It's more dangerous there. The police are there. They've killed my friends. We don't risk it that much anymore."

The gang seems to have settled down in two rooms at the Pensión Lusitania where the owner sometimes overlooks the fact that they have not paid for a few nights. I sit in the room Corre and three of the remaining seven call home. It is decorated with a poster of a pouty Pamela Anderson Lee in shorts and cowboy boots and one of the face of a child with long blond hair and a teardrop rolling down his cheek. Taped to the walls are snapshots of birthday celebrations, of Corre's beauty contests, and of clients who have fallen in love with them.

During the day they sleep, have lunch, clean the room, and do laundry. Often they rearrange the furniture, but the two mattresses are always left pushed together so they can all have a slice of bed. At night they look for rent money. The ideal is to make at least fourteen dollars so they can get two rooms instead of one. It can get pretty tight when they all sleep in one room. Anything over fourteen goes toward the next day's lunch money. With the new market realities, the division of labor among the surviving members of the Fourteen Locas breaks down as follows: Those who passed through adolescence with their good looks intact continue to make money selling sex. Those who didn't are now thieves, grabbing watches, gold chains, leather jackets, and purses, slashing uncooperative victims with a knife. They've even added a new member: Jairo, nineteen, who when he is introduced makes sure I know he has never worked in prostitution. *"Yo soy serio,"* he says, *"soy ladrón."* He extends his hand politely. "We try not to kill," says Pinocho, who has grown into a stocky young man with little charm.

Corre is full of it. His delicate features have matured. With a cheap wig, a little lipstick, and some blue eye shadow, he looks like a soap-opera star. It bolsters his ego, he says as he hands me the snapshot, and might get them some money. I comment on how beautiful he looks. He simpers and tells me that he doesn't feel like a woman in those clothes. "I actually feel like I can outdo them. I can put myself together better. I feel so good like that. It is my moment of being someone. When I put on the makeup I know I am beautiful. Maybe even more beautiful than a woman." Corre's comment does not surprise me. He has never been modest. But I realize how ingrained our machismo is, how even among the sectors that our society marginalizes and disposes of, being a woman is not anything they would want to be.

"So who are your clients now?" I ask.

"Same. All types. Young, elderly, poor, well-fixed ones. They have their wife and families and, you know, they pick one of us and they don't know we are sick."

"Don't you tell them?"

Corre dodges this question by explaining that the gang try to prostitute themselves less but "we have to eat and pay for this room. We are where we are because we suffered on the streets."

When they feel sick, they can go to the Hospital de Dios, but they prefer smoking crack instead. "If we wake up feeling bad, we'll smoke some crack. We get high so that we can live in another world. Being high, we dare do more—to prostitute ourselves, to steal. Being high makes us lose our fear. We take drugs to forget. Wouldn't you?"

Whenever Corre sees me standing at the door of the Pensión Lusitania he cannot remember my name. *"Ah, la que vive en Nueva York"*—the one who lives in New York—he cries out and rushes to kiss my cheek. But it always strikes me that Corre is more important to me than I am to him. To me, Corre is the face behind the statistics. His life history encapsulates all the issues that trouble me about our sexual culture, and yet Corre transcends all our standard and inadequate images of the victimized poor. Corre, with his affectionate charm alternating with street-smart savvy and seriousness and pain beyond his years, is often in my mind and in my heart. I look forward to spending time with him. I wonder, who am I to him? To him I'm probably just someone who makes an occasional appearance, a temporary phenomenon, like most things in his life. Today I am the instant answer to the daily problem of locating lunch. He may forget my name but Corre is always happy to hang out with me. When I leave him, Corre lingers in my thoughts, admiration of his courage mingling with concern for his situation. I recurrently think about his words spoken in front of my video camera:

"I want to work but I have no papers," he responded when I asked what it was he wanted from life. "I want a home. I want love from a boyfriend. You know, something that I don't have to give to someone so that they are with me. Even the foundations that help us, they live from our ribs. They get funded because they help us, but even there we don't feel accepted.

"We are *desechables*—we are gay, we are from the street, and we are prostitutes. The police rape us, just as they rape the prostitutes, but what can we say or do? They are the police, and the police are the police. You know here in Colombia it is normal. They take us, drive us around, take us on the *vuelta* and kill our friends. It's normal here to kill, to kill someone and leave them on the street. Left alone in the grass. They don't feel a thing about doing that."

Last time I went to the Pensión Lusitania, the *parche* were getting ready to pay a visit to the grave of La Chiquita, who they claimed had been shot twice because "she" had refused to get into a car with a client. When they went to claim her at the morgue, "she had no kidneys and they had stolen her eyes," Corre says, alluding to the practice of organ trafficking. He asks me if I would like to go along.

The cemetery is a few blocks from the Pensión and the Terrazas, probably the five most dangerous blocks in the world. As we walk out, Corre asks me to give him my watch, a stainless steel and gold Cartier, a watch of great sentimental value. "You don't want to walk around here with it." I slide it from my wrist and give it to him. "You are with us. Nothing will happen to you." I walk down avenida Caracas next to Madonna, emaciated and sullen. Pinocho and Corre walk a few steps ahead. Jairo walks behind me. I am surrounded by malnourished, HIV-positive boys and yet I feel safer than if accompanied by a team of trained bodyguards all looking like Steven Seagal.

Madonna is the young transvestite who had told me how hard it had been, at first, to allow a client to penetrate him—he was saving himself for the man of his dreams. He tells me now as he walks next to me that he is no longer a transvestite, that he has stopped taking hormones. They were making him sick.

Madonna tells me he ran away when he was fifteen, when his father abandoned his mother and she could not feed all her children. He was her least favorite. "She could tell I was a homosexual." Madonna knew it too.

It was hard to get into prostitution. When he first took to the street, he would stand at the door of a gay bar, afraid to walk in. The owner did not want to let him in because he looked so young and frail. But because he was pretty, she allowed him work as a *ficha*. His job was to dance with clients and get them to buy an entire bottle of liquor. With friends he made at the bar, he started going to work in El Norte, the more exclusive area. Corre's gang were always too heavy: "I was scared of them." But Madonna always saw them, because when she became a transvestite around the Terizas, they would compete for business. When her AIDS test results came back positive, they joined forces.

Outside the Cementerio gates, street vendors sell everything custom requires for a visit to the deceased. "We have to buy some flowers," says Corre, turning to me and searching his pockets. I give him a bill and they choose the ones they like: gladiolis.

Two types of people are buried at the Central Cemetery: members of Colombia's patrician and political families, and the very poor and marginal. They show me the statue to Luis Carlos Galán, the presidential candidate slain by drug cartels in 1986. The afternoon is cold and they all button their jackets as we walk past the mausoleums of important Colombian families. I was expecting solemnity and sadness, but they stroll as if in a park, acting as my tour guides. They point out the important names and the fanciest graves. They like the tombstones of marble, but they prefer the ones with large statues of angels. They would have liked to have given La Chiquita an angel.

I follow them to where the elegant and airy resting places give way to a labyrinth of stucco walls with little drawers where the bodies of the Colombian poor lie. Jairo and Pinocho and Corre disappear, flowers in hand. I ask Madonna where they went. They like to play hide and seek. "They have more energy than I do. I was in the hospital last week." Madonna explains they get outpatient treatment but they have to buy their own medicines. "The only way is by selling ourselves."

"Do you wear condoms?"

"Most clients don't want to," Madonna tells me, "so no, not really."

When I try to lecture, Madonna stops me. "*Ay mami, que se va a hacer,* we cannot lose the client, we let them do it. At the pension they sell them for cheap—"but I'm sure not going to pay for one."

We continue our walk in silence and I wonder if Madonna is thinking the same thing I am. Will he be buried soon—killed by the police or by the syphilis that his immune system is having difficulty fighting?

IV.
A Love Story

Nada se parece mas al infierno que un matrimonio feliz.

(*Nothing resembles hell more than a happy marriage.*)
—Gabriel García Márquez

"Magdalena had a fluorescent statuette of the Virgin and she slept holding the Virgin in her hands every day of her life," says Gustavo Correa, the sixty-four-year-old father of a virtuous young woman who followed the rules of her church and her culture and is, as a result, now dead from AIDS. He is a retired military man with doe eyes and skin that is as white as the plaster image of the Virgin Mary, mother of God, that I can see from where I am sitting in his living room. "*Magdalena fue una niña de principios muy cristianos,* a very spiritual, Christian person, always a friend of *la Virgen.*"

His chest swelling with pride and with pain, Gustavo Correa tells me that his daughter arrived "pure" at the altar, meaning that she was a virgin the day she married the type of man she was brought up to marry. Three years, almost to the month, after her wedding at the old Iglesia de San Nicolás, her father, her mother, her siblings, her husband, her relatives, and many of the same friends and curious acquaintances, hundreds of them, that had witnessed her saying yes to her groom, went back to stand vigil over Magdalena's body. She was twenty-nine years old.

"My wife is also a good friend of the Virgin Mary. As you can see, she is the most important thing in our home." Señor Correa points to an indoor garden next to the living room where he and his wife, Alma, have agreed to receive me. My gaze follows his finger. In a bed of plants, surrounded by thick green leaves and candles, stands the same *virgen de yeso* I saw, as a girl, in convent schools, chapels, and neighbors' gardens. Mary and Joseph, her terrestrial husband, sat on thrones in the hallway that led to my grandmother's bedroom. My grandmother would pause and kneel in front of them, kissing the statues' feet when she passed by. She would ask me to do the same, and I would, but it never felt comfortable. When I go to visit her now, I see my cousin's four-year-old daughter doing the same, and it still feels as uncomfortable as ever listening to Señor Correa's words. I have never felt close to the Virgin.

I am here to ask hard questions of a couple in mourning, to ask about their daughter. Before I walked inside the Correa home, all I knew about Magdalena was that she had married Manuel Flores, someone I vaguely knew, someone who was considered the catch of Guatemala. I also knew that Magdalena had left a daughter and that both the baby and Manuel were also HIV-positive. I knew this because it was the *chisme*, the gossip of the moment, what everyone in Guatemala talked about. The story had spilled over to those who knew Guatemala's landed gentry in San Salvador, San José Tegucigalpa, Managua, Panama, and San José. The tragedy was the first time AIDS had entered this privileged Central American world where pretty girls of good last names marry handsome men of good last names. The particulars of the story were spoken of in secret with shimmers of malice and morbid curiosity, at parties, in telephone conversations, and across bridge tables at the clubs. There were various suspicions and speculations about who infected whom, about what Magdalena's family was feeling, about what Manuel's family was saying or not saying. The versions, as always with gossip, were mostly vicious and degenerated truths. Some gossips whispered that Manuel had married Magdalena knowing that he was either gay or HIV-positive. The only common denominator among the various stories was that Manuel was being demonized, while Magdalena was made a martyr. Manuel was invariably cast as *un loco* who had spent a lot of time in the United States, that land of dangerous freedom. "Freedom," of course, referred to parties, drugs, and sex. Little was said about Magdalena other than that he had infected her—*pobrecita,* poor soul.

I understood that by simplifying the story of Manuel and Magdalena into broad categories of good and evil this segment of upper-class Guatemalan society could preserve the illusion that AIDS does not happen to *gente decente,* decent people. And no one could be more *decente* than Magdalena, than Manuel, than their families. By refusing to consider what they shared with Magdalena and Manuel, they too increased their risk of contracting the virus that causes AIDS. By making the scenario extraordinary, *gente decente* could go on thinking that AIDS only happens to homosexuals, prostitutes, and deviates. If it happened to Magdalena and Manuel, it was because they must have done something too different, too weird, or too wrong. They must have sinned in some big way. But because AIDS is linked to sex, then it had to be something Manuel had done. In this world, only men are allowed to have a sexual life. Manuel's sexual life was open territory, discussed left and right. "I heard that when he lived in Boston, he was wild," someone said. "I think he even had a black girlfriend." And thus racism also entered the mix of ignorance and censure that fought hard to defend this oasis of good manners, good behavior, and good names against AIDS. *La gente bien* needed to believe that it would never happen to any of them. The irony is that it was exactly because Magdalena and Manuel followed the traditional patterns of our sexual culture, of their class, and of their religion that AIDS entered their pristine, privileged, and loving home. Magdalena and Manuel's story is not a *chisme,* as people have made it, where Manuel is a villain and Magdalena is a virgin. Manuel is not a villain. He was simply told from the day he was born that, as a man, he could do whatever he wanted to do. Magdalena is not a saint—as most girls think they need to be. She simply was not given enough information about sex. She was, instead, educated to be the woman that our Catholic Church has promoted since the beginning of our republican era.

When, in the late 1800s, the first publications directed to women appeared in Bogotá, the purpose was to educate women, not because as individuals they had the right to an education, but because mothers exerted influence over their children and because their husband would find them more interesting. It was also a way to guide them and to save them from tedium. Most of the reading, however, concentrated on religion, morality, customs, and marriage. The list of publications was extensive and their names a dead giveaway: *El Hogar* (The Home), *La Mujer* (Woman), *Biblioteca de Señoritas* (Library for Young Misses), *La Caridad* (Charity). No article was published without the approval of a cardinal or a bishop. "What is a real woman?" an article in *El Iris*, another one of the publications, explored in 1867. "It is a weak creature, ignorant, shy, and lazy, who could not survive on her own; a word can cause her to pale, a stare can cause her to blush; she is scared of everything, she knows about nothing, and she acts, nonetheless, guided by a sublime instinct, by an inspiration that is worth more than any experience." One hundred thirty years later, these are words that resonate in me. I heard them growing up. Sitting in the Correas' living room, I feel that they could apply to this household as well.

As I sit on a sofa next to Señor Correa and facing his wife, who has not said a word except in greeting, I think about all the gossip and chatter—is Manuel living in Miami? is the baby going to die soon? do Magdalena's parents hate him?—and I wonder why I never hear anyone talk about the prevention work that Gustavo and Alma, with the help of Manuel, have begun doing after their daughter's death.

I learned of it from reading a Guatemalan weekly magazine. The title "I Have a Daughter in Heaven" caught my eye. I thought it was another story about people who talk with spirits, the fluff that fills the pages of our popular press. But there was nothing phony about this story. It was very real. The subtitle read: "AIDS has come to the family of Gustavo Correa: His daughter is already dead, his son-in-law and his three-year-old granddaughter are infected." The story didn't mention Manuel and Magdalena by name, but it seemed likely these were Magdalena's parents. In a color photograph, Gustavo sat in the foreground holding a poster that read TO WORRY ABOUT AIDS IS NOT ENOUGH. BETTER TO DO SOMETHING. His wife stood behind him—as she has done for more than forty years of marriage—with her right hand on his right shoulder, as a sign of support for him and a well from which to draw her own. With her left hand she is not really holding but merely touching the poster. She does it so very lightly that it is obvious she feels uncomfortable. Just as she would prefer not to have to receive me in her living room, she would rather not have had to pose for this picture. But she knows that as a wife she has to support her husband and as a Christian she has to help others. This is not easy charity, though, like feeding the starving street children or bringing toys to the orphans at Christmas.

The picture touched me because the Correas have allowed, in this land of *familias de bien* where people talk only about triumphs and not about tragedies, that their good names be used. They have agreed to be photographed. My culture, unlike North American culture, is not a culture of the confessional. No one writes books or goes on television to talk about their struggles with drinking problems, depression, incest. The recovery movement is not for us. Good appearances are very highly guarded. Seeing their picture was like seeing my grandparents' picture. They are a couple in their mid-sixties, from an upper-class family in a provincial city where mothers assume their daughters to be sexless and fathers provide money to their sons for obligatory visits to the brothels. I can tell that this is the hardest thing either of them has ever done in their entire lives. I can only imagine how difficult it must have been for Gustavo Correa to utter the words I read in the article: condoms, genitals, venereal disease. He, who in all the years of his marriage probably never discussed sex with his wife—he later tells me that his mother had many children but he was never permitted to see her while she was pregnant—is adamant about speaking of it. "We need to break the myth that we must not speak about sex, or about genitals or about AIDS," he told the magazine. "We say, yes, we must talk. Mothers and fathers must talk with their children. We cannot continue like my generation. Our generation was a generation of lies and we must now continue with the generation of truth."

I look at the Correas and my admiration grows. I can only picture what it would be like for my grandmother to have to hold the poster Alma is holding, for my grandfather to talk like

Señor Correa. Gustavo and Alma share their background and have similar cultural and religious attitudes. My grandparents sent their daughters to live in convents where the word "sex" and all talk of men was prohibited. When their young male cousins or brothers or uncles visited them at La Enseñanza, they had to speak to them from across the room through a *torno*, a heavy wooden revolving window. My mother and aunts spent their teenage years promising their parents good behavior and *ejaculatorias*, brief and fervent prayers to the Virgin. If they behaved and prayed, they were rewarded with sweets. But for my mother and her sisters, even candy had special names. Caramel balls known everywhere else as *huevitos de caramelo*, little caramel eggs, to pious convent girls were *suspiros del Niño Jesús*, sighs of Baby Jesus.

I have not been here half an hour, but I can tell that Magdalena grew up in similar surroundings, forbidden to ask or even mention anything related to sex because, like the Virgin Mary, good girls don't have sex, don't even think about sex. Her mother never explained to her that she would start menstruating. Like me, she was told that babies were brought by a stork from Paris. Like me, when she learned how babies were actually born, she had already started menstruating. I was fourteen when my mother called me into her room, and I had been getting my period for more than two years. Magdalena's father read to her and to her sister an explanation from an encyclopedia. Her schooling was stricter than mine. While I went to a coed, nonreligious school, she was educated at El Colegio de la Presentación, the exclusive Catholic school for the girls of the privileged founded at the turn of the century, where sexual education has been, *in saecula saeculorum,* taboo. Yet this school is described in a historical account of the region as "the proper environment of discipline, moral principles, and ab ovo education according to Christian sentiments that has been received by our mothers, our wives and daughters and other beloved members of the feminine population." These words were not written, as one might suppose, for the *bello sexo,* the fair sex, in the period of *El Iris* but in 1979 by a historian, a member of Guatemala's provincial aristocracy—a man, of course.

La Enseñanza's mascot is a bee and the motto is "Knowledge, Virtue and Work." But the school's much-praised curriculum concentrated more on their conception of Virtue than on Knowledge; more on *economía del hogar*, home economics, than on charts of supply and demand or any macroeconomic explanations of balance of payments. And as for Work, it really meant housework rather than paid work, or work as in a profession or a career. Nothing in the school would suggest to a girl of La Enseñanza that she could be anything other than an *ama de casa*, a wife and a mother.

To graduate, girls needed to present not a final thesis but a *canastilla de bebé*, a layette complete with embroidered diapers, crocheted baby shirts, and knitted bootees. Both parents and students believed this a worthy project. The nuns would donate the beautiful baskets to needy mothers in the poor barrios or to orphanages. And the girls prepared themselves to become what they were intended to be—the wives of the next rulers, the mothers of babies who wore ornate cloth diapers. None of them would ever have to wash them—the servant girls would. And the girl-wives would remain under the hypnotic and dangerous illusion that they had fulfilled their roles in life.

I flew to Guatemala, a country known for its Mayan temples and its colorful weavings, for its placid lakes and political turmoil. This country is where the term *banana republic* was coined because of the influence that one American-owned banana-growing company—the United Fruit Company—had on its history, the politics, and the daily lives of its citizens from the turn of the century to the late 1950s. By making alliances with the ruling elite, the UFC, *la frutera* as it was known, basically ran Guatemala. It controlled the jobs of forty thousand Guatemalans; it owned the country's telephone and telegraph facilities; it administered the country's most important harbor and monopolized its banana export. It also paid no taxes. When Jacobo Arbenz was elected in 1953 and tried to change the terms for the *frutera*, the United Fruit Company aggressively lobbied Washington and the press to see Arbenz as a Soviet sympathizer. They were successful. Because he initiated an agrarian reform intended to redistribute the country's land—two percent of Guatemalans owned seventy-two percent of the land—the United States branded him a Communist, backed and armed his opponents, sent planes in, and got Arbenz out.

Today, the United Fruit Company has moved out of Guatemala, but land is as unequally distributed and much more bloodied. For the past two decades, the army, the right-wing paramilitary, and rebel forces have massacred each other. When I arrived in Guatemala City in 1994, there was talk of cease-fires and peace negotiations. I resisted my temptation to report on politics. I even decided to forgo the obligatory visit to Antigua and Chichicastenango. I was there to talk to the Correa family about Forjar, the organization that Señor Correa created to do AIDS prevention and whose name means "to forge," as with metals, which to him means "to grow from pain."

I arrived at their home in the residential neighborhood of Santa Clara late one Sunday afternoon. The moment I walked inside, the house felt as familiar as their photograph. The Correas were getting ready to go to Mass. I could hear the blender in the kitchen making the juice a maid would later offer me. I sit now in the living room with the Viennese furniture of bentwood and beautiful woven straw, and the same Capo di Monte and Limoges porcelains, the Lladró figurines I have always disliked in the homes of my grandmother's sisters.

Next to the altar that Gustavo Correa is pointing at, my eye catches the many picture frames on a console with a pink marble top and gilded legs. From where I sit, I can make out that the largest frame on the table holds a picture of Magdalena on her wedding day. I want to ask the Correas if I might walk over and see her, meet her, get a sense of the woman whose privacy I am invading. But Gustavo is talking, his wife is silent, and I am incapable of moving in the face of their screaming pain.

"My daughters' dream was to have never been touched by a man other than their husbands. For me, it was immensely pleasing to hear the words of Manuel, Magdalena's husband, to hear him say how he had received Magdalena in front of God's altar. I gave her to him *pura*, unstained, as he himself confirms it." Many times during our conversation this gentle man, whom I have a hard time picturing in a military uniform, has to close his eyes tight and stop talking so as not to break down. He makes fists with his hands before opening his eyes to continue telling me about his beloved daughter. Not to embarrass him, I look at Alma who, still silent, rocks herself back and forth, harder now, in the Thonet chair with as much dignity as sufferance. Her husband recomposes himself and continues talking. Alma clearly wishes he would not.

"Manuel said it with full pride in the eulogy because, you know, in his life there were many women and in Magdalena's life there was only one man. So he recognizes that he infected her. He infected what he loved the most, *lo que más amaba.* And he also infected the fruit of their love—my little granddaughter, who still lives, and that is a miracle from God."

The ability of faith and prayer to soothe the believers does not cease to amaze me. It is clearly very important for him to clarify to me that it was Manuel who infected Magdalena with the virus, but Gustavo's words about his son-in-law are spoken without a trace of anger or reproach or resentment. Many people, including members of his family, he says, were very hard on him. Many of their friends and acquaintances showed more interest in gossip than in supporting them in their difficulties and in their sadness. The scorn and the curiosity were such that after everyone knew she had AIDS, Magdalena and Manuel moved to Miami, where she could also receive the best medical treatment. "She died there," he says.

But he confesses that while she was alive, it was hard to acknowledge to others what it was she had. He said his daughter had leukemia. Today, the metal desk in his office at the hardware store he owns is stacked with pamphlets and videotapes with the words AIDS visibly displayed. He has embarked on a one-man AIDS-prevention crusade. Manuel sends material from Miami—"we have seventeen tapes, we even have tapes from Harvard"—tapes that mention the use of condoms, literature that discusses the risks of vaginal sex, oral sex, anal sex, intravenous drug use. He tells me he goes from classroom to classroom talking to young men and women about the risks of AIDS. Even the nuns at La Enseñanza have opened their doors.

"Manuel, who is a brilliant man, very well prepared and capable, an intelligent man who speaks five languages and has a heart that is bigger than him, wanted to do something to help people out of their ignorance, to stop the spread of the epidemic. Manuel believes that condoms are not a magic wand that cures everything. It is only a part of prevention and sex education. And in reality to really help our brother what we need is education," he says.

I am trying to imagine Señor Correa talking about sex to the girls at La Enseñanza, and I think how brave he is. But for all his good intentions, when he starts elaborating, his prevention work disturbs me some. "It is important that we talk about sexuality because sexuality belongs to God. Jesus of Nazareth had genitals just like mine—and my genitals are not horrible, they are not dirty," he says softly. "God created man after His own image and likeness. So *that*"—he means sex—"needs to be spoken of with dignity because God gave us genitals for the beautiful process of Creation. We are tools to give Life. The other"—he means desire—"well, that's not God's."

Gustavo Correa is, alas, trapped inside the religious and patriarchal models that dominate our sexual culture.

The grief of the Correas is as palpable as the small round marks that the woven bamboo is leaving on the backs of my legs as I sweat from discomfort. How can I ask tough questions in the midst of so much pain? Cowardly, I stop myself from voicing my doubts about the way he is conducting his prevention campaign or about the way he is treating Magdalena. But I notice I reject his arguments. He can now talk about AIDS but he still will not accept his daughter's sexuality. And isn't it exactly the shrouding of a young woman's sexuality with shame that has sent her "to Heaven"?

I choose to listen instead to how they have reacted so Christianly to their tragedy. Señor Correa is telling me how he and his wife never turned on them, not on Manuel, much less on their daughter. "We reacted with tears but with solidarity for them. We could not understand how a couple that was so happy would only face darkness. That three of the people we loved most in the world were infected with something worse than leprosy. Manuel's family did the same."

"The suffering for all three of them was very cruel because all three were infected. Yet there were no reproaches between them. There was no 'you are the one to blame.' There was something in her principles: accepting God's will. And my daughter's love for Manuel was such . . . and his for her . . . and where there is love there is no room for anger, for reproaches. Their problem was this: the seed of their love was infected. The only thing for them to do was worry about what could be done for their child. Theirs is a love story."

I want to tell him that, for all the support and the love they as a family were able to provide to Magdalena, it is more a cautionary tale than a love story. What happened to Magdalena and Manuel is not God's will, but a deadly reality in a culture where men have all economic, political, and sexual power, where they like things as they are and women rarely question them. Señor Correa talks about the importance of sex education, but it is an education that reinforces our traditional class and gender roles. "Our families have known each other for years. *Es gente muy bien,* the best of Central America. They were all educated in the best schools, and then he lived in Europe, in the United States. A young man, Manuel, very dedicated to his intellectual pursuits. *Muy leido pero muy vivido*"—very well read but quite experienced. "He lived with many women, he says he even lived with an African girl." I now start to understand the basis of some of the rumors and wish he had not mentioned the African girl. Has she become the scapegoat? Have they found a reason to blame something foreign—and black—and not see that the more likely cause is right inside their homes?

I listen attentively to his words, trying hard to wear a neutral expression, the one I was taught to wear early on in life when I felt that I could not speak up, that it was better for a girl not to have opinions. I feel my compassion slip away, replaced by something fierce and critical. I call him names in my mind—racist, sexist, zealot, religious fanatic—just as I would when getting into political arguments with my father and friends during my first years of college.

"Manuel fell in love with my daughter because she was a *zanahoria.*" *Zanahoria* literally means "carrot," but in Colombia for some reason it is a symbol of good behavior, prudishness, and modesty. For Gustavo Correa, as for most parents, it is an honorable thing for a woman to be. He would never understand if I told him that the high morality that he is so proud of is what keeps us from knowing how our bodies and our countries work—to be a *zanahoria* is to allow others to rule over us, in sex and in politics. And today, in the era of AIDS, to be a *zanahoria* is life-threatening.

"Manuel was a worldly man, a man of many women, many easy women. Women he invited to travel with him, even to live with him, or just spend a night with him and then it was like nothing's happened here. But he came up against a *zanahoria*, and when he asked Magdalena to live with him, she replied to him, after we get married, after we receive the blessing at God's altar. She told him that she was not capable of doing that to her parents."

I looked at his wife, a woman I've never met but I feel I know. She reminds me of the women her age I see walking to the Iglesia de la Torcoroma or at my own family gatherings—simple yet distinguished, educated in convents but unread. Devout aging matrons with white hair and with the important last names of Colombia's Atlantic coast, who wear little makeup, simple dresses of small flower prints, and a modest gold cross or *medallita* or rosary dangling between their tired breasts. Women who spend their lives bringing up the children, obeying and standing beside their husbands, supervising the servants, going to Mass, reading prayer books, organizing novenas, doing charity work. I want to turn to her and tell her that it is her rocking silently, the rosary between her breasts, her submissive attitude toward her husband, her denial about her daughter's sexuality that needs to change. But I watch Alma take out a white handkerchief she keeps close to the cross dangling on her chest. She wipes her face softly, first the sweat, then the tears. She sighs a little louder than she meant to and pushes the heel of her shoe against the stone floor to make the rocking chair go faster and her husband's words easier to bear. Alma's chair, I notice, is the exact same one my grandmother uses to whisper the rosary every evening at six surrounded by the half-dozen servants that live with her. Again I decide to say nothing.

Despite her obvious distress, her husband continues. "Before, Manuel would just ask and all the women would say yes. My daughter said no." There is pride in his voice. "Manuel says that he was impressed by this. He liked it. He is a very spiritual man, a romantic. He reads a lot of poetry. You know how we men are, when the woman says no, that motivates us men. In the modern world of today, there are many women who say yes. My daughter said no."

Like Magdalena's father, our culture would commend Magdalena for repressing her sexuality. But I want to tell her grieving father that this macho attitude our culture espouses has killed his "precious flower," as he refers to his two daughters. It is an attitude that puts women at risk of premature pregnancies, of dangerous abortions, and of contracting HIV. He is telling young girls in Guatemala that sex belongs to God, but is he able to see the risks imposed on a woman who is not educated about her body in a way that recognizes her sexuality? By telling a group of Catholic girls that sexual desire is ungodly, he is reinforcing the fears and repression that turn girls into ignorant young women, leaving them as exposed to the risk of contracting AIDS as before. His insistence on mystifying Magdalena's virginity, her purity when he "gave" her to Manuel on the day of their marriage, is as dangerous as having unprotected sex, as sharing needles. How can I tell him that it is preferable to be less devoted to leading the life of the Virgin and to know that sexual desire is a natural development for all human beings, men and women, rich and poor, something we must acknowledge and be responsible and educated about? I had thought that that was what he was talking about in the article I read. Today, the highest praise he has for his beloved daughter is that she was a virgin until the day she got married at twenty-six.

"What was Magdalena like?" I ask, turning to Alma. She has been silent during my visit and I want to include her.

She tries to respond, but her voice breaks. I tell her it's okay, maybe I can come back another time. She nods. "I'll show you her photo albums," she says faintly. As I have many other times when sitting in people's living rooms or bedrooms reporting for this book, I feel the split between what I'm doing and why I'm doing it. I am touched by their commitment, I want to respect their mourning, and I also know that I am going to write harsh things about the way they brought up their daughter. Nothing can be harder for these parents than to open up their daughter's private life. I want to honor her memory, but I also need to point out that she is the victim of an epidemic that has rocked their world precisely because of the ways in which they so carefully built it.

Alma keeps checking her watch. It's almost time for the six-o'clock Mass. She wants me to go not only because she wants to get to the church on time but because she wants to stop feeling pain. I don't want them to miss it. But mostly I want to run out because I know that I've wrung them enough emotionally. I get up from the sofa. Gustavo grabs my elbow and walks me over to the table with the pictures. He hands me the one of Magdalena on her wedding day. She is a radiant bride. But my eyes wander down to the table and I notice a smaller frame with a picture of Magdalena wearing a red and black plaid double-breasted suit. I want to ask him if I can hold that frame, but I don't.

I don't know what to say. I think maybe I should say she is beautiful, but I don't know if that would bring them more pain. I say nothing but thank you.

Alma stays behind and Gustavo walks me to the door.

"If we have let you into our hearts," he says, standing on the threshold, "it is with one end and one end only: that God grant many people be saved from this. Because what happened to my family could happen to yours. There is no one, no man, no woman, no child, who is immune to this, to this epidemic that instead of diminishing is increasing. That we with the pain we live with in our own skin, *en carne propia,* that we have opened the wounds by telling you this is so that there are lessons learned, no other reason, no?"

"Yes," I say obediently and step outside.

He closes the door behind me, and I notice a sticker posted on the wooden front door: WE ARE CATHOLIC. DO NOT TRY TO CHANGE OUR RELIGION.

Forgive me, Lord, for I am about to sin.

On the way back to my hotel room, I zigzag between the families returning from a Sunday at the park, the screaming children in colorful outfits, the Indian women sitting on mats selling *huipiles* to the blond tourists. I notice a father buying drinks for his children, and I remember how when I was a girl, the same age as the children I am facing, my father would also take us out and buy us drinks. I remember not the *refrescos*, the carbonated drink that I never cared for, but the *agua de coco*, the coconut water that I liked so much. The vendor would chop off its top with a rusty machete and stick a paper straw inside so that I could sip the tangy, cold liquid.

I returned to El Rodadero, the beach where my family used to vacation when I was a child. I bought myself a coconut and the process was the same, but the green round fruit felt smaller in my hand and the place less magical than when my father would carry me on his back and walk me into the deep sea. The water where I played, rolling in the surf, holding the bottom of my swimsuit so that I wouldn't lose it, looks frothy and murky. I stare at the black-sanded beach, at the new and ugly condominiums one glued to the next, at the uncollected leftovers from the day's picnics and the cars parked where they are not supposed to park, and I see the chaos of a country that profits from violence, corruption, favors, inequalities between the rich and the poor, the men and the women, the real and the unreal. Standing here, it feels the same.

This is where I come from, places like El Rodadero, homes like the Correas', and today they all feel so remote—and so confusing, because there is, after all, something warm, comfortable, and safe about the coconut and the rosaries.

I am still thinking about Magdalena. Her father described to me what could have been one of the soap-opera heroines that all the women of our households—*la señora de la casa* and her help, regardless of their ages—sit and watch during every spare moment, morning, noon, and night. Magdalena could be Esmeralda, Topacio, Cristal, María de Nadie, a virginal beauty that kisses *el galán*, the love of her life, with her mouth closed, as a good girl should. Gustavo Correa wanted me to see Magdalena on her wedding day looking delicate and "pure" and *completamente plena*, so completely fulfilled. And from listening to the *chisme* and to him, that was the picture I had created in my mind, that was the picture that corresponded with Magdalena, the twenty-six-year-old woman who had saved her virginity for her Príncipe Azul, her Prince Charming.

But I am more interested in the picture her father did not show me—the one in the smaller frame where she does not look like the *zanahoria*, the demure girl that Señor Correa described to me. I was not able to observe it close up, but from where she stared at me, she exuded vibrancy, strength, and independence, even something sensual. Not a woman I could ever picture sleeping with a statuette of the Virgin.

Was it really the Virgin who gave Magdalena the self-control that we all lacked? She was born just a year after I was, of my generation, a generation that felt the ripple effects of the bra-burning days of the 1960s, even if long distance in dubbed American television shows. And if we were protecting our chastities as much as we could, we were all having some sort of sex. After all, didn't we all feel weak in the knees when kissing our *traga*, as we called the boy we had a crush on? There were jokes and terms for permissible sex, sex that would not compromise that treasured hymen— not that we knew what it was called or where to find it. Hard, wet kisses were allowed. It was called *martillar*, to hammer. Breasts could be touched, kissed, with or without clothing. There was what boys called *el brochazo*, the brush stroke, genitals stroking each other, usually in parked cars and with underwear on. Many times the stroking led to some penetration, which was theoretically stopped at that exact moment when it still could be, before *oops!* it was inside and then *oh!* the blood and then the damage was done—and you thought you had to be forever and ever with the boy you bled with. The boys were less courteous about our concerns. As boys, they just knew they wanted to get in. Who in Barranquilla has not heard the joke about the three biggest lies in the world? The first: "Can you lend me some money? I'll pay you tomorrow, for sure." The second: "Come on, *llave*, one last drink.

I promise it's the last one." And the infamous third: "Don't worry, my love, *déjame,* relax, I promise *sólo la puntica,* just the tip."

Big lies. Huge lies. There were plenty of insertions, and judging from the number of pregnancies, it was not just *la puntica.* Talk about push and pull, about the conflict between come-here and go-away, about love and desire mixed with guilt and remorse. And though many—I would say most—were really not sure of what had happened, so many had to announce they were getting married because *mami, estoy embarazada,* I'm pregnant. But the mothers seemed to prefer to organize a quick wedding, before it started to show, rather than to teach us how to be responsible and avoid making mothers and wives of sixteen-year-old girls.

It is easier for parents to see us as sexless than to see us as responsible about sex. When my friend Ana's mother found a pack of vaginal capsules in her dresser, she wept for a week. "How can you do this to me?" her mother kept repeating while practically locking Ana in her bedroom and absolutely refusing to let her, who had graduated from college by then, see her boyfriend again. Another young woman in Bogotá recalls that when her younger sister confessed to her that she had had a clandestine abortion, she asked her mother what contraceptives were available to her. She wanted to avoid having to go through what her sister had gone through. But all she got was the very stern answer "How dare you be so disrespectful to your mother." Her mother did not speak to her for weeks. And a young woman in Barranquilla, who says her mother was more open-minded than most, was constantly reminded that "the worst thing she could do to her mother was to get pregnant." Her mother never explained, however, how to prevent that from happening.

Not being able to turn to mothers or to teachers, we turned to no one. We were left alone with our ignorance. None of our mothers suggested a visit to the gynecologist, and there was no equivalent of Planned Parenthood in our rich Catholic neighborhoods. For poor girls, it is not much different. In the northeastern coastal city of Recife in Brazil, poverty and the presence of sailors mean that many young women enter prostitution. As a result, Recife has received wide support from international public health agencies. There are free family-planning clinics available to all young women. Studies show that only a few go to them. Most fear their families will find out and question their virginity.

But isn't it ludicrous for mothers to believe that girls' sexual urges just don't start until their wedding nights? Weren't they girls once? It is a process that starts the day we are born, and it cannot be stalled by holding a statue of the Virgin. Any of us would rather hold our boyfriends.

Typically in Latin America, pregnancies are unrelated to female sexuality. When an unmarried girl gets pregnant, it is blamed on the man—*la perjudicó,* he harmed her, he "ruined" her. And the maternity aspect of the event further overshadows her sexuality. She immediately becomes a mother, and mothers, like the Eternal Mother, are ethereal and uninterested in sex, as if that were a virtue. Birth control is too much of a bold statement. It claims for women something that is only allowed to men.

Men, by contrast, are expected to know about sex and to experience as much of it as possible, to never turn it down, to always want it, and to teach us about it once we are theirs in the eyes of God. Our parents and our pop culture tell us that the man should teach us and guide us. While our female role models are virginal, submissive, loyal, ingenuous, fragile, understanding, dispassionate, incapable of initiating the sexual act, and prepared to obey, the man that is presented to us as the ideal is a trophy hunter, a warrior, a conqueror, and a hero. At a mixed focus-group discussion about sex in Guatemala, one of the men said the husband should be the one to open a woman's eyes to sex. A woman agreed: "It is the man who should orient us." In Haiti, women insert special lotions and potions inside their vaginas—it's referred to as dry sex—so that men will not feel that they are enjoying it. "Women have been brought up to not ask questions, to not be active, to not have self-determination particularly in things related to sex," says an AIDS worker in Costa Rica. "Women remain in silence and it is men who decide when and how to have sex."

But such norms, as romantic as we are taught to believe they are, only inhibit women from becoming knowledgeable about their bodies, about their sexuality, and therefore about STD and HIV prevention. There is nothing romantic about thinking that vaginal itching, discharge, and abdominal and back pain are an inevitable part of womanhood. Romance and religion limit our ability to make informed decisions about our sexual behavior and our sexual health. Brazilian women reported mistrust of condoms because they feared that if the condom came off inside the vagina, it could travel to the throat. A street girl in Colombia feared the same. A young woman given condoms at an AIDS workshop threw them out before someone would find out she had them. In Uruguay, after a day-long workshop about sexuality, a twelve-year-old girl asked if it was true boys could not get pregnant.

Still, whether young women go to see a gynecologist or not, whether they have sex with or without guilt, with or without a condom, one thing is certain: Girls, like boys, feel sexual urges. More often than not, exploring occurs. As a safeguard to virginity, in Barranquilla there is the brush stroke. And often when unmarried couples let their exploring go further, it leads to anal sex, which also protects a young woman's virginity. While the brush stroke is rather harmless, anal sex is by far the riskiest behavior when it comes to contracting HIV. In the age of AIDS, treasuring virginity and encouraging women to be shy about sexual matters is the same as exposing them to the threat of a fatal illness.

I sit on a bench, sipping from the can. The sky looks cloudy and turbulent. Nothing seems clear today. I smell the grilled corn from the street vendors, the eucalyptus trees, the beer, the rum, and the tutti-frutti. It is the smell of families in the park on a Sunday. Mothers hold on to the children while the husbands walk a few steps ahead, exhorting the women to hurry up. Men ogle the women and let out the *piropos*, the compliments, usually crude, crass, and creative. *"Quisiera ser la brisa que levanta tu falda"*— I'd like to be the breeze that raises your skirt. The girls, coyly, giggle and wiggle.

I feel a pang, a pang of longing and loneliness because there is a place inside me that is used to such flattery and actually likes what in my New York world would be seen as borderline sexual harassment. And there is also a part of me that understands that this dynamic within families, between single men and women, between married couples like Gustavo and Alma, between the anonymous couple on the street, is all part of what I am criticising. The Sunday-at-the park smell that brought on my nostalgia turns into a stench of inequality, of power for men and submission for women. And it is this inequality that has brought me back here today. I understand Gustavo's need to hold on to the image of pure Magdalena, but at the same time I want to take his hand and explain to him that it was exactly this stereotype that rendered her helpless in the face of HIV.

I listen to his words, now that I am not in his presence and need not feel apprehensive about seeming insensitive: "We have been invited to many schools, and we show them films and slides of infected genitals so that they can remember that they too can be infected if they don't take care of themselves, if they do not love themselves, if they do not respect themselves."

Simply showing these audiovisuals to the young women at La Enseñanza is not enough. How do I get Señor Correa to understand that women are vulnerable to the risks of HIV exactly because of cultural factors like the ones he is glorifying? What he needs to understand is that these values—the ones that insist that Magdalena must be pure, that men can't respect women who say yes to sex—need to change before the screenings change anything. He can show these tapes a million times, but if he does not talk about a change of attitudes, about the knowledge and the skill and the sense of efficacy that women need to negotiate and practice safe sex, it is an exercise as futile as praying as a form of birth control.

I go over his words: "In today's world, there are many women who say yes. Sex is something ordinary these days, one finds it easy. In my day, women were more difficult and there was prostitution. So today we must have sex with respect, with the security that everything will be okay, that we will not get infected. But when one is drunk and goes to bed with a drunk woman who will not remember what happened and one falls asleep without washing, like a pig, well, one is exposing oneself to disease. If I pay a hundred dollars to a *puta*, nothing spiritual is left."

As a good Christian, he knows repentance: "That's what I was like. I don't even remember their names, but thank God I was always a good friend of water and soap. Because in my life, I have been a sinner. No one can throw the first stone. But if I can, today, at age sixty-four, give any advice to young people, it would be so *lindo*, so wonderful, that their sex be linked with love and that it have something spiritual and not purely commercial."

As a follower of his culture, Señor Correa had very different parameters for his two sons when it came to sex. "With that pair of flowers that God gave me, I cared for them as flowers of my garden with fervor and love. But in our culture, something exists. When I talked with God I would tell him: 'God, if you are going to punish me, I'd rather have a daughter who is a *puta*, a whore, not a son who is a *marica*, a faggot.' That was my world. I considered that it was a punishment from God that he would give me *un hijo marica*, a homosexual. So, as a man and a *machista*, with that education I was given, I would see that my sons would have a sexual encounter early, very early. But with water and soap, my son. *Con cuidado.* The first relation of my young son was with a prostitute. He borrowed my car and he asked for money. The woman was already in the car and he stopped in to ask me for the money. I told him: What you are about to do is normal; just be careful."

It is admirable that Señor Correa can now see the inequalities between the sex lives of men and women, that he can now talk about his sex life and that of his two sons as wrong, albeit seen under his Christian lens. But he has a ways to go. For all his eye-opening, his limitations are patent. Little will change just because he can now preach to young men to have, instead of paid sex, sex with love, spiritual sex. Until he can speak equally openly about boys going to prostitutes and about girls having desires before their wedding night; until he can see Magdalena as a woman with a sexual dimension before her marriage; until he understands that women should aspire to be educated, assertive, able to say yes and no, rather than a *"zanahoria,"* the epitome of the good girl, naive about sexual matters and chaste before marriage—until then, women will continue unwittingly to be at risk. I want to run back to his office and confiscate his tapes, even those he is so proud of because they come from Harvard.

*   *   *

I had two purposes when I called Manuel and asked if I could talk to him. I wanted to get to know Magdalena better. I was not satisfied with the image that her father had painted. It did not match the woman I caught a glimpse of in the small photograph. But I also wanted to hear his side of the story. If he had been so worldly, so sophisticated, if he was so "experienced," what made him want to marry a beautiful but provincial woman who had never been to college or to Paris, who lived with her parents and worked, just mornings, taking care of her friends' children. I wanted to know what about Magdalena had appealed to him, why he chose to marry a woman who resembled a character out of a Victorian romance novel rather than an independent, well-traveled, sexually assertive woman like those he had been involved with for most of his adult life. After my afternoon at the Correas', I could understand what about him would appeal to Magdalena—he was *un buen partido*, a catch, a heartthrob, a Flores. He symbolized stability and power and prestige.

Matches like Manuel and Magdalena are praised by our parents, by our popular culture, and by our literature. Magdalena, the beautiful princess, proper and provincial. Manuel, the handsome, sophisticated heir, a man who in Guatemala because of his birth was entitled to be powerful—like all the men of his family.

In 1885, a great-grandfather fought on the side of Justo Rufino Barrios, who ruled Guatemala and believed in a united Central America. His grandfather, César Flores, was a personal friend of Rafael Carrera, the caudillo who held on to the presidency for over twenty years, governing on behalf of a tiny land-based elite of which Manuel's family were prominent participants. The two men were so close that the president named Don César ambassador in Europe. Manuel's father was, as one would expect, a political figure early on. In his late twenties, he served as governor of Retalhuleu, the province on the Pacific coast where the Flores family were the largest landowners. He then served as congressman, subsequently as senator, and was also named minister of agriculture during the last years of the dictatorship of General Jorge Ubico, a military man from an aristrocratic background who attended school in the States. It is said that General Ubico compared himself to Napoleon and surrounded himself with busts and prints of the Emperor. By the time Manuel returned to Guatemala, his older brothers had already entered politics—one was a congressman, another a senator. His history and privilege made Manuel the man that women like Magdalena dream of marrying.

It was virtually a version of *Esmeralda*, the soap opera that I most remember because Barranquilla came to a halt the day of the final episode. School was let out early so that our teachers could get home in time to watch José Armando, the Prince Charming, a dashing young man with riches and power, save Esmeralda, the simple, blind woman who has agreed to marry the doctor who restored her sight, a man she is grateful to but does not love. Esmeralda is in love with José Armando and suffers before he decides to bring her everlasting happiness.

Our songs, like the saccharine ballads of Rocío Durcal, and the fiction of Corín Tellado in the women's magazines are equally "romantic"—women praying to God to give them the man they quietly love or women so emotional about losing a man's love that they are delirious.

Today the soap operas and the songs seem more racy. The heroines have careers and do not throw the hysterical fits that characterize these melodramas. But even when the women are portrayed as more liberated, they stop short. These are the words of one of these new characters: "Love is a corny romance, I know. It is the main enemy of our liberation but, regardless, it is eternal. And a breakup is able to leave me like an old rag."

Shakira, a twenty-year-old from my hometown who made the U.S. pop charts last year with her CD *Pies Descalzos* (Bare Feet), is the new role model. She has abandoned the antics of women ballad singers. No more singing melodramatically about abandonment or dreamily about love, her woman is more in touch with the world; she sings about alienation, about drugs and abortion explicitly—not just about romantic love. But regardless of how much her image is different, the message is the same. "People close to her dare say," read a feature article about the star, "that she will only give herself in body and soul the day of her wedding." And when I turn my radio on, I hear another wailing female voice: "You tell me you stayed late working / And I will pretend one more time / And in the kitchen when I'm left alone I can cry / I will ask myself should I love or should I fall / I can smell your perfume of bar and brothel."

Our women's magazines, *Vanidades* and *Buenhogar*, knockoffs of *Glamour* and *Good Housekeeping* except less racy, if that is possible, now give us a few hints about how to dress for the office and travel tips on European museums. But most articles still focus on how to get love from a man, for that is all we need. In a single issue of *Vanidades*, I counted eighteen: how to get it, how to keep it, all you need to know to make him happy. Love—meaning the love that will make you a wife—is the only goal women are told to have. "It is unthinkable [for a woman] to live without love," writes Florence Thomas, a French feminist psychologist and anthropologist writing about Colombia, where she has lived for more than twenty years. "Love is entirely the responsibility of women, and they have to 'get it' at any price," she writes in *Los Estragos del Amor* (The Ravages of Love) which is a study of how the media perpetuates gender roles in Colombia. Regardless of the apparent liberation, we continue to believe the old idea that female identity is activated only when attached to a man's. While men are encouraged to buy action and power, we can only buy love. An unmarried woman is a marginal component of society. The only way out of this predicament is to fall in love. And to tell us how to do it well, we have *Vanidades*, *Buenhogar*, ballads, *fotonovelas*, the purple prose of Corín Tellado, the soap operas of Delia Fiallo—both of whom are surely richer than Barbara Cartland.

Except these "love" stories are being shattered by the HIV/AIDS epidemic. AIDS really is the starkest way of unmasking what our culture considers love between a man and a woman. As long as men do and women don't—sexually and politically—the results are tragic for both. There is nothing romantic about what our soap-opera heroes show us or what our sappy ballads purvey as love. At the risk of being called unsentimental and cold by those who were close to Magdalena, I say there is nothing romantic about her death. Her father says that her body died but her soul gained Eternal Life, the Life of Richness. "She is happier than you or me," he says. "She has no problems. No trouble."

But I really doubt this would be the choice of a woman not yet thirty years old.

Women are being infected by the ignorance, by the inequality that our culture glorifies and mislabels as romance and as love. There is nothing romantic about being *abnegada, resignada, dada* to one man. There is nothing romantic about economic, sexual, and political servitude.

Gustavo Correa painted me a romantic picture. Magdalena and Manuel's marriage is a love story, he said. But to me it is a story that portrays political disempowerment, not love. It is the continuation of what in Barranquilla is called *la ley del embudo*, the funnel law: the wide brim for some, in this case, men, the narrow end for us. It is a story about the dangerous connection between the glorification of good girls and the absolutism of men in power which perpetuates the inequalities of our societies. Women of good stock are expected to protect their virginity, to go to school but not to be highly educated, to make some money but not too much, to be well spoken but not outspoken, to be alluring but not overtly sexual, and to work hard only at conquering a man to marry—a man, preferably, with Manuel's background, a man who will join, very early on, the ranks of power, a man who will decide the laws of his home and those of his country.

To do that, we need *cultura general*, which we get in short stints abroad—finishing schools in Switzerland, a year or two of learning English in the United States or French in Paris. Girls of my generation and of my class on the Atlantic coast of Colombia were rarely encouraged to get an education to become financially independent. We were given education not to find a good job but a good husband. All we needed to know was how to keep house, entertain, and be well dressed. As women, our success in life is measured by who we marry. All that matters is catching someone like Arturo—*un ministeriable,* a member of the exclusive clique of privileged men who make the deals and rule the country. While they lunch together at the exclusive clubs—the Jockey Club in Bogotá still does not accept women as members—and discuss the latest privatizations, plan joint ventures with American multinationals, and exchange friendly business favors, their wives organize lunches and *tés* at each other's homes and discuss their families, their diets, the latest painting on the wall, and their clothes. We are trained—be it in Barranquilla or in Guatemala— to marry these men of power, the ones who govern the country's economy and make the deals with the multinationals. We are supposed to catch one of these men who, right out of college, become *patrones*—men who in their early thirties can be made ministers. We marry them and become their wives, *señoras de.* But these desirable husbands are the same men who strongly believe that there are good girls and there are bad girls, that there are mothers and wives at home and prostitutes outside, and that they as men are entitled to have both while we as women are one or the other. The same men who are advocating free-market economic policies are the ones who are dictating our social policies and our legal rights. We are to be pretty and elegant at a social gathering, cultured enough to know about Stravinsky but not about stock markets, interested in children but not in politics—women who, in short, would never threaten their authority.

In *Una pasión impresentable*, a novel set in Barranquilla, a mother advises her daughter on her wedding night: "Your duty is to always be available, but of course not when you are menstruating and don't do anything prohibited by the Church. Having sex is like eating a ripe mango: you get all smeared eating it but you actually feel you've eaten nothing. Fortunately it doesn't last very long. What is important is love and respect and obedience: no one better than your man to know what is good for you, and men, my daughter, will always be men. You have the good fortune to be marrying a serious man, an old dog, with wealth and position: you will find happiness if you make him happy."

Men of important last names like Manuel are encouraged to experiment with everything—education, travel, sex, power—for everything is available to them. But to settle down they always prefer a nice girl. The image that Señor Correa painted to me of Magdalena is the same portrait of a woman that Catholic publications of 1870 encouraged men to marry: "Young Christian: You want a decent lady that will be a Christian wife, a good mother to your children? Well, do not seek her where a foolish and vain world flaunts its precious beauties as in a bazaar of slaves. Do not go looking for her either in public showing off brazenness and self-confidence, nor at a street party weaving in polkas, nor in schools or academies being a know-it-all. The Christian lady loves darkness and retreats instinctively; in the best example of the Queen of all ladies, María, mother of Our Savior, she has well learned that only in the valley are lilies born.

"And do not let fear make you grieve that, because this flower of Christian virginity that we are searching is hidden, it will be impossible to find. Do not fear; modesty, virtue, purity . . . are difficult to find but he who knows how to choose shall find."

Why would he want this? I wanted to know if it was true, as Señor Correa had suggested, that he was attracted to Magdalena because she said no. Did Manuel feel that not being able to make love to his girlfriend was romantic?

I wait for Manuel to pick me up outside one of the buildings on Brickell Avenue, a lush boulevard of palm trees and glossy condominiums that, I venture to say, are at least ninety percent owned by Latin Americans.

Miami feels familiar. I have been coming here almost as long as I can remember. I must have been thirteen or so the first time. Miami felt like it was a supersonic city of the future. Labyrinths of highways, stacked one on top of the other, made me feel like I was riding with the Jetsons. It was the home of Disney World, malls, corner stores that sold colored notebooks and Milky Way chocolate and Bazooka bubble gum, things that in Barranquilla made me feel privileged to have them. During my college years in Michigan, I would feel I had already gotten home when I arrived at the Miami airport to make my connecting flight. Today, I feel uncomfortable in Miami.

I have heard many say that Miami is not really the U.S., that it is the entrance to Latin America. It is. It is a Latin America with comforts; it is Latin America with a working infrastructure. As such, it is a prolongation of all of its contradictions, a continuation of the ills of our corrupt and patriarchal societies. Wealthy aristocratic families, nouveau-riche merchant ones, former presidents, corrupt or not, keep apartments here. Miami has been a haven for deposed dictators—Fulgencio Batista and Anastasio Somoza are buried here—and a source of money for presidential candidates—Mario Vargas Llosa, Violeta Chamorro, Jean-Baptiste Aristide all held fund-raising events. Even Fidel Castro raised money in Miami in 1959. It is also a place to seek refuge from political turmoil. A former Colombian president hid in his Key Biscayne apartment after receiving death threats, and a group of businessmen and politicians plotted to depose President Ernesto Samper, who was allegedly implicated with drug money, from here. I have heard the wives of the rich tell their husbands they *need* to come to Miami to shop. Mothers and daughters make special trips to buy wedding gowns and trousseaus. Women walk Dadeland Mall, the more sophisticated ones go to the Bal Harbour Shops, buying annual wardrobes and the expensive creams that promise wrinkle-free maturity and shampoos to make their hair healthy, like American hair—blonder, straighter, better. Miami offers safety, state-of-the art medical treatment, fancy shopping. Children can be taken to Disney World and everyone can escape corruption charges, political turmoil, or simply the tedium of our lives in the countries that the owners of these condominiums help shape, countries that have unreliable public services not to mention other more serious deficiencies such as justice, education, or welfare.

A brand-new four-door silver BMW pulls up. Manuel steps out, walks toward me, and kisses my cheek. He suggests breakfast at Gianni's, the small open-air café a few streets down. Brickell Avenue really is the dream boulevard to any wealthy Latin American—green lawns, glossy skyscrapers, clean streets, smooth roads, tended tennis courts, and a beautiful waterfront filled with pretty yachts. Everyone speaks Spanish, drives an expensive car, and dresses to the nines. This is what rich Latins wish their countries looked like. The waiter says hello in French and Manuel orders coffee in perfect French.

Manuel feels as familiar as the Correas did. But with the Correas, I was not able to let out that side of me that has lived outside Colombia. With Manuel it is easy to be the woman who speaks half in Spanish, half in English, who is highly educated and well traveled, who pays her rent and has a career, who has relationships, sometimes good ones, sometimes not, who keeps condoms in a white ceramic box at the bedside, next to the small cross her grandmother always kept on her night table.

Like me, Manuel was sent abroad during his teen years. Like me, he spent a lot of time traveling while getting a college degree from an American university—though a minimal percentage of Latin Americans, mostly male, are educated abroad. Manuel also spent time living in New York, Boston, Miami, Paris, and London, seeing the world as an elegant-mannered *bon vivant*. We exchange information and realize that, although we didn't know each other then, we had many friends in common. He went to the University of Miami and then transferred to Boston University, where I had lots of friends from Barranquilla. We figure out that we had both been at the same party in the fall of 1980, at Adams House at Harvard, where a bathtub was filled with champagne and guests swam naked in the pool. He had even had a torrid affair with one of my close childhood friends.

If I was surprised and terrified when I first heard my American schoolmates talk about sex, Manuel tells me he was delighted and ready to indulge in the newfound freedom of American culture. For the first time in his life, he met girls who consented to have sex. He didn't have to struggle to decide whether a girl was the kind that stops at kissing or the kind that can be taken to bed. Gringas had sex and drank beer and, much to his surprise, roommates conferred with one another on who would get the bedroom on what nights. He was in heaven. His apartment—he was one of the few freshmen with his own off-campus apartment—was a revolving door; girls came and went constantly.

He spent weekends in New York, where he knew the doormen at the famous discos. The bouncers at Studio 54 and Xenon recognized him, and he knew the correct password to get into Club A. He lunched in London, partied in Mallorca, and sailed in the south of France. He had girlfriends—"all the time." In Boston, he had a "a girl from Istanbul, a redhead, a black girl from Nigeria, and the exuberant Brazilian who drank caipirinhas in the morning." He liked the Brazilian the best, and once flew her to Portofino for the weekend.

For nine years the world was his playground—parties around the clock, weekends spent in faraway places. All he needed was an American Express card, a telephone, his address book, and airports. His friends were the monied and cultured European aristocracy, Guatemalans scattered around the world's capitals, and his wealthy collegemates. Life was like an unending country fair. Money was always available—from *papi*—to pay for the next joyride as soon as the last one ended.

In 1989 he decided it was time to return to Guatemala. He went back to Retalhuleu and became involved in administering the land that his family had owned for more than three generations: thousands of square miles of fertile land on the Pacific coast. Manuel's family's holdings are so large they probably equal the entire state of Rhode Island. "My ration of city boy was saturated," he says. "I wanted to return to Retalhuleu, to the countryside. It seemed exotic, the countryside. There I was the owner of it all."

As he faces me, I notice his green eyes, his full upper lip, his fine linen shirt, his impeccable table manners, and I understand why Magdalena would have found him irresistible if not a little intimidating. I had imagined him taller and in some ways less interesting. He is handsome, sophisticated, articulate, charming, and quite smart. I am sure she had never met anyone quite like him.

While I renounced the role that I had been born to as a Colombian woman and returned, at age twenty-four, to New York where I still live, Manuel eagerly assumed his corresponding role. It was time to settle down, to *coger seriedad*, assume seriousness, take charge of what had been carved out for him, generations back. By returning to Santa Clara, Manuel was responding to the call of duty and to the attractions of having been born landed. He went back to a place where he was to direct the work of the more than two thousand men who picked the coffee beans his family owned: men who would call him *patrón*, master. Manuel had never worked in agriculture and knew as much about crops as I knew about sex at fifteen. But he was boss to these men whose subsistence wages supported more than five thousand men, women, and children. It was their work that allowed Manuel to study in Boston and frolic in Paris, London, and New York.

The Flores family has long owned some of the best coffee plantations in the Caribbean. When the United Fruit Company was expanding in the late 1800s, it came to Guatemala. There it followed the lead of its founder, Minor Keith, who in 1897, when expanding operations, married the daughter of a former president of Costa Rica and became known as the "uncrowned king of Central America." Keith understood the benefits that could be reaped from alliances with the local landed aristocracy. In Guatemala *la frutera* befriended men like Manuel's grandfather. My family was the region's potentates, the *mandamás*, the bigwigs. We've always been friends to the Americans," Manuel tells me as we drive down Biscayne Boulevard to his office, an import-export company. "You know when in 1960 the U.S. was obsessed with overthrowing Fidel Castro, President Yaígoras was asked to set up an air base and a training site on our land. We did." Keith was expanding at the right time. Land in those days could be bought for almost nothing, and the local elites were ready to sell at any price. By 1899, the United Fruit Company owned more than 200,000 acres of land throughout the Caribbean and Central America. In the early 1900s, Guatemala's strongman, Manuel Estrada Cabrera, granted the UFC a ninety-nine-year concession to finish constructing and operate the country's rail line and the right to manage the entire mail system.

I notice we are surrounded by the skyscrapers built with the billions that Latin America's businessmen and politicians prefer to keep, not where they make them, but in the United States. Although I see the importance of pacts and friendships between powerful businessmen and the landed aristocracy, the politicians who do not believe in agrarian reform and workers' rights have benefited not only their own elite class but foreign interests as well. Men like César Flores may have been offended by the term "banana republic," but that is in fact what he was acceding to. Driving around Miami, I link the friendship between Manuel's grandfather and the Americans with Magdalena's fate.

When César Flores died, Pedro was a graduate student at the University of Miami. At his father's funeral he met his future wife, Dolores, a convent girl at the Rosarian Academy in Palm Beach who came from Santa Clara. Her mother was a Velasco, the most venerable name in the region; her father was a diplomat. When he married Dolores Suárez Velasco at the cathedral in Retalhuleu, Pedro Flores entered Guatemalan society.

Pedro started a coffee export company in Miami, and Dolores gave birth to two babies. At age twenty-six, Pedro Flores returned to his vast holdings. Within a year he was appointed mayor. Soon Pedro Flores was established as a man of the land and of politics, and his wife as a woman of the Church and the mother of his children. She had nine; Manuel was the fifth.

The phone rings in his office. It is his father. He asks Manuel to accompany him to Fort Lauderdale the next day to see a yacht he is interested in.

"What was he like?" I ask.

"Always busy. I rarely saw him, but he scared us when we got to see him once a month. He was very distant and very *seco*—very dry." He intimidated Manuel, who always wanted to please him. "But he was so demanding."

Dolores was exactly the opposite. "She was born for her children, not to develop herself," he tells me. I wonder if he is he saying it to please me? "She was born with the Christian concept of sacrifice. Every day she talks to all of her nine children. Everything revolves around her children, her husband, and the Church."

I have come to Miami to explore one family tragedy. But each detail shared with me by surviving members reveals the ways in which personal beliefs and biases have political implications. It is impossible, I think, to fully understand the story of Manuel and Magdalena without examining the history and political culture that made their tragedy inevitable.

I am tracing it all to bananas. When, in 1870, Lorenzo Dow Baker bought a few bunches of bananas in Jamaica and sailed them back to Cape Cod and sold them immediately, he never could have foreseen that, by bringing a new fruit to American tables, he would be reinforcing the way the men and the women of Latin America relate to each other. But bananas reinforce the machismo that has forever existed. Almost since the day in 1899 when the Boston Trading Company merged with the Tropical Trading and Transport Company to create the United Fruit Company with control of eighty percent of the banana industry, the Flores family has had business links with the American company—a company that was able for an entire century to influence the politics of Latin America, a company that gave meaning to the term that today describes a corrupt nation dominated by foreign interests and a ruling elite: banana republic. In Guatemala, in Honduras, in the Dominican Republic, in every country where the United Fruit Company acquired land, the company had the power to make laws, to set prices, even to elect the president—or to overthrow him, as in the infamous coup of 1954. "The yellow banana," feminist historian Cynthia Enloe writes in *Making Feminist Sense of International Politics: Bananas, Beaches & Bases*, "symbolized America's new global reach."

Banana plantations were developed as a result of alliances among men of different but complementary interests: businessmen and officials of the importing countries and landowners like César Flores, and government officials of the exporting countries. But this new way of conducting business, I am now realizing, affects the wives, the daughters, the women of the exporting countries.

It was probably in Guatemala that the UFC exerted the most influence in national politics. Guatemala's small size enhanced the alliance between the UFC, the local landed elite, and the central political power, making it tighter. Here the UFC controlled the largest segment of the economy, two percent of landowners owned most of the nation's arable land, and the percentage of politicians who were landowners or supported them was quite high. The triumvirate was mutually beneficial, with the government giving the UFC all kinds of fiscal breaks, and the UFC agreeing to keep wages low—as low as fifty cents a day—so that other landowners could keep paying such miserable pay to peasants. Under this government, landowners could fly to Miami for the weekend while the annual income of an agricultural worker was eighty-seven dollars. "We've been coming to Miami forever," Manuel boasts. "The Flores have lived on Brickell before any of these skyscrapers were built."

It is traditional in Latin America that our governments have been presided over by strongmen with considerable wealth and extensive business interests, men who are in power to protect their holdings and those of their friends more than to govern with social conscience. To modernize Guatemala or the Atlantic coast of Colombia or any of our countries would require an attack on a system that allows the concentration of land in a few hands—an attack that would naturally be vigorously resisted, by creating death squads, if that's what it took, by those who had benefited from landownership for so long. Regardless of efforts at land reform, today in Colombia three percent of the population still own seventy percent of the arable land. In Guatemala it is equally disproportionate.

Manuel is part of that tiny percentage. When he went back to Santa Clara, he was "happy and proud" to follow in his ancestor's footsteps. Magdalena fitted his new life like a glove, just as his mother had fitted his father's. Magdalena was brought up to marry a landowner who gets involved in politics, the type of man who rules the land and his home and the country.

"He runs the country as if it were his own *finca*" is a common saying about our political leaders. When the Mexican caudillo Porfirio Díaz wanted to thank his dentist for his dexterity in tooth extraction, he appointed him to parliament. Up until a decade ago Colombia's governors, senators, and mayors were appointed. Those appointed were men like Porfirio Díaz's dentist, friends of men of power, men like Pedro Flores, landed men who could gesture across fields, as I saw my grandfather do, and proudly say: "All this land you see from here to the mountains far away on the horizon, this all belongs to you, my boy." I was standing next to my brother and I did not feel included. Our leaders have been men who are raised in our tradition of absolutism, men who are told they can ask for and get whatever they want—a favor from friends in government; a *tintico*, a coffee, a glass of water, or sex, from a maid or from a wife. Just as these men open the doors of local and often federal government, of businesses, of the U.S.

representatives in Washington, they also feel that they can open the legs of any woman they want. They grow up feeling invincible, indestructible, invulnerable. Anything different would not be considered manly—the first thing a Latin man needs to prove.

While men have the right to everything, women are permitted as much as the men think they should have. In Latin America, a woman who expresses her sexuality is a slut and a man who does is a god. Listening to Manuel talk about his upbringing, his education, his sexual initiation is like opening one more window on the sexual practices of our landowning elite. He is a man of power who is told, from the day he is born, he needs only to be macho. *We* are told that we are only half a person unless we marry one of these men. He grew up as the son of a landowner in Guatemala, but it can be no different from the upbringing of the son of a landowner in Colombia, Panama, Peru, or El Salvador. They are the men who make the rules in our banana republics— and here I am not playing to the anti-U.S. sentiment that is attached to the term. Banana republics have been about CIA covert operations and hand-picked dictators, yes, but they are also about the perpetuation of the cult of machismo. Banana republics need a macho mentality to survive—foreign companies need patriarchal societies as much as plantation owners need multinationals to buy their bananas. But in all the discourse about banana republics, the fact that they are as abusive to women as they are to banana workers seems unnoticed. Banana republics are unfair, violent, dangerous, insensitive to all except the handful of men who make up the rules, rules as arbitrary concerning the rights of the women they marry as of the workers they employ.

Washington says it is proud of Latin America today. President Clinton, on his first trade and investment tour of South America, said that the hemisphere is "a new world in the making," characterized by free elections, free markets, and an easing of all sorts of government regulations of the money-making process. We have so-called democracies because we have freely elected presidents in every country—except for Cuba. Plantation economies are in competition with neoliberalism and the forces of the market. Today our countries sell their bananas not just to the UFC (now called Chiquita Brands) but to Dole and others as well.

And our leaders have found the answer in *maquiladoras*, export-processing factories that are supposed to be the miracle drug to the problem of poverty. Now, apart from growing bananas, coffee, cotton, sugar, and tobacco, Latin America assembles clothes, baseballs, microchips, and cars for American corporations. Along the U.S.-Mexico border, maquilas employ over 500,000 workers, at least half of whom are women. Maquilas offer health insurance, social security, and higher wages than what they can earn as maids, the only other opportunity for poor and uneducated women. Still, assembling products for consumption in the North does not mean women are treated fairly. Maquilas require women to take pregnancy exams as a condition of employment and deny them work if they test positive.

Bonita, a 28-year-old woman who assembled radios for General Motors, recalls being sent to a clinic before being hired. All that she was administered was a pregnancy exam. Paula, also 28, says she was given the test by a doctor at the plant in Tijuana where she was applying for a job. The same happened to Graciela at a Panasonic plant and to Rebeca who worked sewing elastic in Fruit Of The Loom underwear.

What place, if any, do these women's rights have in the agendas of our male leaders, the ones who negotiate the fiscal terms that they believe will bring foreign investment and thus prosperity to our countries?

In Colombia our regional politico is called a *cacique* (chief), a *jefe* (boss), a *líder* (leader). Maybe they are being elected, not appointed, maybe they even have instituted land reform, but they are still men who believe that as men they have different rights than women. When there has been land redistribution, it is men who receive land titles. Banana republics might be entering the so-called globalization era, but they are doing so while patriarchy remains.

"This feeling of wanting to live outside the law, or to change it to serve narrow interests, encourages private and public corruption and creates a state of widespread skepticism, fear of others, impotence and anger." These words were written by a group of Argentinian bishops who have taken on the task of bringing back credibility and legitimacy to their justice system. It is the public institution that Argentinians least believe in. Judges, reported the *New York Times*, are the biggest lawbreakers. It has become almost routine to hear about another judge who was secretly videotaped demanding or accepting a bribe. Argentina as a nation is feeling impotent and angry because a few feel above the law. But the words of the bishops are much like the words I have heard from women in Nicaragua, Mexico, and Colombia as they describe their relations with their brothers, their fathers, the man next door—and of course, most of all, their husbands.

Corruption is not only an Argentinian problem. Stories about Latin America in the past year's international press have portrayed the whole region as riddled with corruption and cronyism. In an assessment of corruption levels in fifty-two countries as perceived by businesspeople, Latin America was prominently at the top of the list. Colombia was named the third most corrupt country in the world, Mexico the fifth, Bolivia the second. In Argentina, the study group was concerned about how rapidly it is increasing. Corruption, as defined by the economists and sociologists at Göttingen University who put out the study, is the misuse of public power for private benefit. The index assesses the degree to which public officials and politicians in the particular countries are involved in corrupt practices—bribes, kickbacks, and the embezzling of public funds. The report also acknowledges that most of the bribes are paid by foreign multinational corporations to businessmen, and that although the United States has the Foreign Corrupt Practices Act with tough criminal penalties for international bribery, it is, alas, the only one.

In Panama, President Ernesto Pérez Balladares announced that his choices for the board of directors that will run the Panama Canal after the United States hands it over in 1999 included the son of his own foreign minister and four members of his family—a first cousin, a son-in-law, and the spouses of two other cousins. As in the perfect movie of banana-republic-and-U.S. machinations, the American chairman of the Panama Canal Commission gave a response that was boilerplate. "I know almost all of them, and I couldn't be more pleased," he told the press. "In a nation of under three million people, there are many relationships among the established families. But I think the key is the quality and the background these individuals bring as successful businessmen and bankers already involved intimately in the business of the canal." Sure. It is easy for them to be involved. They are intimately involved because they are the only ones allowed to be involved, the only ones given the opportunity to be involved.

I attended the first Iberian and Latin American presidential summit, held in Guadalajara in 1989, as a stringer for the *New York Times*. Searching for a quote about the summit from one of the presidents there, I found a circle of cameras trying to get comments from the president of Uruguay, who was being escorted by his PR firm exactly for this purpose. The cameras shone on him as he concentrated on his answer. I elbowed my way next to the president and asked him if he thought this summit was a step toward that unity that Simón Bolívar dreamt of and that the talks of regional trade agreements like NAFTA and MercoSur were advocating. He answered my question perfunctorily as I saw the deeply thoughtful face he had worn in front of the klieg lights turn into the most flagrant smile of flirtatiousness. The president of Uruguay held my hand, pulled me toward him, kissed my lips, and walked away leaving me with one last word—*"preciosa"*—and with the humiliation of being treated that way because he is a man in power in this land where men are only powerful and woman are only pretty.

And that sense powerful men grant themselves, the sense that that they are above all, they grant themselves at home and in their relationship to women. Our men grow up being told, by their fathers, their mothers, their teachers, their priests, their governors, that they are exempt from the rules. As men they can. And they can because they are men. They grow up feeling powerful, feeling they have the right to whatever. Our governments are corrupt, our justice systems operate mainly with impunity, our economies are shared among a few friends and families, our policemen rape us because we are ruled by men who grew up in a society that granted them impunity from the day they were born. They consider themselves above the law because they believe they *are* the law. For what other reason can the presidents of Argentina, Brazil, Panama, and Peru have the arrogance to redraft the constitutions of their countries solely because each of them wants to stay in power longer? None of these countries permitted reelection. Yet none of these men felt the constitution was beyond their reach— not when it came to doing something they wanted to do.

Democratization entails rewriting of constitutions—talk of the rule of law, of human rights, even of sex education and women's rights. Since 1993 in Colombia the Ministry of Education requires sex education in public schools. Yet in Colombia our politics are still driven by strongmen in a system built on "clientelism." These are relationships of mutual benefit where the chief, the boss, the leader allocates jobs or other material rewards in exchange for political support. It is quid pro quo among the chosen few, among men who know they will soon inherit their turn to govern.

Six months after Manuel Flores had arrived in Retalhuleu to oversee his family's fields, he was voted (not appointed, as his father was) councilman of the town, a place where he had never lived or even spent a single night. It was not surprising that the political leader of his father's Party approached him and asked him to run for *concejal* on his ticket. His last name and the number of hectares attached to that name, plus the number of votes he could amass with two thousand employees on his *finca*, guaranteed a victory. "He is a brilliant politico," he tells me. "He knew I was the son of the most important agricultural businessman in the region. With me on the ticket, he gained at least five thousand votes."

"Did you like it?" I asked. "Were you always interested in politics?"

"It was part of the movie I was living when I went back. I was the same age as my father when he was councilman. I wanted to follow in his footsteps. And I really thought I could come in with new ideas, fresh ideas that could help *la gente de mi pueblo*, do something for my people. You know I am open to everyone, *sin diferencias,* without discrimination."

"How were you going to do that?" What he thought was going to take an hour, two at most, has taken all day. We are both enjoying our talk, which feels more like two people getting to know each other than a journalist and a source. From his office we have gone to his doctor's office for a routine checkup— "I have T-cells to play with for a while," he jokes as he walks out rubbing a small cotton ball on a vein in his right arm—and we are now sitting outside another trendy café, sipping sparkling water, on Lincoln Road.

He started preparing himself, he tells me, by rereading *The Prince*, by studying the biographies of his country's political leaders. He mentions the governments of Ubico, of Ponce as examples. This is the first time that I feel the same contradictions I felt with Señor Correa. And this time, too, I am unable to point them out. I let him continue.

"But they served no purpose. I was very naive. I thought I could really do something, but when I started my speeches, everyone laughed. People want rum and money, not promises or speeches."

Regardless of the democratization process that the U.S. touts, in regional politics clientelism and nepotism rule. It is still the descendants and the friends of political families who get elected. Even the name used for political slots connotes power and connection and privilege. Congressional seats in Colombia are referred to as *curules*, campstools with carved legs reserved in ancient Rome for the use of the highest dignitaries. In the elections of March 1994, a twenty-seven-year-old second-rate soap-opera actor with a powerful last name returned to his hometown to run for Congress. He received the second highest number of votes in the history of his home state. Twenty-two of the congressmen elected that year were sons, grandsons, brothers, or nephews of previous politicos. Ironically, nepotism is beginning to work for daughters too—two of the twenty-two were women. The same seems to be true in Guatemala.

We can talk all we want about democratization and free elections, but if these elections are decided by favors and connections, a practice that has been institutionalized in Latin America from Mexico to Argentina, practiced by the left, by the center, and by the right, will anything ever change? How can a constitution eradicate the vices of our political customs when it is a fact that customary law has always been greater than constitutional law? Votes will continue to be exchanged for money, for a *mercado*— literally for a bag of groceries—for some rum or for the promise of a job, a piece of paved road, a scholarship, or at least a good letter of recommendation for a son, a brother, a nephew. The candidate running for the senate on Manuel's ticket offered jobs at the Flores plantation.

As councilman Manuel was given an office on the square of Retalhuleu, the same square where there is a plaque commemorating his great-grandfather. Manuel speaks with disdain and anger of his political experience. He could not stand going into that office because all that happened was having a long line of people asking for jobs.

"Was this your full-time job?"

"For many people it is. But, you know, councilmen do not get paid. They don't get a salary but they know there is the *serrucho*, the saw." Manuel gesticulates as if he were sawing the trunk of a tree. In Guatemalan as in Colombian politics, "to saw" is the expression used for kickbacks and bribes. In Mexico, it is called *la mordida*, the bite.

Our banana republics, now disguised as democracies, will continue as long as men continue to be the lords of the manor. And as long as the *niñas de buena familia*, the girls with the right last names, the European features and the light skin, don't realize that they are supporting this unequal system and that this unequal system buys them trips to Miami but not rights. As long as the same men who build our bridges and dictate our trade and tariffs agreements and our minimum salaries continue believing that women should carry the possessive *de* in front of their names when they get married; as long as our politicians continue to take their boys to the brothels when they reach puberty because that is the only way to make them into real men; as long as husbands continue to keep a *casa chica*, which means a small house but in the institutionalized jargon of machismo means the house where he keeps his *querida*, his mistress. It is not uncommon to hear boys recount the story of bumping into their father, or their uncle the senator, or the mayor at the classy brothel.

The sex lives of our politicians are in the public domain. A Venezuelan president lived with his mistress in the presidential palace. Former Mexican president Carlos Salinas's mistress was a high official in his cabinet. After his fall from grace he left his wife, and he now lives with his mistress in Dublin. During an official trip to the United Nations to deliver a speech about street children in Guatemala, ex-president Jaime Serrano slipped into Stringfellows, a strip joint, with his entourage—including his teenage son. The press in Guatemala focused their story, not on the fact that he was there with his son but that Serrano was an avid evangelical. In Brazil the right-hand man of impeached Brazilian president Gustavo Collor de Mello, Pedro César Farias, was charged with embezzlement of public funds. When he was asked in court about his sex life, he said his first sexual experience had been with a prostitute at age sixteen. Six years later Farias, who had been married to the same woman for more than forty years, was found dead—naked in bed with a mistress. "We wouldn't have governments in Latin America if our standard was that there should be no extramarital affairs for politicians," a Latino woman told the *New York Times* when asked about the alleged sexual liaison of President Clinton with Monica Lewinsky.

But the most outrageous example of male chauvinism run riot in government is Pedro Adum, former minister of mines and energy of Ecuador. In print, Adum gloats about his fortune, amassed over the course of the previous twenty years. Telling his rags-to-riches story to a local reporter, he explains how, while he held public office, his private company became the biggest builder in the province, building roads and schools. In his comment there is no trace of awareness of any conflict of interest. Adum goes on to explain how, while minister, he disregarded airline security by refusing to leave a gun behind when boarding a plane. He also nonchalantly tells how he threatened a banker that he would withdraw millions of dollars belonging to the state oil company if the bank didn't hurry the papers for his acquisition of a personal helicopter to "tour the thousand of hectares of land, shrimp farms, and cattle ranches" that he owns.

While his best friend, President Abdalá Bucaram, fancied himself a disco king lip-synching with go-go girls in miniskirts, Adum claimed to long to be a Cro-Magnon man. "If I could, I would like to go around naked," he told the same reporter. "Sometimes I say that the only difference between the Cro-Magnon man and Pedro Adum is clothes. I would like to have lived in prehistoric times, to run around naked. There was more freedom, less prejudice. If I liked a woman I would grab her by the hair and take her to the cave and I would have her. I would satisfy my sexual appetite and my biological appetite, because in those days you just took women."

Two months after the interview was published, President Bucaram and his cabinet were deposed. Adum is under investigation for having taken more than thirty million dollars from state coffers. He is also accused of having knocked out two Texaco executives at a business meeting, of punching a congressman, and of striking the daughter of Ecuador's most important oil family, who worked as his right hand.

"I have been everything in my life. I have tried everything in my life. I have gambled at cockfights and at the racetrack. I've played poker, twenty-one, and roulette in casinos. I have enjoyed porno shows, I've enjoyed good food. I've liked to hunt, to scuba, to fish. Perhaps my hobby is to be a hunter. I have been a very good hunter."

Manuel went back, albeit unconsciously, to continue the Flores tradition, to behave as the Flores men have behaved in the fields, in the halls of power, and in bed for the past two hundred years. Like his grandfather, Manuel is still one of the few privileged men who, because of his birth, can promote and prolong what is the only way of governing that we in Latin America know. Ours are republics that operate through elites—U.S.-educated ones—that allow multinationals to overthrow our elected leaders and organize our coups. Our governments, mostly comprised of men of his background, crush our workers when they demand that their rights be respected, when they demand to be paid more fairly by a foreign company. As in the days of the UFC, multinationals need alliances with the men who think it is to their advantage to continue paying miserable wages to the women who work the *maquilas*, the neoliberal answer to our economic disparity. These are the men considered to be the good catches, the dream men for women like Magdalena to marry. We are supposed to marry men who crush, who exploit, who do politics by exchanging favors with friend or foe, men who think they can treat women the same way that they treat their workers. Has this crossed any woman's mind? Or am I the only maladjusted soul who feels that these *partidos* we are supposed to work hard to snare are the ones who, if they do not care about workers' rights, likely would not care about women's?

Because Manuel's sexual intitiation was probably the same sexual initiation any boy of his class would have had, I ask him how he lost his virginity. By now I feel comfortable asking him almost anything.

"*Con las mantecas,* of course," he tells me, thinking he will make me laugh by choosing a term from back home. But sitting under one of those green umbrellas that sophisticated outdoor cafés have, the term feels out of place. *Manteca* means lard, cooking oil, but spoken in *costeño*, the relaxed slang of the Atlantic coast, *mantecas* refers to the maids, the half-literate women who work in our homes. Part of their job is to serve us, the children of the *patrones*. As a girl, I would ask to be fetched a glass of iced water, or a pencil I had left in my room upstairs. Manuel had Ilva, the scrawny young girl his parents took to Bogotá at age fifteen to work for them, bring to his bedside a glass of Milo, the Colombian equivalent of Nesquick. My father felt proud that he was sending Cata, our maid's daughter, to school. But every day after she came back from classes she had to quickly change from her school's plaid skirt to her white uniform and serve lunch to my young brother, who was also returning from school.

"*Ey, marica, y es que tu no te comes a las mantecas de tu casa?*" his cousin Mauricio asked, startled. Translated literally, Mauricio asked: "Hey, you faggot, don't you eat the lards at your house?" But what Manuel was being asked was if he was having sex with the help. That he didn't implied that he was not a man but a *marica*, a faggot. Mauricio instructed him on how to start being macho. Manuel can't remember clearly if he was thirteen or fourteen.

He started right away. He tells me that he was having sex with three out of the six maids who worked for his family. The stories of boys having sex with the maids are so common that I believe he was, even if having sex with three of them feels a little exaggerated. For his first time, he chose Elba, the youngest of the six, the one who brought his glass of milk up to his room. On Fridays as he got dressed for the evening she helped him blow-dry his hair.

"I called her up to my room and told her that I needed a *sobo*, a rub. My knee was hurting and I ordered her to go get the jar of Vick's Vaporub from my mother's bathroom. As she was rubbing my knee, I touched her thighs, and she laughed, pretending to be mad, but I knew she was flirting and she says to me, '*Ay, Don Manuel, no sea atrevido,*' don't be bold, don't tempt me."

Manuel tells me he and Elba had sex all the time, under the dining room table, in his bedroom, in the small downstairs bathroom reserved for guests at dinner parties. Before he went out in the evening, while Elba held the blow-dryer and he brushed his hair straight, he would lock the bathroom door. While the blower was on, he pulled Ilva's skirt up, his pants down. "We would have great sex."

As Manuel says this, I feel there was something passionate, not forced, about these young bodies discovering their sexuality. Manuel tells me that was so, and that girls like her—meaning poor girls, *las niñas de pueblo*—are much more in touch with their sexuality than the girls from the Club Santa Clara. But then he adds that whenever there was penetration with Elba, it was mostly anal. She, too, was protecting her virginity.

Manuel was a testosterone-filled and erupting volcano. He seduced the cook and another one of the young housemaids his mother had brought from the countryside. He tells me that all he could think about was sex. Elba would serve the food that the older woman who he was also having sex with would prepare. I try to recall what I was thinking about at age thirteen or fourteen. I wanted to be romantic with boys, to have them want to marry me, not want to have sex with me.

"Were you also going to prostitutes?"

He likes my question because he has a story he wants to tell me. When he started having sex with the maids, he knew he could gloat in front of his friends from Guatemala, he knew that having sex with the maid was mostly done on the Pacific coast and not in the more formal capital. Sitting around with his friends one day, soon after he had come back from Santa Clara, the conversation turned to solitary sexual release. Manuel stared at them and, savoring each word, he said, "I don't need to jerk off."

"Oh yeah, sure," the rest of the gang cried out at the same time, *"no venga a tirárselas."* He had always had that smart-ass, know-it-all attitude.

Ray, who already had hair on his chest and wore his shirts open, let out his secret too: "My dad takes me *donde las putas."*

"But mine is for free—*bueno, bonito y barato."* Good, pretty, and cheap. Manuel was always trying to stay one up on everyone.

Ray had a car and more pocket money than the rest. He promised he would take the guys to the brothel his father took him to. He told them they would be treated like kings because his father knew the owner—intimately.

The following Friday, Manuel rushed home, got out of the gray pants and burgundy tie he wore to school, and changed into his Friday outfit, the clothes he had bought in Miami, the bell-bottom pants, the platform shoes, and the sleek, one-hundred-percent polyester Nik-Nik shirt that adhered to his childish, hairless chest. Six-packed in Ray's Renault 4, they were nervous children, puffing away on cigarettes and trying to act older. When Madame opened the door, she welcomed them in and said to Ray: "Your dad called to say you were coming. He wanted to make sure we treated you boys well." For years to come, going to the *putas* on Fridays between six and eight became a routine. Those who had girlfriends had to hurry. At eight o'clock sharp they had to be on the doorsteps. The *novias* were waiting to be picked up.

Manuel drops me off and we agree to resume tomorrow morning. As he drives away, I feel that his stories are the counterpart to mine. I have enjoyed every minute of my time with him. Manuel and I spoke in Spanish, and in English, but mostly in Spanglish, a mixture of the two. We sprinkled our conversation with French and Portuguese and Italian, showing off what we've picked up in our travels. When we were college students, my friends were friends with Manuel and his brothers—popularly known as *los lords*—so I recall their names being mentioned many times. Although our paths were pretty similar, they never crossed until today. We have enjoyed our talk because we complement each other's experience. Because we both left our countries early on and absorbed the openness that being in the United States gave us, we can talk about sex, and about our *política*, with less reservation. I feel a betrayer, a voyeur of my own people. We are intellectualizing our upbringing, and that feels comfortable for both. We are sharing anecdotes to complement our analysis and that has been fun. He laughs at my stories. I laugh at his.

Manuel is a dream of a source. He is smart and savvy, charming and articulate. He talks with candor yet with caution. He is well read, and with his fantastic imagination he sets great scenarios and dialogues for me. I know sometimes it must be confusing for him. He has opened up his private life to me. I can only trust that he is telling me the truth. He can only trust that I will write only what he would like to read. But I feel I have not done half of what I came here to do. I have learned a lot about him. I have learned little about Magdalena.

Manuel didn't have to have lived in Guatemala for people, especially women, single women and their mothers, to know exactly who he was: one of the men at the top. He was a Flores, the grandson of César, the son of Pedro the mayor, governor, congressman, senator, and minister. He was also single. The moment he arrived, he was the town's heartthrob. Everyone wanted to land him.

That was fine with him. There he was, ready to play the hand his birthright had dealt him. He knew that to do it right, to really settle down as the man he was brought up to be, to establish himself in Guatemala, he needed a *novia*, a serious girlfriend. He also knew it had to be one of the good-family girls, one of the girls from El Club Santa Clara and La Enseñanza.

Although his good looks and prestige made him the town's catch, it was not easy to find a woman he enjoyed even going to the movies with. They were all too small-town for him, he tells me. During his first six months there, his sister had set him up with all the pretty possibilities at the Club Santa Clara, but even the ones who had traveled some, spent a year abroad learning English, were still, he says, not only provincial and unsophisticated but *mudas*, mutes. "You take them out and they don't say a word. You can't have an interesting conversation with them—they've never read a book in their lives."

Apart from not finding a girl, Manuel thought the transition from jet-setting to just settling was going to be hard, but he was actually enjoying the life of the country gentleman immensely: "Back to the province where I am the owner, the master of the countryside." He moved into the one-bedroom apartment his family owned in one of the luxurious condominiums of Santa Clara, where the rich *guatemalteios* live, and commuted to Retalhuleu. And he would fly on the family Cessna to the province where he was the lord of the manor. In a matter of months he went from being the irresponsible *hijo de papi* traveling the world to being an important player in the daily life of a sleepy town where feudalism was alive and well. He was enjoying the privileges and the elegance of colonialism. He was one of the few men in the world who still could enjoy this luxury. His European friends marveled when they visited and saw his setup: a large house amidst luscious groves; jeep rides through land, *his land,* that included beaches, thermal waters, pristine brooks and streams; shirtless workers who, for a daily pittance, would pick beans, carry a machete, and uncover their heads to salute him with their straw hats as he drove on open roads in his four-wheel-drive with his walkie-talkie in hand and Helga, his Rottweiler, in the backseat. He enjoyed being called *patrón*, master. The old feudal lifestyles of British India or French Africa were still alive.

His European friends liked to visit Santa Clara. Like him, they found the girls with the good last names, the lighter skin, and the clothes from Miami boring and provincial. But they simply adored the girls with the browner skin, the darker hair, and the clothes made locally. While the good girls were staid and proper, *pudorosas,* these were sensual and amusing. Manuel's voice is confidential. He sees me as someone who has been exposed to more and who would also find these girls boring. Manuel knows I want to hear juicy stories about El Carlín, the high-class brothel where he had more fun than at the Club. He also tells me, with nonchalance tinged with braggadocio, that he knew that to complete the part of lord of the manor, he needed a country club girl as a wife and many Carlín girlfriends for fun. Anyway, those girls from El Carlín understood the deal. "They were very respectful," he tells me. "If you ran into them at the beach or on the street, they would never say hello. They knew better than to compromise the important men of the town."

"So what was it about Magdalena?" I asked him the next morning as we sit at one of the second-floor tables at a Borders bookstore in a glitzy mall in Coconut Grove. We are having more coffee, and his daughter is with him. She is tiny for her age, she talks a ton, and she asks even more questions. She wants to know who I am and he tells her that we are talking about Mami Magda. He buys her a chocolate drink, grabs a few children's books, and sits her at the next table. She opens up the story of Babar, a gray elephant with a golden crown who is happily married to Celeste, another gray elephant with no crown.

"Did she read?" I ask.

"Oh, no," he says, "when I met her she didn't. But after we started going out, she did. That's actually how we started dating. It is a very romantic story."

With a smile, he tells me the story of how they met, how he had been irritable all week, wondering if he could actually go through with it. He had spent the longest hours of his life taking these girls out, and he could not face another attempt at conversing and being answered with fluttering eyelashes and flat monosyllables. This Sunday morning, his sister had said she would be at the club with Magdalena, a girl she wanted him to meet. He stared out the window. How he missed those Sundays when he would sit at a chic restaurant with a lovely and interesting woman next to him—having eggs Benedict at the Elysée Matignon if in Paris, or drinking bullshots at Gino's in New York. The reality was that now all he could do on Sundays was go to a club filled with uninteresting and mostly unattractive people who wore clothes that, even if expensive, offended his elegant sensibility.

It was a sunny day; if he stayed indoors he would feel worse.

He decided that driving a few blocks to go see this girl was not such an effort. At least he would not have to endure another of the conversations that, after six months, he could recite by heart. He would ask about school, meaning college, but they all said La Enseñanza—as a way of letting him know that they were of good stock. He was sure Magdalena would be like the rest, so as insurance against a boring conversation, he grabbed a book. He could read while getting some sun—he liked being tanned.

Manuel was surprised by Magdalena's beauty. She looked more European than most of his previous dates. She didn't have that chubby Latin look that Manuel found too local and too ordinary. She was tall, taller than most girls in Guatemala. He noticed her long legs and her almost blond, flowing hair, which was dyed but was not of the blackness that showed too much Mayan roots. He liked her.

As a conversation starter, he asked her what book she was reading. "I don't read," she replied, "I work." She did not read, she said, because when she was at La Enseñanza the nuns had made her read Miguel Angel Asturias, their Nobel laureate, and she had found it too confusing. Manuel tells me he sensed something different, a *chispa*, a spark, a curiosity and a desire to learn, to explore.

"As homework," he said to her, "I would like you to read this," he said handing her his copy of *Love in the Time of Cholera.* "Maybe we can discuss it sometime."

She must have been enraptured by Manuel's gallant way of asking her to read a book. Just as with sex, we are made to believe that men are the ones who should show us and teach us. Manuel must have felt to her like a *galán de la telenovela*, a soap-opera hero who walked out of the television set and into her life that Sunday afternoon at the beach. Couldn't she envision herself, looking like a *reina de belleza*, walking down the aisle with him? She probably imagined a majestic wedding like the ones reserved for European princesses and beauty queens. A Miss Colombia had the church specially air-conditioned for the event. She was probably told, as I was, that the most important day of her life would be the day of her marriage. *El día que te cases,* the day you marry, was an abracadabra, words that opened up a whole world of riches, of excitement and adventures. Things would start happening then and only then. And it was not just about sex, although our mothers, our fathers, the ladies who play cards every afternoon at the club and gossip about which girl is good and which one is loose do expect us to be asexual up until then. As Augusto Pérez had told me, "Mothers want to believe their daughters are playing with Barbies till their wedding nights." But it was also about what happens to women as individuals, what happens to a young woman's place in society. We stop being daughters and begin being wives. We go from being *la hija de* to being *la señora de*.

Marriage under machismo is the only way for a woman to feel she has a self. Time spent before marriage is all preparation for that day, to the moment that marks the beginning of ourselves. Until that day, we go to school or take jobs, not looking for financial security but for a way to amuse ourselves and earn a little pocket money, enough to buy fancy clothes but not enough to be independent. Good girls are not supposed to know how to make it on their own. After marriage wives get their own checking accounts where husbands make monthly deposits so they can keep house. They acquire responsibilities such as going to the supermarket, ordering the maids around, telling them what to make for lunch and dinner. The servants stop calling them *niña*, girl, and start addressing them with respect, using not *tu* but *usted*, not *niña* but *señora*. I am six years older than my cousin Rosanna but, to the help, I am not as much an adult as she is. She is married and a mother; I am neither. She is Señora Rosanna, I am still Niña Silvana.

When Magdalena met Manuel, her life, at twenty-three, was a very acceptable life, the life that society, her parents, her friends, maybe even she, expected. She lived with her parents, worked in the morning "cleaning the pee and poo of other people's children"—Manuel's description of her work. Manuel, even if speaking with condescension, has a point. Most of the girls who went to La Enseñanza take jobs related to child rearing. Most women, Magdalena included, receive no special training, yet it is assumed that as women they naturally know how to take care of children.

Just as the jobs available for poor women in Latin America are in domestic service—in Colombia 96.9 percent in 1995 worked as maids—middle- and upper-class Latin American girls work jobs that are related to their condition of being female. I am quite sure that the day-care centers of Guatemala or of Colombia do not have any men on their staffs. Good girls from our clubs who do not work with children take jobs in travel agencies and in decorating, which are also "feminine" jobs. A few work as officers in savings and loan institutions, in banks, or in insurance companies. Those from families with political connections get mid-level jobs in government offices. As a case in point, statistics show that eighty percent of the jobs in design and financial services are held by women, women like Magdalena. They are hired because they are paid less than a man. But the real figure that matters, according to the Colombian report on the status of women prepared for the Beijing Conference, is that women who actually hold a job with any independent decision-making ability comprise less than two percent. "The problem is that the structure of machismo is so ingrained in our mentalities that the only way to change it is through training and education," says the woman who supervised the study and presented it at the UN. But just as I get surprised when I see the "de" included in my friends' names, I wonder why she, a woman working on a report that exposes the situation of women in Colombia, uses the particle that makes her a possession of her husband. Granted she is married to one of our political bosses, a leader of the Liberal Party, whose last post was as minister of communications. But how can you talk about training and education if you are doing the opposite of what you are training and educating people to do? Why does she accept being identified by her husband's name and writing "de" every time she signs her name? Is it because her husband will not accept her *not* using it? Because a man of power, a man who is one of the prime movers in running my country, believes that a woman should belong to her husband? Or because she is validated as a woman if she can tell the society she is speaking to that she is married and to whom? Is she more successful if she tells us who she belongs to?

It was exciting, I suppose, for Magdalena to meet Manuel, a man who would not only open up a life for her but one that would include Paris, London, and New York. Few men in Santa Clara could offer her that. I am sure she wanted to see him again, tell him that she had read the book, listen to Manuel talk about his trips. She had never met anyone who had been to so many places, anyone who spoke about Europe as routinely as a banana worker complains about the price of school uniforms for his children. Maybe if she read, if she did the things he wanted her to do, they could get married, her life would begin, and he would take her to see Paris. Manuel tells me triumphantly that Magdalena read *Love in the Time of Cholera* in one sitting. "She wanted to be prepared for when I called her. Isn't that so romantic?"

I too once treasured Arturo's gift of *The Prince* and found that his words when he gave me the book— "This is so that you learn about the world"—were romantic. Today, they feel like arrogant orders. I liked that he talked to me as if he knew more than I did. As I sit and hear of Manuel's gallantry toward Magdalena, his words feel like Arturo's, words that both men and women expect from men. And while I know that there is not a cabal of Latin men sitting around conspiring to use flattery and affection so that they can control our thoughts, the way we dress, what birth control we use and whether we use it, what we say, who we speak to, and so on, the reality is that that is what happens. It is what they have learned, it is how they have seen men talking to their mothers. We women contribute to it too. We encourage the myth of being demure girls, pretty and shy.

"I could not believe how lucky I was. She could be the mother of my children as long as she was willing to learn about my world. We could grow together. I could give her some of my world. It could be the repetition of my parents' story. I liked that."

Soon after his first dinner with Magdalena, Manuel tells me, he was *timbrando tarjeta*—the literal translation is "punching the card"—the local expression for the official and expected daily visit to her house. All of the city was talking about how Magdalena Correa, *la hija de Alma y Gustavo,* and Manuel, *el hijo de*

Pedro y Dolores, were *novios.* There is no casual dating in Santa Clara. Manuel courted Magdalena as he knew he should. When he was there, they watched television, or talked, always with her parents present. Manuel didn't mind, He really liked Gustavo, and he liked the fact that Alma and his grandmother were cousins. He enjoyed being included in family gatherings. To be alone with Magdalena, he took her out for an ice cream or a *jugo,* a fresh fruit juice. She would never go to his apartment. It would ruin her reputation. Good girls do not go to their boyfriends' flats, especially if they live alone.

"Magdalena was a change from the European and the American women, but a change for the better," he answers. "And I loved her uniqueness. I didn't think that there were still girls who believed in the myth of virginity. I couldn't believe I had a girlfriend with the moral principles of the seventeenth century. But it fitted perfectly with the movie I was living then."

His answer feels cold. Magdalena's life seems to be summed up as just fitting a role in other people's lives. To her father she is the exemplary daughter; to her husband she is the Victorian heroine. But I am also interested in learning why he decided to choose her for that role. I am ready to ask, to pry, to find out as much as I need to know about Magdalena. It feels wrong, though, to talk about the intimacy of someone who has died—especially in these cold surroundings, neon lights announcing foamy cappuccinos— and even worse as I look over at the pigtails of her orphaned daughter waiting patiently for Papi to finish talking about Mami.

"So what about her did you like?" I ask.

"I knew she would give me stability and tranquility if I wanted to start a home. She would be the perfect mother. She was far removed from my crazy life." He means the travels, the parties, the girlfriends in Europe and the U.S., the things he needed to leave behind in order to become the Flores man he was.

Manuel was happy to play Pygmalion. "And she would listen to me. It was great." He wanted a blend of a somewhat assertive and cultured woman with one who depended on him for her independence. I am starting to understand what Manuel saw. Magdalena had the potential to learn to be a little like the women he had met abroad, yet she also had the place in society he needed to be accepted by Santa Clara's elite. Magdalena was different from the other girls because she was curious and willing to learn and explore. She listened to him and she absorbed. To me, it all sounds like a young woman with a great desire to live. He didn't want her to work at a nursery "cleaning the pee and poo of other people's children," so he wrote a resume for her and helped her find a job at an insurance company. He wanted her to dress differently, so he bought her new clothes. Unlike most men there, who prefer that their girlfriends and spouses dress conservatively, he wanted her to show off those long legs he liked so much. He bought her miniskirts. "She was feeling much more secure about herself," he tells me. "Her world was opening. She was brought up to get married, and I was telling her, I want more from you. I was telling her about the history of the world. She had never heard of Alexandria in Egypt, about the Crusades. She was fascinated. I wanted her to explore her intellectual capacity, to develop herself."

I am starting to see Magdalena in her red and black suit.

Sometimes it was hard. When he had friends over from Europe she would feel insecure. She didn't speak French, and the girls who were visiting seemed so free to her, so sophisticated. When at the pool they took their tops off, she would throw a jealous fit—"You must have had something with her or else why is she showing you her breasts?" She wore the short skirts he gave her, but she could not go so far as to take off her top at the beach. What if someone *conocido*, someone from the Club, saw her?

For him, she was perfect. Being with Magdalena speeded his entry into the political elite of the region. Society would stop seeing him as the debauched single man. She would get him accepted, invited to the dinner parties where local politics are made. It looked good if people saw him in public with Magdalena when he was running for councilman. To have a serious girlfriend implied that he was a serious man, *un hombre serio,* like his father.

"Were you sleeping around?" I finally decide to ask Manuel directly.

"Sure. Every day. You know if my stiff girlfriend from the Club Santa Clara would not put out, I had to go find it somewhere else." Manuel's crassness shakes me a bit. I feel I should be allying myself not with him but with Magdalena. But I also feel some complicity forming between us.

"Somewhere else" was everywhere else. He often stopped at El Carlín for a drink before heading home for the night; sometimes he would go straight after having dropped Magdalena off.

"It was like being at the Club Santa Clara except it was more fun," he says. "There was always someone I knew, there would always be an uncle, a friend, a business partner. You discuss a little politics, a little business, sitting next to an *amiguita*, that kind of a friend. They are not like a prostitute you pick up on the street and don't even ask her name, you know. Here you sit with her, you are a gentleman with her, you buy her a drink, you dance with her, you flirt with her while you talk to your friends. If you are a *político* you promise to pave the streets of her hamlet if she gets her friends to vote for you."

Then there were the girls at *la plantación*. Almost daily after work Manuel would meet up with one of these *muchachitas del campo*, the girls from the fields, and take her out for a Coca-Cola, a meal, or a ride in the jeep for a sexual tryst. If the good girls didn't put out, these girls—the daughters, the wives, the nieces of the men he employed—would feel honored to have sex with the owner's son. His secretary, Tomasa, a strong *morena* descendant of Jamaican slaves whose family had worked on the land since the days of the gringos, provided him with a different girl every day.

They had devised a system together. Manuel would call the main office where Tomasa worked and ask her where and when he could pick up *el repuesto*, the spare part—the password they used to refer to the young woman who would satisfy *el patrón*'s sexual appetite. The scenarios and the women were multiple: a sixteen-year-old girl from a nearby hamlet who would wait for him at the office, a divorced schoolteacher, women of all ages and of all shades and racial mixtures—"all of them feeling lucky" if chosen to spend one evening with *el doctorcito*. Rarely did Manuel see the same woman twice. Depending on his mood, they might be taken to the main house where they could get a nice dinner, before or after sex. But sometimes he felt like just having them in his jeep, *plantación adentro,* or by the riverbank. Sometimes he had all the time in the world to revel in their company, and sometimes he had to rush back to El Rodadero by eight, for he was frequently due to attend a family dinner at Magdalena's or a political meeting.

"*Esa negra* was so efficient." He laughs.

This was Tomasa's way of paying back all that Manuel's family had done for her. Her father had picked Flores coffee his whole life. Now she had it good. If I could read her mind, I know she would think of the Flores family as good people who take care of you if you stick with them. She would be forever grateful for the job she was given. She worked at the hacienda, taking care of administrative stuff—better than working the fields. I bet she voted for every Flores who ever ran for office.

She was a woman of about fifty, and she knew when she saw Manuel that she could do something for him. He was a *soltero*, a bachelor, and she knew that men needed women in a certain way, in a way that those girls from his world would not be able to provide. She knew this because she had done the same thing before for the other boys. But she also knew it because it is simply a fact, a given.

The girls that *la cholia Tomasa* provided were "funny and quite good in bed. They don't have as many hangups as the girls from La Enseñanza and I am the *doctorcito*. They would do anything just to be with me, all in the hope that they might get pregnant." He has a point. Men in Latin America are always joking about never knowing how many children they really have. Wives are always wondering about the number of *hijos por la calle*, the children born out of wedlock from casual encounters. In the days of our grandfathers it was common to have children out of wedlock—and to marginalize them. Manuel tells me his grandfather had twenty-three "natural" children. Manuel's grandmother referred to them as *tizones del diablo*, the charcoal of the devil, and they were not even allowed to enter her house. My granduncle had one. He worked for him as an overseer of the fincas. And he was allowed to come to the main house. He ate lunch with my granduncle and they discussed the cotton and the cattle. But my grandaunt would not join them and he was never invited to family gatherings. He greeted my mother and her sisters with the respect that any other peon would, always removing his straw hat. He saddled my horse for me many times and I never knew he was a relative.

In legal terms they are *hijos naturales*, natural children, a strange word to refer to children born out of wedlock. Such children are not only marginalized by our societies but up until 1974 fathers had no responsibility to take care of them. Today fathers have to recognize them, but there are still laws that discriminate against illegitimate children. What makes a child illegitimate? I have always wondered. At most Catholic schools, *hijas naturales* are not accepted. How can the Catholic Church label a child, any child, illegitimate and yet preach the message of universal brotherly love?

In Chile, for example, where divorce is illegal, more than forty percent of children are "illegitimate." By law they cannot be military officers or high police officials. This is a country whose economy is the envy of all the region, a prosperous society where there is room for artists, fashion designers, trendy restaurants, and every other sign of cultural sophistication, and yet its social policy makers still have not made divorce legal, although half of the country's married adults are separated. When I mentioned this discrepancy to a male Chilean friend, a worldly banker, he disregarded my concern, saying, "It doesn't matter that the law exists. Everyone in Chile gets divorced because they have found a loophole in the law."

My friend might not understand the imperative of making divorce legal because he is male, a male in power, a male that knows how to bend the rules to make them work for him. When Congresswoman Mariana Aylwin introduced a divorce bill in the lower house, polls showed that seventy percent of Chileans supported the bill. So did President Eduardo Frei. "We cannot continue with the system we have now. . . . It is absolutely despicable and dangerous, and it leaves women and children totally unprotected," he told the *Washington Post*. But the bill was defeated. The Catholic Church in Chile, as in most countries in Latin America, exerts great influence in the country's politics, and its demand that Chileans adhere to the country's tradition of strict marriage laws does not go unheard. It is the voice of men like Senator Hernán Larrain that will be law: "It serves no purpose to our society to destroy the institution of the family. We cannot stand by and watch the moral integrity of this country decline." As of today, divorce in Chile is still illegal and Mariana Aylwin just lost her reelection bid.

With Manuel's entrance into politics came a new temptation to add to his brothels and feudal entanglements. The political rallies were also a breeding ground for more sexual adventures. Magdalena never accompanied him to a political rally. At these gatherings, as Manuel has said, there was more rum and music than talk of political programs. The local band would start playing before Manuel could finish his speech. "No one cared what I had to say about what I would do if I was elected," he says. "They were there to party for free and to get favors from us." But it was exciting to feel the drums playing and the musicians singing your name; to hear the *"viva, viva el doctorcito Flores"* directed at you; to have everyone want to shake your hand; to walk the dusty streets of a poor hamlet surrounded by throngs of *gente humilde*, poor people; to be a big shot just like General Flores, just like his grandfather, just like his father; to be seen as the *Adonis blanquito* by the local women.

After the unfinished speech, he would be pulled down from the podium and made to dance with the wife of the owner of the house, then with the string of girls who were there hoping he would notice them. "At every rally I would have one of these girls." Comments like this can sound like posturing, and I am sure he is taking some literary license, but they are believable. I have seen it happen, I have heard plenty of such talk. He might be embellishing the stories. Maybe he did not sleep with a woman at every rally, but I am sure he did at many. Maybe he didn't make love to a different girl on the riverbank or under the mangrove or inside the banana plantation every afternoon, but he *was* having sex with girls from the fields. And he was not having sex with the woman he loved.

It must have been hard for Magdalena. In a small city like Santa Clara it was impossible for her not to find out about her boyfriend's cavorting. There were the phone calls. Manuel would find her in tears, many nights, huddled in her mother's arms. He would know what had happened: another anonymous phone call with a woman's voice calling Manuel a *bandido*, a womanizer. "I am not a girl from the Club but I make love to Manuel Flores" or "Your boyfriend is a wonderful lover" or the one that I suppose must have hurt the most— "*Que delicia,* it is so delicious, damn virginity, you don't know what you are missing."

Manuel would comfort her by telling her they were calumnies, plain lies from envious people. "They do it just to hurt you. Look at me, how would I have time to do anything? Look how busy I am."

I cannot tell if he feels any remorse. For two days he has told me stories with generous details, but he has also been removed emotionally. I am also thinking how frustrated I would feel if I could not make love to the man I loved. Manuel admits that the novelty of her behavior wore off after a few months. He was in love with Magdalena and yearned for the intimacy and the deeper connection that a sexual relationship adds to a couple.

After a year it became unbearable. "I told her, Magdalena, there is something I need, there is something missing in our relationship so that I feel whole. I would ask her to make love and she would ask me for time." They would kiss, mostly in his car before he would drop her off for the night—long hard kisses, even passionate ones—or at the discothèque on weekends. Sometimes she would have an extra drink, but even then she always made him stop. She was never too drunk to keep saying no, and she had been clear with him: She would not make love with him unless they were married. For that whole year, she was relentless.

Finally, confused and frustrated, he wrote Magdalena a note: "*Yo que camino cojo, que camino cojo?*"—"I who walk limping, which road do I take?"—and went to visit his ex-girlfriend for the weekend. This was a woman a few years older that he had felt strongly for. They had always had a potent sexual and intellectual connection, but she did not fit the image of the demure woman he needed to marry. Today, he is married to her.

Magdalena was devastated. She knew what it was all about.

Manuel and I are talking like close friends now and I feel I am going too deeply into Magdalena's intimacy. I can never ask her for her side of the story. But I keep asking.

Upon his return that Sunday, he ran into her. "I went in with my dog Helga and there she was, having dinner with her sister and a cousin. I could tell she was *desbaratada*, devastated. She looked as if she had been crying all weekend. I went up and said hello and she was trembling, her mouth was dry, she was that seventeenth-century girl who could not utter a word."

Manuel could be writing the scene for a soap opera—the woman in love who only musters her courage when she is threatened with losing the man, for that would kill her. She was brave and told him she wanted to talk to him. He said he would call the next day and did. Manuel was surprised when, the next week, Magdalena insisted on being taken to his apartment.

Sixteen months after they had started dating, it was the first time Magdalena had been there alone with him. She was risking her good reputation, one of the few valuable assets a woman should have. She had been there once, when they had started seeing each other, in the afternoon and with her sister. She had shown up unannounced, giggling nervously, as if they were doing something very risqué. The visit had been very short. Manuel had a picture of an old girlfriend near the television set in his room, and when Magdalena saw it, she ran out in tears. Now she wanted to go back, alone with him, at night. He was startled.

"I want to make love," Manuel tells me Magdalena told him.

"What, just like that? What happened?" I ask.

"We got there, I had a bottle of champagne in the refrigerator—reserved for another occasion," he jokes.

"What was it like?"

"Pure happiness. The ultimate devotion."

"Good sex?"

"Amazing."

As Manuel tells me this story with its familiar romantic trappings I begin to get suspicious. I am surprised that their sex was amazing—wasn't she terribly nervous? What happened to her virginal resolution? Who has amazing sex, the first time? From that day on, they continued a sexual relationship. Manuel told her to go to the gynecologist and she did. I am starting to see

Magdalena's complexities. She, as I had intuited from the small photograph, was responsible, very organized and methodical about her birth control pills. She was also very reserved, her younger sister, Marta, recalls. She says they were best friends but they never shared the secret of sex. Only when Marta confided to Magdalena that she thought she might be pregnant did Magdalena tell her that she too had sex with Manuel and that she was on the pill. Marta was not pregnant that time around, but she continued to have unprotected sex with her boyfriend until, of course, she did get pregnant.

"Did you stop sleeping around?" I ask Manuel.

"No," he says. "I was too weak. I thought it would all stop the day that I got married."

Magdalena's wedding was just as she must have dreamt it would be. True, there were some organizational hitches. Manuel kept changing the date. First February, then June. They finally settled on September. Then Manuel refused to get married in the cathedral because he wanted to break with all provincial tradition. He wanted to be different and have the ceremony at the church near where his grandmother had been born. To the Correa Vives family that was not elegant enough. Still, Manuel got his way—it seemed that with Magdalena at his side, he always did.

The wedding was at the church he preferred and it was splendid. The entire town came out to the street to salute the *novios*. Their wedding vows were blessed by the bishop of Guatemala with the help of four priests. Governors, senators, landowners, matrons in their new dresses, all the important men of the country in their tails flocked to the Club Santa Clara where they danced to the waltzes and the mambos of an eight-man band and ate smoked salmon on little pieces of black toast and drank vintage champagne. The President made an appearance. The newspapers devoted full pages to the wedding. The Flores and Correa families were ecstatic and proud. Manuel and Magdalena were too. He was becoming the man he was born to be. She was becoming the wife she was brought up to be. They spent their honeymoon in Mexico and Miami.

*   *   *

Upon their return, Manuel and Magdalena moved to the condominium his father had bought for them. Manuel opened an office in downtown Guatemala—at the insistence of Magdalena, who had asked him to stop going to the hacienda. She wanted him away from any temptation, and Manuel was trying hard to fit in. He joined the Group of Young Executives and the Group of 25, so called because each of its members possesses one of the twenty-five "best" family names in the region. He attended the lunches with the men, and the dinner parties with the wives. He had decided to play by Santa Clara's rules. But it was never easy.

"I forbade Magdalena to leave my side during social engagements." He would sometimes sit with the ladies, doñas at twenty-something dressed in smuggled Irish linen, and listen to them talk about their diets. Or Magdalena would sit with him as the men got excited over sports and politics. "As the scotches increased, so did their volume and the nonsense of their conversations," Manuel says, and I smile back in shared superiority. We both know the routine when dinner is served, usually buffet-style. The wives go to the dining room, while the men don't make any move to get up. The wives wait in an obedient line holding two plates. She serves one for herself, the other to take to her husband. Only after dinner would some of the wives join their husbands, and maybe by then there would be some dancing. "The only contact between men and women," he says.

As expected, Magdalena left her job at the insurance company, spent her time setting up their new home and, less than two months after their marriage, was expecting a baby. She had a smooth pregnancy. It was again Manuel who set the rules about how to be pregnant. Magdalena was to listen only to classical music so that the baby would be born with a cultured ear. She gave birth to a girl. They decided to name her after the sister of Manuel who had introduced them. "When I walked into the hospital room," he says, "she was surrounded by twenty women—grandmothers, grandaunts, mothers, sister, cousins, friends—sitting on her bed, the floor, the few chairs in the room."

Everyone stopped to admire the beauty of Manuel and Magdalena's baby when the nurse took her out for her daily stroll in the old-fashioned dark blue English baby carriage. She was a chubby pink doll fed with bottles of milk shakes made with green bananas, always dressed in hand-embroidered dresses, wrapped in blankets and sheets that all of her aunts, cousins, and relatives spent months knitting and buying for her.

Everyone was also commenting on how easy it had been for Magdalena to lose weight after her pregnancy. The extra pounds, which for most women are so hard to shed, had disappeared overnight. As a matter of fact, people were telling her she was losing too much weight and was looking skinny. She didn't mind. Manuel tells me he thought it was sexy. But she had no appetite and she was finding handfuls of her hair on her hairbrush. When she woke up with white spots on her forehead, she went to see the doctor, who told her it was nothing serious—some inconsequential skin fungus that could be cured by an over-the-counter cream. Her blood test showed that her white-cell count was a little low, but again, the doctor told her, nothing to worry about.

She continued to feel weak. The doctor then tested her for lupus and leukemia. When those tests came back negative, the doctor suggested an AIDS test to rule out everything. When Magdalena told Manuel, he was indignant: "How disrespectful of that doctor to suggest such a thing. Is he crazy?"

Magdalena took the doctor's advice and went to the only laboratory that at that time, in 1991, offered AIDS testing. She felt no apprehension, and indeed made a day trip out with her mother, who seldom got to go anywhere out of the house. After the blood exam, they did some shopping and saw some friends.

Magdalena called for the test results the following Saturday, as the doctor had instructed. She was alone. Manuel recalls that she had spent the morning relaxing, washing her hair, preparing for a dinner party that night. He was out with his father looking at some land but was expected back for lunch. She dialed the doctor's number as casually as if she were making an appointment at the hairdressers.

Doctor Tapia got on the phone and, after the proper hellos, he asked her if she was a promiscuous woman. Manuel reconstructs that conversation for me.

"*Perdón,* doctor. Am I what? I didn't understand. What did you ask me? Am I pro—what?"

"Pro-mis-cua," repeated the doctor. "Are you promiscuous?"

"What are you telling me? I don't even know what that means, doctor."

"Well, it means that, well, that you have sex with men other than your husband."

She wasn't following him. "Doctor," she said, "I've only had sex with my husband. Why? Why are you asking me this?"

"Well, because if you are not promiscuous, then your husband is promiscuous."

The doctor explained that her AIDS exam needed to be confirmed but that she had tested positive. "Call me on Monday, I'll have confirmation by then, but the important thing is to get your daughter tested. If you tested positive, most likely your daughter will test positive as well. You should get your daughter tested and your husband tested because I think the three of you have AIDS. Have your husband call me on Monday."

"Yes, doctor."

Manuel found her in her bed trembling, *tendida en mocos,* wailing inconsolably. In between her sobs, she told him what the doctor had said. "I told her it was definitely a mistake." His tone is paternal as he tells me this, the same tone a parent uses to tell a child not to be scared of the dark, that thieves and ghosts don't exist, and still the child knows that they do. "From where are you going to have AIDS, I told her. AIDS was something that only homosexuals got. I told her to calm down, that I would call the doctor."

Manuel had a way of comforting her. Just as she had believed him when he told her that the phone calls telling her that he was being unfaithful were lies, she believed him this time. "I will talk to him, and you will see it was all a mistake," he said, holding her tight.

Monday when the maid was serving him lunch, Magdalena brought the cordless phone over to the table. His hands shook as he dialed the number. When Magdalena saw his face, she understood that the doctor was telling him the same thing he had told her. Manuel hung up the phone and with no emotion in his voice told her to prepare the baby and the nurse. They were going to see Dr. Tapia, the only doctor taking care of HIV-positive patients in Guatemala. His office was at the best private clinic, where the city's elite went.

"But what are we going to say if someone sees us at the clinic?"

"We will say that you have cancer."

When they arrived at the doctor's office, they turned around. "The waiting room," Manuel tells me, "was filled with men with faces that spelled AIDS."

They decided instead to go and consult an oncologist who, when they said they wanted an AIDS test, told them what they had been wanting to hear: "Don't worry. I don't think a young and decent couple like you would get AIDS."

The oncologist was wrong. A week later, while Magdalena waited in the car, Manuel got confirmation of their fear: the three of them, Manuel, Magdalena, and their one-year-old daughter, were HIV-positive. "I felt a piano hit my head," he tells me. "I asked him what that meant, and he said that it meant that in one month or maybe two or three I would die. Then he said that he thought nowadays people were living a bit longer." The doctor also told him that he could not treat them, that they had to go see Dr. Tapia down the hall.

Magdalena reached out for Manuel's hand. "Ay, Mañe," she said, "this is turning the color of ants."

Magdalena's love story was rapidly turning into a nightmare as pitch dark as an endless tunnel: black like the color of ants. She had no reason to think she would ever have to worry about an epidemic that, as far as she knew, was the product of aberration, of things that homosexuals and prostitutes did, not anything that she who had resisted the temptation of sex for so long would ever be exposed to. Manuel tells me he felt a piano hit his head, but what did she feel? Did she hate him? Did she want to scream and curse and hit him?

The sad and harsh truth is that, in Latin America, the probability of contracting the AIDS virus is higher for a woman like Magdalena—who at twenty-nine had had sex with one man, her husband—than it is for a prostitute from El Carlín, the brothel her husband visited frequently. After a decade of AIDS prevention campaigns, high-class prostitutes are somewhat more aware of the dangers of unprotected sex and many require that their customers use condoms. Despite the unexpected phone calls from strange women, the serious signs of infidelity, Magdalena never thought she had to worry about AIDS. Like Manuel, she associated AIDS only with *maricas* and *putas*, faggots and whores. And Manuel admits to me that, for all the sexual experience he had, it had never crossed his mind to wear a condom.

As of July 1995, Colombia was ranked third—after Brazil and Haiti—among Latin American countries in cumulative numbers of AIDS cases. As in Brazil and Haiti, more than half of the documented HIV infections in Colombia were occurring among young adults between fifteen and thirty-four. And in the fifteen years of the epidemic, all three countries have seen the exponential increase of women testing positive for HIV. According to the U.N. AIDS Report, in Brazil, the male–female ratio of AIDS cases has dropped from sixteen to one in 1986 to three to one as of December 1997. In Colombia, the gap was considerably wider. In 1987, the ratio was thirty-seven men testing positive for every woman. In 1988, it was twelve to one; in 1994, it was eight to one. Dr. Ricardo García of the Colombian Ministry of Health revealed in an abstract he presented at the AIDS conference held in Vancouver in 1996 that on Colombia's Atlantic coast—my hometown—the ratio decreases to four to one. The study also found that the number of HIV infections transmitted through heterosexual contact went from 40 percent in 1987 to 68 percent in 1994.

In Guatemala, the statistics are similar. While in 1984 the male-to-female ratio was eleven to one, by 1994 it was two to one. And according to a study presented at the same AIDS conference by a group of doctors working at the Guatemalan Association for the Prevention and Control of AIDS, the ratio among adolescents is alarming—it is one to one. The study concluded that the new HIV-positive cases indicated that primary mode of transmission is sexual and that the virus had been established in the heterosexual population. Of the 309 cases of HIV-positive people treated at the San Juan de Dios Hospital, 72 percent were heterosexual patients.

But when Magdalena was diagnosed with the virus, neither she nor Manuel, world traveler, graduate of an American university, reader of novels, trendy and informed, had ever heard that AIDS was something they should be thinking about. He had gay friends in Paris and in New York who had AIDS, but it was nothing he thought would ever touch him. *Gente decente,* he tells me, decent people from sleepy Guatemala, were supposed to be immune.

"Doctor, please tell me what to do. I just hired someone to change the floors of our new apartment from tile to marble and it's going to cost me a fortune. What should I do?" Manuel tells me he asked Dr. Tapia soon after finding out the results of his exam. "Am I going to die soon? That other doctor told me that one dies very quickly from AIDS, like in a month or two."

"*Por Dios,* Manuel, please, what is in that head of yours?" Magdalena snapped at him.

Manuel tells me that after the diagnosis Magdalena was much more level-headed than he was. At first, he was a mess and she was filled with equanimity. For the first time I get a sense of Magdalena as a mature, self-possessed individual, not just a woman living up to her husband's and father's saintly and sanitized images. The tragedy is, this newly confident woman is carrying a deadly virus.

Sadder still is to listen to Manuel tell me that, from that day on, their love grew and so did their communication and their sexual relationship. He says that he even acknowledged that, up until that point, he "had led a very irresponsible life." But the cruel fact is that, by then, her T-cell count was as low as 300. His was three times that. While Manuel was jogging every day, Magdalena was withering away. Giving birth had depleted her immune system.

Manuel and Magdalena made a pact. They would keep their HIV-status a secret until one of them became noticeably ill. It was hard work to keep it up. Right after they received the results, the baby had to be hospitalized twice in a matter of months. The first time, they said that she had been bitten by an insect while the nanny promenaded her in the park; the second incident was disguised as food poisoning. When her parents visited, they hid the bottles of AZT. But Magdalena's lack of health was apparent. Cancer, they kept telling everyone, but claimed no doctor seemed able to diagnose which kind.

Pedro Flores suggested a plan: He would take them to Europe—

Paris, Brussels, Madrid, a short stop in Sevilla for a peek at the World's Fair. Magdalena and Manuel were to fly to Miami first, where Magdalena would be seen by the prominent doctor who had treated every Flores for decades. Panicked at the thought of Magdalena being examined by the family doctor, Manuel concocted another story. He told his father that he wanted Magdalena to be seen by a prominent oncologist, world famous, who happened to live in Paris. Wouldn't it be smart to make an appointment to go see him while they were there? Of course, said the father. Manuel tells me he then called his father back and said that the doctor was leaving for Saigon for a conference and that he was only available to see them the week that they were planning to fly to Miami to visit *su médico de cabecera*. Could they meet in Paris directly?

Magdalena got to see Paris—"as a couple in love," Manuel says, another attempt to turn this tragedy into a love story. "I wanted to show her Paris before she died." Magdalena went to the places she had seen only on postcards and in the movies. It was lovely, says Manuel almost too excitedly, it was always lovely. There were moments, I'm sure, when reality must have hit harder than Manuel chooses to remember. For example, at the Deux Magots when they sipped espresso and watched the models and the intellectuals and the beautiful people and then took their pills and injected the baby. Or in Brussels, when Magdalena was getting so tired she would oversleep every morning until Dolores admonished her: "One doesn't come to Europe to sleep." Or the time in Sevilla, almost at the end of the trip, when Pedro toasted and promised another invitation, in five years' time, for the next fair. Manuel tells me that Magdalena smiled at him and they shared a knowing laugh. "It was funny to hear any talk about the future."

Rightly so. There was little future left for Magdalena. Upon her return, her body yielded to the virus. Her T-cell count was as low as 200, which is almost the same as having none. By Christmastime, Magdalena was in the hospital, having had her first convulsion. A few weeks later, staying with her parents in Santa Clara, she had a second one in the middle of the night. Her parents called a doctor. When Manuel saw that he was going to draw blood from Magdalena, he asked him if he wasn't going to use gloves. "I don't use gloves," the doctor answered as he inserted the needle into Magdalena's arm. But a contraction from Magdalena sent the needle flying and blood splashing all over the room. Desperate, Manuel cried out, demanding that the doctor wear gloves. Calmly, the doctor looked at him and asked, "What is it with you, is this AIDS or what?"

"No, doctor, no, but please wear gloves."

The night Magdalena and Manuel returned to Guatemala, the phone started ringing incessantly. The first call came from a friend of Magdalena. She was discreet in her questions, he was short in his answers.

"How are you, Manuel?" she asked.

"Divinamente," he replied. Perfectly fine.

"You sure?"

"Yes, I'm sure."

"And how is Magdalena?"

"Divinamente."

"Sure?"

"Sure."

"And *la nena?*"

"Equally fine."

The phone rang again. It was one of his best friends.

"Mañe, I am your friend and I am going to tell you that everyone is saying you have AIDS. Mañe, is that true?" she asked.

"No, it is not."

"Mañe, tell me the truth. I am your friend, Mañe, *tu amiga de siempre.*"

"Who are you going to believe," he asked, "your friend of forever or the *chisme* outside?"

"Well, I do want you to know that, outside, the *chisme* at all the parties is that *el Flores* has AIDS."

As much as Magdalena and Manuel wished they could, they couldn't continue to hold up the sky with their two pairs of hands. It was time to confront their families with the truth. Manuel called his parents in Miami. It took call after call, three days of talking, before Pedro Flores acknowledged what Manuel was trying to tell him. It was true, it was not a rumor: His son Manuel was HIV positive. When his mother flew back to Guatemala to face the reality, she brought Manuel the handful of books about AIDS he had asked her to buy for him. Before packing them in her suitcase, she covered the books the same way children cover their textbooks. She did not want to be seen with those books when the men at customs opened her luggage.

Religion had not protected Magdalena from AIDS. Arguably it contributed significantly to the death she was now facing. But when it came time for her parents to be informed, she once again allowed religion to intercede for her. She invited her parents to visit.

"My wife and I went," Gustavo Correa remembers. "One afternoon, they invited a priest, a friend of theirs, to lunch. We all had lunch together and afterwards the priest called us into one of the rooms. Magdalena and Manuel stayed out in the living room. The priest told us that the three of them were infected. We cried. *Lloramos mucho. Mucho. Mucho.* We hugged and we continued to cry."

Magdalena died in Miami at home, surrounded with much love and much serenity. Her parents were there, her daughter was there, her husband was there, her sister was there. Señor Correa tells me that when a priest went to see her on her deathbed, he commented that he had rarely met a young woman with such internal peace, a young woman "so prepared to die."

Her body was flown to Guatemala, where she was cremated as she had wished. At the Iglesia de Gaira, Manuel stood in front of all of Santa Clara and in his eulogy, which he addressed in the form of a letter from his daughter and him, he called his wife "the most beautiful star in the universe" and "the great Heroine," and said good-bye to his "Adored Queen, while you prepare our rooms, receive a kiss as big as the sky and our Perpetual Love."

A few days later he flew back to Miami, where he now lives, and married his former girlfriend, the older woman with whom he had always felt a strong connection. He returns to Santa Clara every summer. He wants his daughter, to whom he is selflessly devoted night and day, to see Magdelena's family. At times people come up to him and look at him as if they had just encountered a ghost. Some even comment: "Hey, man, we were told you had already died." When he is there, Gustavo organizes meetings for him to lecture on AIDS prevention. Last time I talked to him, he was writing his memoirs; he had just returned from Santa Clara, where he and Gustavo had spoken to a high school class.

It was Marta, Magdalena's sister, who spoke about Magdalena in the most real way, not as Magdalena the virginal daughter, the perfect Catholic wife, but Magdalena the best friend. "When Magdalena died, I felt like I had lost an arm," she says, sitting in the same sofa her father sat in while he spoke about his "precious flowers." Sitting next to Marta is her sister-in-law, married to their older brother. She and her husband live in the same three-story building that Gustavo Correa built, in an apartment one flight down from the Correas. Marta, her husband, and her three children live in the same apartment as Gustavo and Alma. They are both full-time mothers and housewives.

Marta looks somewhat like Magdalena except she is blond and more outgoing than Magdalena, from what the stories suggest. Marta is comfortable talking about her sister and brings her to life in a way neither her father nor her husband were able to do. She says that Magdalena was methodical and organized, responsible about taking her birth control pills; that she fought tooth and nail when Marta and others wanted to cut off Manuel after Magdalena was diagnosed— "I saw Magdalena's reaction, and I understood that if we were in any way to create opposition toward Manuel, we would never see her or the baby"; that it was Magdalena who gave strength to Gustavo Correa during her last days; and that it was Magdalena who organized the details of her funeral and of how her daughter was to be raised. She asked Manuel to take her to Mass on Sundays and "to redo his life." Marta said she trusted Magdalena because "Magdalena knew what she was doing. I remember one time I saw her eating from the same spoon that she was feeding my daughter with and my heart stopped, but then I thought if Magdalena is doing it, she must know what she is doing."

Marta, surprisingly, also talks about sex in a way that is neither repressed nor romanticized. Like Magdalena, her sister and sister-in-law both went to La Enseñanza and have slept only with the one man they married. When asked whether her Catholic upbringing got in the way of her sexuality, Marta is straightforward in her answer: "No, *m'ija,* I was already twenty-six, so I was a little grown up, don't you think? So in that sense, perfect! On the contrary, I think sex is very important in a marriage, and I guess one can stand other things if there is good sex. When Magdalena fell ill, I spent two months in Miami and I was climbing up the walls, I so missed making love with my husband."

Her sister-in-law, much more modest, blushes at the question, and reddens even more at Marta's answer. It is the first time these two women, sisters-in-law who live in the same building and have known each other for more than ten years, mention sex in a conversation. "Everything I've learned," the sister-in-law says quietly and proudly, "I've learned from my husband. I never speak with any of my friends about sex, not even with my best friends."

After Magdalena's death, Marta and her sister-in-law must see their husbands differently. "My husband flirts a lot with the *pelaitas,* the younger girls," Marta offers, "but he does it in front of me. Still, I don't put my hands in the fire for him, I'm less trusting *now.* And I tell him that if he cheats on me, I will turn around and do the same, you will see. I also talk to him and I tell him that I don't know what it's like to sleep with another man. We communicate a lot. I tell him that it must be cool to try something different. You know, we who have only been with one man, well," she says, looking over at her sister-in-law, "you too, you've only been with my brother."

"Me too," she replies. "But what are you saying, what do you mean? I am not curious, it's not really something I would like to do. How different can it be? My husband is serious and stays home, *es más bien casero,* but I wouldn't put my hands in the fire either. One is more conscious now."

"I think that what happened was a lesson to people," Marta says. "People were saying if that can happen to Magdalena, it can happen to anyone. We've lost other friends to AIDS, but when that happens people start saying that he had been a drug addict or a bisexual and like that. But when that happened to Magdalena, many people were in shock and started to be more careful."

She uncrosses her legs and tugs at her purple linen shorts. "But you know, after a while everything is forgotten, and although people paid attention at the beginning, slowly, *poco a poco se vuelve a ser como antes,* everything goes back to how things were."

V.
Northern Ladies

*As a woman I have no country. As
a woman I want no country.*
—Virginia Woolf, *Three Guineas*

For weeks I kept the ad that I had clipped from *El Diario*, New York's Spanish-language daily, inside my desk calendar next to the taxi receipts, the pink bank deposit slips, the unused ticket to *Miss Saigon*, the flyers announcing foreign policy panels or book readings on the Lower East Side. At the start of each day, as I opened the black appointment book, I would contemplate calling the Centro de Cirugía Plástica to see if my suspicions were correct: that sexist attitudes are not left behind, that they cross the border along with the millions of immigrants from Latin America.

I had found the plastic surgery clinic in the paper's classified pages. Under "Family Planning," next to advertisements of abortions for as little as a hundred dollars, a small box in Spanish offered to make you into the perfect Latin American woman: face-lifts, breast implants, liposuction, permanent makeup, electrolysis, and *reconstrucción del himen*—hymen reconstruction. Two phone numbers were listed, one in Queens, the other in Brooklyn.

When I first saw it, I laughed. But after a bit my face stiffened. Is it possible, I asked myself as I stared at the price list and the sketch of a rose in full bloom, that we Latin women immigrate here and continue to believe that we need to have the body of Miss Venezuela *and* la Virgen María all in one?

When human rights activists reported the widespread practice of female genital mutilation in Africa and among African immigrant communities abroad—a hundred million women worldwide have suffered or are at risk of undergoing the removal of the clitoris or all of their external genitalia—it captured the attention of the media and women's rights groups in this country. With a woman's organs of pleasure removed, the idea was, a husband could feel in complete control of his wife. The woman would have only marital sex and then only for reproduction. No matter that female circumcision is an abominable violation of a woman's freedom. Nor that it puts her health at risk—the rate of infection is quite high—and, at times, her life. Women have died from bleeding or from pure shock.

The procedure was outlawed in the United States in 1997. Recently, owing to a new report indicating that more than 160,000 girls and women in this country may have been victims, or are at risk, the issue is again on the front pages of newspapers. The study, published in March 1998 by the Health and Human Services Department, reports that immigrant communities of African descent will go to such lengths to keep tradition alive as to perform the operation themselves or fly in practitioners from their ancestral countries.

Secretary of Health and Human Services Donna Shalala has been very outspoken in denouncing female circumcision. "It's illegal, it's inhumane, and we've got to be clear about that," she told the *New York Times*. "At the same time, we have to be culturally sensitive in explaining to those immigrants who might put their girls at risk that the practice has harmful physical and psychological consequences." She has ordered educational material to train health professionals who may encounter such cases.

I would like to see Secretary Shalala do the same for the girls and women who seek, or are pressured to undergo, hymen reconstruction. But it is unlikely to happen. She is probably unaware of the existence of the procedure in this country. Although hymen reconstruction is advertised every day in the main New York Latino newspaper, it has gone unnoticed by women's rights groups.

When I saw the ad, I contacted a human rights group—to alert them, to see if they were interested in writing the same type of reports they had prepared about the same practice in Turkey, a faraway place with unacceptable human rights violations. They listened attentively to my story, and were surprised to hear that hymen reconstruction is an abuse committed not only in foreign lands but right here, but politely I was informed that it would not be a priority for them as it would be a very hard case to argue from a human rights law perspective. I was told that, in the case of clitorectomies, the operations were generally forced on the women—mostly preadolescent girls. Hymen reconstruction was more like breast implants. "It is an invasive procedure but it is not the worst," a human rights lawyer explained to me. "It is not deadly or damaging to a woman's health, and it is more voluntary than genital mutilation is." Women were walking into the clinic uncoerced.

"Of course, I am against it," she continued, "but ultimately it doesn't matter what it is—genital mutilation, breast implants, hymen reconstructions. The issue here is not to create a debate over which procedure should be legal or illegal but that they exist at all. The bottom line is that it is all about control over women."

I could understand the lawyer's argument but my outrage did not subside. I determined to investigate for myself. I remained curious and angry—and I slipped into the sadness and confusion that frequently beset me when I confront aspects of my culture that are so backward, so unjust, and yet so familiar. Still I was not ready to stop. I knew these are not useful feelings when investigating a story and I set out to, alas, prove my fear right: the women of Latin American descent who come here with dreams of freedom, of economic prosperity, of *una vida mejor*, are not free from male expectation and domination. They might leave the land of God and men behind but not its rules. The same outdated prejudices, the same antiquated practices come into their new homes, into their new lives in this new land where other rules—ones that offer more choices, other role models—are possible. I wanted to understand why any woman would walk uncoerced to the Centro.

In the right-hand corner, the ad offered a free consultation and a twenty-four-hour phone number. I dialed from my apartment on a Sunday evening.

A woman answered the phone after the third ring. By the tone of her voice, I was sure I had dialed the wrong number. She sounded as if she was comfortable and at home. She probably was—with call forwarding, businesses these days do not have to miss a potential client. I said I was trying to reach the Centro de Cirugía Plástica and the voice asked me, "How can I help you, *mi amor?*"

I asked for directions. From Manhattan, I was to take the number 7 train from Grand Central to Main Street in Flushing to go to the clinic in Queens on the M train—*"eme de mamá,"* the voice offered—from Canal Street to Forest Avenue if I wanted to go to the one in Brooklyn. Any more questions I had, she could answer. She had worked in the clinic, she explained, for ten years. "What is it, *mi cielo,* that you are interested in?" she asked.

I slipped into a voice intended to deceive. I became a Latin damsel in distress, who needed to be revirginized, made into a señorita again. I didn't only fool her, I fooled myself. I am always surprised how that voice always comes out naturally. Decades of living on my own, north of the border, cannot seem to dispel it entirely. I can always go back and retrieve it, like an old pair of favorite shoes from the back of my closet.

"Esa," said the voice on the other side. I might as well have told her I was interested in having *rayitos* done in my hair. "That one we do very well, *siempre queda más bien. Es bien sencillita,* very simple. It takes about two hours. We do it *muchísimo.*"

"Anesthesia?" I inquired.

"Local," she said. "We have Hispanic doctors among our five surgeons. They all speak Spanish. I can recommend two of them. The cost of the operation is between eighteen hundred and two thousand dollars, due on the day of the procedure, and we take all major credit cards."

"But I need to know more," I said. "Do many Latinas do it?" I asked, feigning nervousness. I was hoping that, to encourage me to have it done, she would provide me with harrowing statistics.

"Of course, *amor,* many Hispanas who like to have that *problemita* taken care of. *Siempre se ha hecho, no te preocupes.* It's always been done. They put everything back together and they make sure to leave an orifice for menstruation."

It all sounded barbaric, offensive, a violation, something that should not be permitted. But the fact that a woman described it to me over the phone as if I had called a beauty salon made it eerier and sadder. She was determined to make the sale and recited the clinic's track record. "Many, many" Korean and Chinese clients; girls who fly from Korea to have it done because there, as she explained, parents of the groom can demand to see a document that attests the bride's virginity. The Chinese girls, she said, usually show up with their mothers.

"How about Americans?"

"*No, las americanas no, no les importa eso.* They don't care about that. Although last week we had one, she was marrying an Arab. But among us," she said, "we've always done it. Don't worry, it will be fine." As proof, she told me about the nineteen-year-old woman who has a child but whose fiancé thinks that she is a virgin and that her baby belongs to her mother. To cover her lies, she paid close to two thousand dollars to have the remnants of her ruptured hymen sewn together.

The voice over the phone was warm and chatty, as only a Latina can be with another Latina, even one she has never met, making it all feel stranger. She even confessed—both as a *confianza* and as a good marketing tool—that she had had breast augmentation. She would have kept talking if I had kept asking. But I felt my cover slipping as my discomfort increased. She gave me her name and told me to look her up when I went in for my free consultation. They were open Mondays through Saturdays from ten to six.

"Thanks," I said.

"*Gracias a ti, amor.*"

"Bye," I said, disgusted and disappointed. Machismo swims across the Rio Grande and settles in, as strong and as determined to work hard and to stay as the millions of men and women who come to this country from all over Latin America. By the year 2000, Hispanics will make up twenty-nine percent of New York's population, outnumbering African Americans and becoming the largest minority in the city. Will this mentality erode by then?

"Bye, *mi cielo,*" I heard in the background. How long, I thought as I put the receiver down, will the Centro be in the maidenhead business? Until when, I wonder, will Latin women here need—or be willing—to submit themselves to such a perverse, ridiculous, humiliating, and deceptive practice? The warm feeling of comfort and familiarity that I got from the SE HABLA ESPAÑOL posted in New York courthouses, from the instructions and advertisements in Spanish on the subway and on the bus, from the racks of dailies and magazines targeted to the Latinos in this city, has now become tinged with apprehension. I used to feel we were making a place for ourselves in America. But are the attitudes that have held women back, harmed them, made them second-class citizens, making inroads with all the other transmitters of our culture?

Deceiving one's husband on the wedding night is part of our lore and our literature. Angela Vicario, the returned bride in Gabriel García Márquez's *Chronicle of a Death Foretold,* had been provided with the tools to fool her new husband: "She recounted how her friends had instructed her to get her husband drunk in bed until he passed out, to feign more embarrassment than she really felt so he'd turn out the light, to give herself a drastic douche of alum water to fake virginity, and to stain the sheet with Mercurochrome so she could display it the following day in her bridal courtyard." Angela Vicario failed to employ these methods, causing the death of Santiago Nasar, killed by her twin brothers for allegedly deflowering their sister. To avenge the shame and clean her name, they slaughtered him with pig-killing knives: "Before God and before men," Pablo Vicario said. "It was a matter of honor." No one in the town denounced their revenge. Even Pablo's fiancée saw it as his manly duty. "I knew what they were up to," she explained, "and I didn't only agree, I never would have married him if he hadn't done what a man should do."

Angela Vicario might be a fictional character but her predicament is anything but a fiction. The value men place on their virginity is understood by Latinas everywhere and from all walks of life—from the clients of the clinic in Queens to the stripper I met in Bogotá one night.

She worked at the swanky Le Palace, an expensive and tacky cabaret and bordello with the same name and the same decor as the one my friends frequented in Panama. A pretty girl, she came from Pereira, a small city southwest of Bogotá known for the many young women who leave it to work as prostitutes in the capital. She went to university, lived with her aunt, and danced two nights a week. Her parents could only afford to send her money for school tuition. As she fixed her red sequined bra, she told me that by "dancing and going with the clients" she could have spending money. While this is the same story I've heard from the strippers at Stringfellows in New York City, hers had that Latin twist. On the nights she danced at Le Palace, she would tell her aunt and her boyfriend that she was studying for an exam. She was not overly concerned that her parents or her aunt might find out the truth. She was petrified, however, of her boyfriend. They had been together for two years and she was hoping to marry him. "If he finds out," she said, "I'm afraid to think what he can do. He thinks I'm a virgin. I know he will only marry a virgin."

To be sure, other men, not just Latin American men, expect and demand virginity in their brides. And procedures that allow women to comply with such demeaning beliefs are readily available in these places, places I formerly assumed to be backward or purely fictional. According to the woman from the clinic in Queens, Korean and Chinese women are important clients. *The Lancet,* England's prestigious medical journal, reports that in Egypt the practice is quite common, and that women come to Cairo from the entire Middle Eastern region, as far as the Gulf States. Egyptian custom demands that the husband show a white silk handkerchief with bloodstains to close female family members waiting outside the bedroom. Nonbleeding brides have been killed in rural Egypt, so that the family can "cleanse their shame."

The instinct for survival has forced women to be imaginative and resourceful. An Egyptian woman managed to withhold sex from her husband on their wedding night—and for the following four months—by pretending she was insane. She was simply saving up for the operation that I had inquired about over the phone, no questions asked, just bring a credit card. As far as I can tell, there is only one difference between the operation they do in

Queens and the one performed in Egypt—in Egypt, in addition to sewing, they leave a capsule inside, filled with fake blood.

In Egypt, hymen reconstruction may be a lifesaving tool that women use to protect themselves from violence or to secure their future like the stripper from Pereira. Police reports show that, in the last ten years, the procedure has reduced by eighty percent the number of Egyptian women murdered in order to cleanse the wronged honors of their families.

To an Argentinian in her early sixties, hymen reconstruction, in her youth, meant sexual freedom. She recalls how the procedure afforded young women in her country a sexual life they were not theoretically allowed to have. When she was in her twenties, she tells me over the phone, she had a friend, a woman gynecologist "feminist" who performed the operation to contribute to the "advancement of women" because, as she said, "it was unfair that men could have sex and women couldn't. This way, women were allowed to have sex too." That was Argentina circa 1948 when women were not even allowed to vote. When I tell her that the same thing is happening in New York in 1998, she laughs hard. Fifty years later, women still need to lie, to be deceptive, to hide their sexuality.

The Centro de Cirugía Plástica is not located in the Dominican Republic where a Spanish-speaking TV show aired a whole segment about the popularity of these clinics, or in Bogotá where the newspaper *El Espacio* advertises abortion clinics that also do *himenoplastias sin dolor*. In the United States, women do not need to worry about being stoned to death or "returned" with shame if they do not bleed on their wedding beds. The Centro de Cirugía Plástica is not located in the Middle East where the rule of the Koran goes undisputed, or in a Latin American village where common law makes women the property of their men and a woman's virginity is not an individual choice but a family affair. The Centro is merely a quick subway ride from Manhattan, where I have chosen to live precisely because here I am free of any of the cultural expectations I grew up with.

Why would a woman in this country feel the need to pay two thousand dollars, and incur the risk of a surgical procedure, to lie to the man she would choose as her life partner? Are women who arrive in Queens from Latin America as fearful of losing their men as the university student moonlighting as a stripper I spoke to in Bogotá? And why isn't the existence of these clinics publicized and criticized by women's groups? Even in Egypt, *The Lancet* reports, the national medical association is trying to clamp down on the practice—taking away licenses from doctors who perform hymen reconstruction. Some have even ended up in prison. Ironically, religious authorities condemn the procedure. But this comes from a patriarchal and fundamentalist view rather than from a feminist perspective—they regard it as cheating. The bride, they contend, has to be a true virgin, not a reconstructed one.

While human rights lawyers, women activists, a congresswoman from Rochester, and the secretary of health are lobbying to stop female genital mutilation, the practice of hymen reconstruction goes on inconspicuously. I have no idea how many of these clinics exist in this country. The Internet had no information. The handful of progressive women's clinics I contacted in New York and on the West Coast, thinking that they might have knowledge of hymen reconstruction clinics catering to the Latino population in California, thought I was inquiring about a procedure which reverses clitorectomies. None had heard of hymen reconstruction.

I could not let go of the need to visit the Centro. I wanted to see the place, the face of the woman I had spoken to on the phone, the faces of the women who would be clients. I remembered the suggestion of the human rights lawyer. These places could be investigated and closed down if the procedures were being done under unhygienic or dangerous conditions or if they were performed by unlicensed doctors.

There was only one way to find out.

It is on a crisp fall Saturday afternoon that I decide to visit the virgin-makers. I look at myself in the mirror and think that my oversize dark blue V-neck sweater over the straight brown skirt and black flats will not do. What I wear every day, to go about *my* life, seems inappropriate, conspicuous-in-reverse for my visit to the world of Latin problem-solving. I could wear different clothes, I say to myself, but as I step toward the mirror, I realize the clothes are only part of the problem. It's my face, the look in my eyes. It's the way I stand, the way I walk. The problem is that someone who wants any of the list of things offered at the Centro de Cirugía Plástica would never, ever, step out of her home as underdressed and as unmade-up as I normally look. But I like my comfortable, unadorned clothes and the way my freshly washed face looks even when my skin turns to a shade of hospital green from lack of sun.

I could do without the dark circles under my eyes. My sister is right, I think. While we were having lunch at a Madison Avenue bistro, she stared straight at me, took a sip of her cappuccino, and remarked, "Work, definitely, does not beautify."

I can conceal the rings with a little cream. I can even wear the de-rigueur black eye liner that I still like to wear at night if I'm going out. Would red or frosty pink lipstick convince the staff at the Centro de Cirugía Plástica that I really need to be revirginized?

I change my unflattering sweater for a spandex bodice of ivory crushed velvet. I even go for some lip gloss. It occurs to me only later that all this worry and preparation is unnecessary. As long as I had the money to pay for the operation, no one would really care what my reasons for doing it were.

The clinic is located in a five-story commercial building on Northern Boulevard, one of Flushing's main arteries. It is not in a back alley but a respectable address where insurance companies, travel agencies, and dentists could have their offices. I was expecting the clinic to be more hidden away, and I am surprised that the area is not as run down as I imagined it would be. The clinic is smack in the middle of what looks like Archie Bunker's neighborhood—a tidy row of redbrick houses, small front lawns, and inexpensive cars parked along the streets—except that the people driving the cars, mowing the lawns, pushing the baby strollers are mostly Asian. I see a few Latinos and absolutely no English-speaking blonds. I wonder if these are the Koreans and the Chinese clients that the woman told me about over the phone. But I am really looking for the lines of nervous Latinas, the loyal believers and clients for the restitching of women's genitals for the purpose of deceit and of salvation.

I expect to find them waiting their turn in the large, posh cafeteria with copper cappuccino makers, smoked mirrors, and purple and silver decor on the ground floor of the clinic's building. But all I find there is a $2.50 cup of good lattè and Korean kids in their early twenties dressed in hip garb—baggy jeans and baseball caps worn backward—having sodas and pastries.

The Center is one flight down.

The white lettering on the door of suite number five reads NORTHERN LADIES. Nothing in the ad indicated that this was the clinic's name, and I'm struck now by its irony. It probably refers to the fact that it is on Northern Boulevard, but the allusion is too perfect: ladies who come north, north as in *el Norte, el coloso, el gigante, el mejor, el lo máximo*, and yet, the newly-arrived northern ladies are still dragging the chains of machismo. They stay tied to rules and attitudes that can be shed, once here.

The clinic feels like the beauty salon where María Alejandra and Regina, dear friends, drag me every time I visit them in Panama City. We have manicures and pedicures, and they absolutely make me have a haircut so that I don't look like a "hippie" while we share story after story, updating each other on the state of our minds, hearts, bodies, and souls—and those of everyone we know. The manicure does not last me as long as the good feeling created by an afternoon of pampering and good company. As I sit on the chintz sofa, I wonder what feelings linger with the women who spend an afternoon in this clinic.

I am the only one here. The waiting room of Northern Ladies is decorated in feminine colors, pink and mauve and touches of gray. The television is showing video clips from MTV Latino—lots of cleavage and that insinuating look we Latinas are trained to give the camera. But the volume is turned off. I wish they had something to read. I miss the old issues of *¡Hola!*, the Spanish gossip magazine that chronicles the lives of Hollywood stars and European royalty, that the Panamanian salon has.

From the window of an enclosed cubicle, a woman in a white smock asks me to fill out a questionnaire. I walk over to the window and explain that I'm there for the free consultation, whispering that I want the *reconstrucción del himen*. She does not flinch and just tells me to take a seat, that the assistant to the doctor will be with me in a while. The doctor is off for Yom Kippur. "But his assistant can explain everything," she says.

I notice framed photographs and posters of women of great beauty behind the receptionist's desk. I am tempted to ask who the women in the photographs are but opt instead to go back to the sofa and sit quietly. Too many questions and I might raise suspicion.

The door swings open and three women walk in. I can tell from their accent that they are from Colombia, *antioqueñas o caleñas,* definitely not from Barranquilla, and that they are grand-mother, mother, and daughter. The two elder ones are accompa-nying the youngest woman, in her early twenties, to a checkup after her surgery. What kind of surgery is obvious. To my disap-pointment, she has those breasts that look like baseballs, with a perfect rise and roundness that only implants can give. The price list in *El Diario* says the cost of an *aumento de senos* is between three thousand and forty-five hundred dollars. Twenty-five min-utes from Manhattan and I am sitting in a room where someone is making loads of money by reinforcing the inequality and the disempowerment of Latin American women.

A man of medium height and olive skin, wearing a short-sleeved white shirt and inexpensive brown trousers, invites me into a wood-paneled room with an imposing wooden desk. He looks smaller as he sits behind the desk and leans over after glancing at the questionnaire.

"Entonces," he says, *"se quiere hacer . . .* you want to become señorita again."

"Yes," I whisper in complete assumption of my role. "What do you think?"

"Well," he clears his throat and leans back. "We just do the operation, we offer no counseling. That is up to you."

"But I'm nervous, doctor. Can you help me understand the procedure so that I feel better? It scares me." I know he is the as-sistant, not the doctor, and I hope that by making him feel more important, he will take the role of knowledgeable—and paternal—doctor.

"Oh, no, *m'ijita,* there's nothing to be scared about. It is very simple, we just sew you back and it's like nothing has happened.

You come and after two hours you go home and the only thing is you shouldn't plan your wedding for one, two months, that's what it takes for the stitches to dissolve."

"Stitches?"

"Yes, yes, stitches. We sew you so that, you know, there will be blood and there will be pain on your wedding night. Just like if you had never . . ."

He could not say sex.

"But, how about . . ."

"Nothing to worry," he interrupts me, "*se cose todo*. We leave a hole so that, you know, the blood from your menstruation comes out. It works very well. We do it all the time."

"Where are you from, doctor? Are you a gynecologist? Sorry to ask so much, but you understand—this is something—I—"

Not an M.D. but he did go to school for a few years, studied gynecology in Ecuador where he is from. He is getting uncomfortable and fidgety. And I don't know whether he is suspecting me of what he should, or whether sitting in the boss's leather chair and telling me "we" could do something he—as only an "assistant"—is maybe not licensed to do is making him nervous. Plus, he stutters every time he mentions the word "sex" and I am asking him now to explain to me—in a diagram—exactly what a hymen looks like. No one, I think, has asked him this before. His patience is wearing thin.

He takes out a pad, and with a plastic pencil with a logo from Harvard he draws two circles, one inside the other. The sketch reminds me of a fried egg.

"This is your hymen," he says, shading the area between the two circles. It now looks like a doughnut. Not at all what I thought hymens looked like.

But I had never really thought about my hymen before, not in a real sense, only as that mythical treasure, the most valuable thing I could protect, something that was so delicate and precious that to think about it too much could make it rupture. Where was it? Who really knew? Did any woman denied sex education and burdened with Catholic guilt really know?!

By the time I first visited a gynecologist, it had been years since I had seen the brown spots on my white cotton undies when

I came home the night I felt a penis inside of me for the first time. My shirt was inside out; my legs were shaking. I sat on the toilet, passed my fingernail over the spot, and inspected the dark goo between my legs, knowing I would never again see the man who had done the thing I was supposed to do with the man I would be with "in sickness and in health," till death did us part. I looked at myself in the mirror and thought, Oh my God, what have I done, do I look different, will my mother be able to tell?

I don't like to remember the night I lost my virginity. It was memorable only because it was the first time. It was not with the man I married as I had been told as a girl it should be. Nor was it with a boy I either knew well, liked, or cared for, the way most of my new friends in the United States were cautiously embracing their sexuality. I dove in all at once, all alone, very late one night while in Panama for a Christmas holiday. I was eighteen and in college.

He was older, a senior, a college friend of a friend, there for a few days. We met at a party. I wasn't particularly smitten, but when he asked me to go home with him, I did. There was something perverse about letting this man, someone I had just met, definitely the man I had felt the least for, take off my raw silk shirt in that room. I had always felt the push to go further mixed in with the pull to stop when I had gotten to this point before with those boys who really did make my pulse go faster and my hands turn clammy when they called. But when, this time, the hands were those of a stranger, a visitor, someone no one knew well, not even I, I decided not to say *para*, not to say no, even if it hurt, even if he was not loving me.

Almost twenty years after my hymen was ruptured without any romance, I still imagined it as a precious thin film that looks like the gauze that covered my legs when, as a girl, I fell and scraped my knees. To me, it was like that white tissue woven in small squares that allow air to reach the wound while keeping all the rest out, to keep anything dangerous from touching and infecting me. Like the cotton that protected my open scar, the veil between my legs guarded my virginity.

When my skin bled, or the gauze got dirty, the threads of the squares unraveled, creating a hole, exposing the vulnerability of my open knee. But I could still run and play, even when my knees were bruised. There was always more gauze. I could always ask to have the bandage changed. But there was nothing that could replace this fragile, priceless veil between my legs. Even my grandmother worried. Whenever she saw me riding my brother's bicycle, the one with the bar across the seat, not the purple Schwinn with the banana seat I had gotten for Christmas, she would scream from the front door, "*¡Bájate de ahi!* That bicycle is not for you. That bicycle is for boys. *Te puedes hacer un daño.*" You could harm yourself.

How could the hands of a doctor's assistant with unkempt fingernails reconstruct that intimate part of me that so many people in my family had spoken of in hieroglyphics and in metaphors, never by its name, fearing that even saying its name out loud would make it dissolve and make me forever cursed? But this doctor's assistant with a food stain on his shirt is showing me that my hymen is not delicate and precious and unmentionable but as banal as an egg sunny-side up and as insignificant in my life as the boy who had broken it.

"When you have, h-m-mm, *relaciones,* h-mmm, *sssee-xxx-uu-a-les,*" he stutters, pressing hard with the pen and drawing a firm line that cuts across the shaded area, "it breaks. But the two parts stay there."

With his pen he shows me how he can "just put them back together again."

Like Humpty Dumpty, I want to say.

With needle and thread, I say instead.

The door opens and one of the other women who work at the clinic, not the one who asked me to fill out the questionnaire, walks in. The assistant looks relieved and asks her to answer my questions. "A woman," he says, "can explain it better." Her voice is toasty, like the voice on the phone, as she tries to reassure me, not with a medical explanation but with a recital of cases. I doubt she is a registered nurse, but I don't ask her if she is. She is telling me about the Peruvian girl, the daughter of the mayor of a small city, who had my same problem. She too had come to school here and had experienced *la vida de acá*—"the life over here." When it was time for her to return to marry her longtime *novio*, she came to the clinic. The procedure, the woman explains, was readily available in her hometown, but she could not risk having it done there. She was the child of a politician; everyone knew who she was. She could not afford to trust the local clinics to keep such a valued secret.

She also tells me about the Colombian woman who had it done twice. The first time was to marry a Colombian, but the wedding was called off. For a while she dated an American, but they broke up too. Now the guy she is seeing, who arrived a few years ago from Latin America, has asked her to marry him. She came back to have the operation done for this wedding night.

"But we have married women do it, too." This is the assistant doctor, who has been quiet while the woman spoke but now interrupts to tell me about the American couple who recently came to the clinic. To celebrate their twenty-fifth wedding anniversary, she became a newborn virgin. That is a whole different matter, I want to say, but I nod instead.

I suddenly feel the strangeness of being in this room. Unlike the ultrafeminine waiting area, this consulting room has all the trappings and the symbols of male power—wood paneling, upholstered armchairs, glassed-in shelves with heavy books, diplomas on the wall. Only the plastic pen is from Harvard.

"I would like you to show me my hymen," I blurt out.

The "doctor" and the "nurse" are surprised at my request, but he tells her to "go ahead, *prepárala.*" He'll be right there.

I cross to the door and stand in front of the "operating rooms"— small stalls divided only by pale pink shower curtains. My thoughts are of back-alley bleeding, of botched operations. What if they have an emergency here? Do any of the women who come here to have their hymens stitched, their faces lifted, or the fat sucked from their hips think of the possibility that they might be endangering their health, or are they so desperate that all concern for safety is overridden?

The nurse takes me into the middle stall and is eager to make me feel comfortable, to show me how *solidaria* she is. "We have to lie to men," she says.

She instructs me to take off my underwear and raise my skirt up to my hips.

"Let me give you some advice," she says. "I don't know how long you've been in this country but, you know, once we come here, we start. And it can be one or two but it can also be very many. So if you already have this problem, you might as well do it right. I always advise women that if they're going to have this done, they might as well go all the way."

"All the way?" I am lying on my back. She is standing next to me. She is a very attractive woman in her early forties with mysterious hazel eyes made more beautiful by the well-applied smoky eye shadow. When I compliment her, she thanks me and goes on to give me a lecture on feminine wiles. "I am married and have kids but I have to keep young for my husband. *Hay que cuidarse, tu sabes.* If not, they leave you for a young one.

"Men are not stupid," she continues. "If you have had many men, they can tell, you know, the walls of your vagina, they change, they . . . expand," she says, making a circle with her thumb and finger, opening and closing it. "As you experience more, the walls are not as tight. So you get them tightened. It's two thousand dollars more, but it's worth it."

She confides that after she had her kids, she had this procedure done.

"In your case it's different. You, you have to cover all your bases. You have to make sure that if you are going to lie, you are going to lie well. There is a test the doctor will give to you. The finger test."

"Finger test?"

"He inserts one finger." She shows me her right index finger. "Depending how easy it is for him to insert it, he'll insert a second one." She lifts her middle one. "Depending on how easy that one goes in, he'll try a third. If he can do only one, then you're fine with just the reconstruction, but if it's more than one we recommend doing the tightening of the walls. Are you ready? Should I call the doctor?"

"In a second," I said. "I am really scared. Can you tell me more? Tell me, who comes to have this done? Can I speak to someone who has had it done? You know, it will make me feel better."

Impossible. She is absolutely sure no one will be interested in talking with me. Secrecy is of utmost importance to the clinic's clients.

I try a different approach: "But who comes here apart from women from other countries? Who that lives in this country?"

"Lots of men around have little on their brains, you know." She taps her forehead with her finger. "When men come to this country from Latin America as adults, it's very hard to change them. When they get married, they want señoritas. It's different for the younger kids, the ones who grow up here. They are like Americans, these things are not important for them."

She sees the brutishness of the men. But does she see her dishonesty? Even if she recognizes the backwardness of such men, she will still tell a young woman lying on her cot with her legs spread open to lie, instead of telling her she is better off dumping that man.

"This is your hymen," says the doctor's assistant, handing me a mirror. I thrust out my pelvis, pushing his hands away, and I raise my torso to my knees. I see an uneven membrane of the same pink and brown color that the anthuriums in my grandmother's patio took after they had been cut and put in a vase of water ready to be offered to the Virgin's altar. There is one on each side of that openness that Octavio Paz describes in *Labyrinth of Solitude* as the culprit of my inferiority when he writes: "Women are inferior beings because, in submitting, they open themselves up. Their inferiority is constitutional and resides in their sex, their submissiveness, which is a wound that never heals."

I stare at the epicenter of what constitutes in the language of macho power the possibility of being torn open by a man, making me less and him more. My hymen is split and it is sturdy. My vagina is not a wound but an open door to my interior, all a part of me, all owned by me and by no one else. It is I who chose what, when, who, how many will. I snap my legs shut.

I walk out disappointed with my reporting skills. I was not able to find out any real facts. I do not know how many hymens they retouch and there is no chance I could talk to any of their clients. I do not know if this man has the necessary license to perform the operations or if he does them at all. The sheets I lay on were not bloodstained and the assistant doctor wore latex gloves, but I have no way of assessing whether they keep up with the sanitation norms required.

As I walk out, I grab a copy of *El Mundo de Hoy*, a free Spanish weekly paper published in West New York, New Jersey. No bylined articles, just a bunch of black-and-white photos of the social and political events of the week attended by the movers and shakers—men and women—of the Latin communities in Queens and New Jersey, a few paid ads by the Latino branch of the Kiwanis Club of Hudson County, photos of Governor Christie Whitman's visit to a charity function for Cuban refugees, and a long list of impounded cars to be auctioned.

The front page highlights the thirtieth celebration of the Committee for Human Values Award: "Dazzling! A Memorable Night at Victor's Cafe 52 and Channel 47 TV." Photo after photo of men in black tie, in business suits, women in sequined dresses, standing behind a podium, speaking into a microphone, shaking hands. As with all special nights of Latino politicians, business leaders, and artistic and sports stars, this one too is celebrated at Victor's Café—the Rainbow Room of New York Latinos—a restaurant on 52nd Street in Manhattan with fancy decor, hearty Cuban food, allegedly the best *mojitos* outside of Havana, and an oil painting of a bare-chested "Mano de Piedra" Durán, the world champion boxer from Panama, sporting a thick gold chain with boxing gloves paved in diamonds dangling from his chest.

The Most Distinguished Politician 1997 Award was given to the mayor of West New York. The Man of the Year was a real estate developer and president of the Kiwanis Club. And the Most Distinguished Woman Award went to the "beautiful and elegant" president of the Centro de Cirugía Plástica Northern Ladies "for the valuable services" she has provided to the community where "hundreds of people—men and women—have satisfied their desires through the work of its extraordinary surgeons and the unsurpassable attention of its assistants."

I stare at her picture. It is not the woman that I met, but it could have been her. They both have that cherished look of the ageless *reina de belleza* that the ad promised—the same smoky eyes, the same dyed blond hair, the voluptuous figure draped in seductive clothes. What a disappointment to find that the person behind Northern Ladies is a woman.

I have kept the picture of Nely Galán in my files since her profile appeared with the headline "Tropical Tycoon" in the pages of the *New York Times Magazine* in December 1994. She smiles at the camera with a *coquetería* and control that I recognize as a Latina trademark—not to be confused with the Latin American look, one that is all coquetry and little control. Her shoulder-length hair is the same Coca-Cola color as her eyes. Her mouth is perfectly delineated in pink. She is wearing the same stainless-steel and gold Cartier watch I wear and a heavy cotton knit sweater that displays across her chest a perfect red-white-and-blue flag of the United States.

I was impressed by her when I read the story. At thirty-one, she had just formed Galán Entertainment and had signed a deal with Fox Television to create Latino-themed programming in which she was to "marry the passionate emotionality of the popular Mexican novela with the language and glossy production of mainstream American television." With that position, Nely Galán had the potential of reaching the twenty-seven million Latinos living in this country and the two hundred million viewers in Latin America. She told the *Times* she was developing stories about a Latina teenager in the United States and about professional Latinas and the issues they face in the workplace. For example: "As a Latina you dress a certain way. You're kind of flamboyant, you don't fit with corporate America, but you're still ambitious, and meanwhile your parents are telling you, 'Why don't you just get married?' " For someone who does not watch much television, I remember being excited by her projects and looking forward to watching the shows when they aired.

Galán continued: "I feel like Latinas in this country live in a tug of war. A part of me thinks: 'I'm every American woman's dream come true. I'm a catch. Any man would want me.' And another part of me says: 'I'm divorced, I'm 31, I'm over the hill. I'm damaged goods.' "

I remember being surprised that she too always heard from her parents that to be anything she had to be a wife and mother. I thought those were the words of a mother or an aunt in Mexico or Puerto Rico, while the story mentioned that Galán grew up in Teaneck, New Jersey. Her parents were from Latin America but had emigrated from Cuba when she was two. She has been here ever since. Why would she still be so sensitive to such expectations? Why would she publicly choose to confess that "in the circle of my family, I'm not accomplished because I'm not married and I don't have a kid"?

Reading this was a revelation. I had thought that in this country one escaped that image, but I could understand how it can be hurtful to feel satisfaction in one's work and yet to hear only that a woman's success is measured by marriage and motherhood. It hit a nerve because, until very recently, I too heard it and heard it. I heard it straightforward from my grandmother: *"Ay, Nanita, y cuando piensas casarte?"* I heard it catty from a close relative who the last time I was in Barranquilla proclaimed to the entire dinner table: "Let's hope that, next time, Silvana comes home not with *ropa vieja y novio nuevo* but with *ropa nueva y novio viejo"*—a comment on my tendency to show up with an unimpressive set of clothes and a different boyfriend. They would rather have me arrive dressed in fabulously fashionable clothes and with the same man.

¿Hasta cuando?

At the same time that Nely and I, and millions of other women of Latin American parents, were growing up surrounded by the expectations of our culture, we were also living in a country that offered less rigid gender roles and an emphasis on knowledge and independence rather than on submission. So it is really up to us to say *hasta* when we, as Latinas who have *chosen* not to just be mothers and wives, decide for ourselves *hasta ya*. It is only recently that I stopped feeling a disgrace because I could not reconcile my life in New York with what my life back home was supposed to be. I am curious to return to Barranquilla, where I have not visited in two years, with this sensation. I want to step off the plane and inhale the humidity of our tropics and not feel inadequate when someone asks me what I've been up to in New York and I tell them only to receive either disapproving or uninterested stares.

I'll confess that I have thought a lot about the fact that I think that I stopped looking like the girl from Barranquilla. After all, last time I was in Cartagena, a *palenquera*, the name we give the black women from Palenque, the poor hamlet outside of this beautiful colonial city, who walk the beaches selling fruits from huge stainless-steel bowls balanced on their heads and offering massages or to braid your head into *trenzitas*, offered all three of them to me in English. When I turned back and, in Spanish, complained about the prices, telling her those were *precios para gringas* and I was not one, she squinted her eyes and said, *"Seguro, mi amor"* sure.

I was more amused than offended, for I figured that I must then have that look that I have so admired in Ana Castillo or Julia Alvarez, two Latina writers who could also be, like me, confused for gringas—for they too straddle both cultures. I've spent considerable time scrupulously staring at the photos on their book jackets, looking for clues to what they are like as women, as mothers, as lovers. I recognize a mixture of knowledge, of assertiveness, and of sensuality that I like. There is something real, something that does not pretend to be what they are not, in their eyes and in their smiles, something I did not see in the northern ladies I met at the Centro de Cirugia Plástica.

I started looking for more of these *norteñas*. I wanted to find out if the split between what our culture wanted from us and what Nely and I wanted was something they too felt. Looking for clues to how they were balancing the two cultures, I stumbled upon *The Maria Paradox: How Latinas Can Merge Old World Traditions with New World Self-Esteem*, a book written by two Latina psychologists who understood the difficulties for Latinas in this country who feel that "the more successful they become in North America, the less successful they feel as Hispanic women." I started reading *Latina*, a women's magazine written by Latinas for Latinas founded in late 1996. Reading both the book and the magazine, I can safely say that, yes, most Latinas feel the pull that Nely and I have felt. If not, *The Maria Paradox* would not have become the success it was—it sold an unprecedented amount for a self-help book for the Latino community. And Patricia Duarte, the editor-in-chief of *Latina*, would not feel the need to write editorials saying "Latinas' lives are still to a large extent controlled by others" or "Work, for most Latinas, is more than just a means of survival. It is the road to empowerment that our mothers who stayed home were never able to take." It is both encouraging and demoralizing to see that in 1997 the magazine still needs to talk about how work "pushes us to have a stronger grip to better handle our destinies." In the Anglo world such phrases were written in the seventies and the Anglo women of my generation writing about women's rights have moved beyond simple issues of self-determination and self-respect. To Naomi Wolff or Susan Faludi the word "empowerment" is a virtual antique. Sometimes, while writing this book, I have felt out-of-date as if I were still singing to the *"Internacional"* and to the slogan of the many demonstrations that sung it—*el pueblo unido, jamás será vencido,* or keeping that poster of Che that adorned my college room.

"Empowerment" is the word of the nineties for groups working with women in the developing world and in the African American and Latina communities in the U.S. In "The Empowerment of Women: A Key to HIV Prevention," an abstract that discusses an AIDS prevention project for young inner-city women, empowerment is defined as the "belief that women own their lives, that they can know what is right for them, and that by working together, they can positively influence what happens to them." The world of foundations and of the World Bank is funneling billions of dollars into programs targeted to "empower women" in ways ranging from giving women access to bank credit to teaching them how to negotiate safe sex. Yet it is curious that, regardless of these efforts, there is still no word for "empowerment" in Spanish. *Empoderamiento* would be the transliteration, but it just does not sound right. It sounds unnatural. I have never heard anyone use it—not even the experts. Is the absence of such a word like the absence of a word that would define, say, hatred of men? "Misogyny" describes the hatred of women and "misanthrope" the hater of humanity, but how does one refer to someone who hates men? "Man-hater"? As far as I know, there isn't such a term in Spanish, and the lack is a measure of how our male-dominated world would just not allow it. Is the word "empowerment" such a foreign and imported—and censored—concept for Latins that there is no space for it?

Latina is a bilingual magazine. They publish the same pieces twice—the Spanish text follows the English version. When I read in Duarte's editorial that "work, for most Latinas, is more than just a means of survival, it is the road to empowerment that our mothers who stayed home were never able to take," I turned to see how she had translated "empowerment." But the sentence was deleted in the Spanish version. Of course, it could have been edited out for space reasons, but it was such a seminal sentence in the editorial. Or can it be that Duarte can only talk about empowerment in English.

Hiding in my air-conditioned apartment from a sticky August night in New York City, indulging in one of my favorite pastimes—staying home with a stack of magazines—I ran across Nely Galán's name in print once more. She had written a piece for *Vogue*. I had never seen the stories she had wanted to produce on television, so I impatiently turned the pages to find out what had happened to her since that profile I had read.

There she is described as a "Cuban-American media maven" working on a book combining beauty and career advice. In her photograph, I can see the changes in the three years since she smiled for the *Sunday Times Magazine*. She is leaning against a rail wearing a simple white cardigan and khaki pants, still smiling, still *coqueta* yet more in control. Her smile is less the smile of needing to please and more one of reserved sensuality. She is more sure of herself and therefore more distant with the camera, more mysterious, more beautiful.

The story is about growing up without any role models for beauty, about how no one told her what to do with uneven olive skin, unmanageable dark curls, and accentuated curves. And although I have fun reading and reminiscing about how I, too, felt invisible when devouring *Seventeen* and saw only tall, blond, hipless, leggy models in the ads for Herbal Essence and Clearasil, I wonder why she has chosen to write about beauty. Nely learned nevertheless, and being the savvy businesswoman that she is, she is banking on it. She says she is proud to see that Latina women—Salma Hayek, Gloria Estefan, Jennifer López, Daisy Fuentes come to mind—are now seen as role models not only for what is beautiful but for what is self-determined and successful. Like the women behind Northern Ladies, she has understood the importance of appearance and beauty in our culture. Unlike the women in Queens who promote and profit from women's stagnation, Nely's project does not seem to promote the submission of women.

Still, success has not made Galán completely immune to traditional cultural expectations. "Recently," she writes at the end of the piece, "I overheard my mom confessing to her girlfriends, 'Who would have ever thought Nelita would turn out to be the real beauty of the family? I just don't understand why she won't pick a husband already and give us some grandchildren.' A husband. Grandchildren . . . well, that part of the equation is another story altogether."

Latina magazine is taking huge strides to rid us of these ghosts. In a recent issue they went for broke, in a sex survey that tackled all the taboos. The questions were as risqué as those one would expect in *Cosmopolitan*, ranging from preference of penis size and sexual position to issues of birth control and HIV. But more risqué than the questions were the answers! Unlike the Colombian women, of whom 75 percent in a survey claimed to fake orgasms, 66 percent of U.S. Latinas said they don't. Women of Latin descent are initiating sex, are telling their lovers what they want in bed, are having and giving oral sex. Forty percent were open enough to confessing having had anal sex. And though 75 percent of the respondents said they came from families where sex was never discussed, 90 percent said they would ask a new partner to take an HIV test.

Further proof that traditional attitudes are being confronted comes in their May 1998 issue. Venezuelan-born actress María Conchita Alonso is asked if she thinks all Latina women were born to be mothers, and she candidly replied: "Motherhood should not be implied by society! The perception that a woman's not fully grown if she's not a mother is bullshit."

Today, as I ride the subway or the bus, I notice the schoolgirls who remind me of myself at that age—wavy hair, backpacks filled with books, lips always outlined in dark brown—and wonder if they will write like Nely or answer like María Conchita. There lurks in me the woman born to be *resignada*, to speak only after men do. I search for this in them, eavesdropping on their conversations, studying their body language, and I am glad when I do not see it. But I know their experience is different than mine. I grew up *allá*—the place their mothers speak about, the place where *abuelos* and *primos* still live.

I can be in my apartment in the Village listening to salsa played on *la mega*; I can go to have an *arepa con queso* on the corner of Roosevelt Avenue and 84th Street in Jackson Heights or to a Cuban rumba on a summer Sunday in Central Park. I am happy that I can have parts of my culture close at hand, that it is possible for me to live in New York with things *de acá y de allá*—even if at times they are hard to balance out and I start only hearing the whispers and admonitions of the past that make me wonder who I am.

I wonder if it is different for girls of Latino parents: if the things of *allá* are as foreign as my first subway rides to work were to me *acá*. For my friend Rosa's daughters, to dance to the *vallenatos* songs that their mother likes is an imposition. Rosa holds on to the culture of the country she grew up in. But Colombia, for Daniela and Claudia and Margarita, is a place they know only through photographs and other memorabilia. They listen to the *telenovelas* on Channel 47 broadcast in a language they understand only if spoken slowly. When Rosa asks the girls where they feel they are from, she grins proudly when they all tell her *"de Colombia"* where they've never been. For as much as Magali wants her daughters to be Colombians, the girls would rather listen to Sheryl Crow than to Colombian-born Shakira. The Colombia they know is as accurate as the map that Margarita, who is thirteen, drew for her school project last spring.

On New Year's Eve, I have seen the three girls stand uncomfortably in the middle of the living room as their mother ordered them to dance to Carlos Vives, the *vallenato* king. When everyone in the room says *guepaje* and gets up, the girls swiftly retreat to a corner. Their uncle turns and twists the *tía* around but the girls' feet slide left, then right, in that rigidity you suffer when things feel foreign. Watching them struggle uncomfortably, I am reminded of when I first had to read out loud in Sister Cherry's

English class at the Academy of the Sacred Heart and I was the only girl in the class who spoke English with an accent. They might hear these songs every day, but the songs will never have the same meaning they do for Rosa, for her sister and her husband, for me. We spin around, singing at the top of our lungs the lyrics that convey messages of accepted male infidelity, of macho prowess, of women who suffer in their kitchens. These are songs from a land where snow never falls as it did that New Year's Eve in Greenwich Village.

I became aware of the dichotomy that many U.S. Latina girls grow up with when I visited the offices of Cultural Exchange in midtown Manhattan and spoke to a Puerto Rican woman, a consultant hired by the New York Board of Education to write "culturally sensitive material" about AIDS awareness for Latina teenagers. Although statistics show that these young people are at extremely high risk, parents of Latino students have been fierce opponents of condom distribution programs.

Now when I go to Rosa's house or I sit next to the cafe-con-leche girls on the subway, I listen to their half English, half Spanish conversation about how they reconcile the differences. *Mother Jones* magazine published a survey about teenage sex that said a large percentage of American girls are sexually active by thirteen. Are they? "These girls are at such risk of AIDS," the consultant told me. "At home, they are told not to have sex, but all their peers at school are. So they have anal sex—that way they protect their virginity."

They are easy to spot, these young Latinas. Many wear flags, made out of plastic beads, of their country of origin around their necks, large gold hoops, much more makeup than the girls their age that don't have Latin parents. I've heard them talk about going shopping after school, about preferring to get jobs as salesgirls for the summer rather than to go visit their *abuelas* in Puerto Rico or the Dominican Republic. I am sure those grandmothers are eager to see their granddaughters, to feed them, hug them, tell them to be good girls. But the gap between granny and *nieta* widens with the years as these girls grow up and become *creaturas gringas*.

Rosa's oldest daughter is seventeen. She has a boyfriend who is also Latino. Sometimes he spends the night at their cramped two-bedroom apartment. He sleeps on the couch in the TV room while Daniela sleeps in her room with her two sisters. Rosa is sure they don't have sex.

When I see them together holding hands, I wonder if it's true that they don't and I hope that they do and that if they do they know how to do it safely and responsibly. When I see him, I also look for hints of what I hope are shared convictions with Emanuel Xavier, a Latino contributing writer at *Urban: The Latino Magazine,* whose poem entitled "Tradiciones" lingers in my mind:

> *I want to break tradition—*
> *about latin machismo*
> *fucking every puta in site*
> *leaving behind nine million,   billion children*
> *scattered thorough out Brooklyn,*
> *Manhattan,   the Bronx,*
> *marrying the most humble,   convenient wife*
> *then cheating on her*
> *left and right*
> *beating her*
> *whenever the gandules are too cold—*
> *forget about the chuletas*

In the fall, Daniela starts college, something no one in her family has ever done. She may marry her boyfriend—or have other relationships. I hope she will meet young men like Emanuel Xavier, men who renounce the oppression of and violence against women that men of previous generations would like them to embrace. Then Karen will have a better chance at a fulfilling life, one that includes knowledge, preparation, and a more fair and loving relationship with a man.

I am headed back to Queens, on a very different mission from the one that took me to Northern Boulevard in Flushing for my visit to the hymen-reconstruction clinic. This time, I am going right across the Fifty-ninth Street Bridge to Woodside, to visit the place where Latinos first go when they feel ready to fully accept their new country: the Latin American Integration Center, an organization that helps Latino immigrants to prepare for their citizenship exam. This, I think as I sip a lukewarm coffee bought from a street vendor and watch New York City's heart pump at the rate of the speed of my cab, would be the perfect place to discover which traditions are easily dropped and which will carry on as today's Latinos cross the psychological border into *el Norte*.

I hail a cab on Thirteenth Street and Fifth Avenue, and the city I have chosen as home flies by my eyes. I leave behind the New School, where, in a cubicle on the fourth floor, I have kept the piles of papers that have become this book. We turn left at Washington Square Park, a place I've crossed on many a spring afternoon, heading for the library alone and happy, or walking next to a man I have felt passionate about. We go up Park Avenue South, taking the underpass that opens into the New York City of power and elegance. The traffic is heavy on stately Park Avenue, of the multi-million-dollar corporations and the rich and elegant residences, this winter Tuesday morning, but we finally turn left on Fifty-third Street and cross over to Third Avenue, where the Citicorp building stands steely on the city's skyline, and I am reminded of the facilities that financial institutions have often provided, knowingly or not, to the placement of squandered millions from the coffers of our man-ruled countries.

Traffic is stuck on Third, and I am surrounded by taxis and trucks. The faces inside the cabs are close enough to mine that I feel as if we are all sharing a dinner table, and yet no one speaks to the person they've been sat next to. I have no option but to play my usual traffic game: study the faces next to mine, watch the people on the sidewalk go by, and guess what their lives are like. I try to decipher their histories, what they do for a living, by the way they walk, their pace, the way they wear their hats and tie their scarves. These Upper East Siders look mostly professional, and in a hurry. I turn to the ads displayed on the sides of the blue and white buses that a Cuban friend describes as wonderful hotel lobbies on wheels, and face the sanitized images of beauty, success, and appearance we are meant to aspire to. And, not far, at Bloomingdale's, where this vision is all for sale, the flags are flapping wildly, inviting the whole world to buy.

I like crossing Manhattan's bridges, impressive engineering feats unknown in my country, where the money for such massive constructions usually ends up in someone's account in a Park Avenue bank. I wonder what Monica Toro will be like. She is the volunteer from the Center that I am going to see. I am just across the bridge and I already feel miles away from the Madison Avenue world I was just surrounded by. Woodside is a working-class immigrant neighborhood where the streets are lined with cheap storefronts, fast-food restaurants, and places announcing *envios a cualquier parte en América Latina*—outfits that for a fee will send anything, from money to clothes to spare parts to refrigerators, to any place in Latin America. Here, ads for The Gap give way to ones for Newport cigarettes.

The cab stops in front of the Center, next to the van from Ecuadorean Tropical Products. I don't think of Ecuador as a tropical country, but I am always amazed how important it is for newly arrived immigrants to have the things from back home with them when they are here—the food, the newspapers, the music, the soccer scores. I was surprised when I found a Manzana Postobón, an apple-flavored soda popular in Colombia, in a bodega in Jackson Heights. And during the World Cup, when I accompanied my brother, *hincha que es,* to El Chibcha, a popular Colombian bar on Roosevelt Avenue that showed the games on satellite TV whenever Colombia played, I was outraged to be charged twenty-five dollars just to enter a place that was jam-packed. But what I am trying to find out is if the need for those things, *todo lo nuestro,* comes attached with attitudes from back home. Which are the men more prevalent on Roosevelt Avenue, the ones who want Northern Ladies or the ones who want to "break tradition with Latin machismo"?

By the year 2050, more Latin Americans will be living in the United States than African Americans, Asian Americans, and Native Americans. The Center is the first place Latin immigrants will come when they are ready to become citizens of the United States. This is the place that teaches them how the Senate and the Congress pass the laws of this country. It teaches them the importance of citizens' rights and civic duties, how to vote, what the colors of Old Glory are, and the names of all the presidents in order. This is their entryway into America's political process.

The Center was founded in 1991 with the support of local business and political leaders interested in helping Latinos become citizens. More Latino citizens mean more votes for Latino politicians. The Center aims to raise the political consciousness of the Latino immigrant community, reaching out to men and women who have lived here for twenty, thirty, even forty years and are incapable of or uninterested in participating as citizens. The Center organizes workshops, hosts prominent Latino leaders as speakers, organizes social events. I am here, however, to see if they also teach them that in this country a woman is not required to marry her rapist, that she is not required to display her virginal blood, that she can have a safe and legal abortion. Does the Center make it clear that, in this country, a woman, if she wants to, can be free from the tyranny of our machismo?

"I don't have to prove myself to South American culture," Monica Toro tells me in the oval conference room at the Center, the American flag prominently displayed. Of all the women at the Center this morning, Monica is the youngest by a good twenty years. She is twenty-seven and she is the only one who was born in this country—in Elmhurst, to a Colombian mother and an Ecuadorean father. Her mother, who arrived in this country when she was nineteen but became a citizen only after twenty years of residency, also volunteers at the Center.

Until 1995, the Colombian government did not allow for dual nationality. When the law changed, Colombians flooded the agency. Monica's mom was one of them. According to the Immigration and Naturalization Service, the number of Colombians who became Americans in 1995 doubled from 1991. And the Center helped many of the twelve thousand Colombians who became Americans in 1995 file the necessary papers for the naturalization test. "For twenty years, my mother always thought she would go back to Colombia. Buy a house and retire there. But here she is, and now that my brother and I are married here she knows she is not going to buy that house she always thought she wanted in Pereira, so she understood it was better to live here with rights," says Monica.

When Monica says "Colombia," her accent is that of a *pereirana*. Up until she turned eighteen, she spent all her summers there. So are her looks: straight jet-black hair, small, elongated dark eyes made longer by black eyeliner, height about five-two. Her looks remind me of Luz, the twenty-eight-year-old widow I met in Bogotá, HIV positive, infected by her husband, the only man she had ever been intimate with. Monica is slighter than Luz but she has the same square body with small breasts and sturdy legs. They are both pretty and plain at the same time. Other than their manes of thick beautiful hair, there is nothing really distinctive about either. They look like a million other women with Andean features one sees in the markets of Bolivia and Peru, or on the Colombian llanos tending small plots of potatoes, or walking the streets of downtown Bogotá, their glances always cast down. But Monica's confidence and mannerisms bespeak a different language.

She is dressed like a proper Catholic Latina girl—a red crew-neck sweater over a white turtleneck and gray flannel pants—but underneath her ordinary looks and clothes is an assertive young woman who is more at ease with the language she took her SATs in—the language that won her a full scholarship to Columbia's dental school—than she is with the Spanish she speaks a few sentences of to connect with *mami y papi* and the *primas pereiranas*.

Her voice is calm and articulate as she explains the work of the Center. "We Latinos have been in Queens thirty years and we still don't have a Latino representative," she says, explaining why she spends her Saturday mornings teaching the citizenship class. The results are not as encouraging as she would like, but she is committed. "If I can get a couple of converts, it's worth it. If I can change the mind of someone who thought they were never going to vote, I'm happy." She says she will inspire a couple of people in each class—two or three out of twenty—to become politically active, but as she puts it, "Every vote counts." She tells me of the mother of a seven-year-old, who is now involved in her son's PTA and recently called to tell Monica she had marched for Ruth Messinger. "I encouraged her. I told her that she is still young, capable of making a difference in her community."

I am impressed by her civic devotion but more curious about

what it's like to work next to women who think differently from her, to have men in her class who find it difficult that she, a woman, is their teacher. I have surprised her with the question. What does that have to do with citizenship? Why am I asking something that can sound so small, petty, and irrelevant when she is telling me about raising the political awareness of so many?

She tells me how she sees people on the subway, people whose faces she doesn't even remember but who stop and tell her that thanks to her they have their passports, that they are bringing their moms over for a visit. But Monica, a well-raised Latin girl, is too polite to keep talking about something other than what I, the interviewer, have asked her.

She tells me about Mr. Rodríguez, who insists on calling her "señorita" in class. His wife is always correcting him—*"Es casada,"* she snaps at him, and he immediately apologizes and addresses Monica as "señora." Monica understands that in Mrs. Rodríguez's world there lies a huge difference between the two and that "señorita" coming from her husband is a sign of utmost disrespect. But Monica could care less if Mr. Rodríguez calls her Miss instead of Mrs. She also finds it touching that when she walks into the room, the men get up to give her their chair. "It's funny sometimes," she says, "they all stand up."

At work, it is less funny. There, men stand up for a different reason—they do not expect the dentist to be a woman. "One hundred percent of the time" they assume she is the nurse. Once, as she was ready to inject anesthetic into a man whose wisdom teeth needed removal, the patient jumped out of his chair. "Bring in the man," he screamed.

I have opened the door to a discussion about her experiences growing up caught between the culture of her immigrant parents and those who come to the Center and the more liberating rules available to women in the American culture. I want to ask her how it is that she—daughter of Latinos, of conservative, Catholic Latinos—feels no allegiance to South American culture, as she puts it.

I ask her what it is like to grow up in Queens and spend the summers in Pereira, where the boys would surely have treated her differently because she was an *americana*, and she responds with a laugh and a story. "Oh, you are the greatest attraction that ever came to town, and boys ask you to do things they would never ask their own friends." She loved getting rides on the back of motorcycles and being asked to go swimming in the river, but whenever she would she would get into trouble, not with her mother, but with her uncles, who felt that—as her father was not there—they, "as the men," had to take control and opine. One of them would yell at Monica's mother every time she rode a bike or walked into church wearing jeans— "The whole street is saying she went to do things with that boy. How can you do this to us? What kind of girls are you raising? I raise my daughters differently, *las están dejando americanizar.*" Nothing that she should be proud of. As a matter of fact, every time she heard her uncle scream about how *mi hermanita* is raising them too American, she felt bad, she felt that her mom "feels like I can embarrass her down there."

Regardless of how much more liberty she had, compared with the girls from Pereira, it was not as if she had a mother whom she felt she could talk to about her feelings for those boys—especially about one in particular, Fernando, whom she met the summer she turned sixteen. "Sex education was taboo at home; a good solid Latino family does not talk about it, you know. You talk about drugs, about hanging out, but when it comes to sex, they would just say, you know that so-and-so are doing this, but that does not mean you should; and you know that you are going to wait until you are married, and that was the end of the sex talk."

But she also tells me that her mom is slowly changing, that she feels that over the years she can talk more to her—even though when Monica told her about birth control, something her mother has probably never used, she told her "just make sure it doesn't mess up your body"—end of conversation. "Who knows," adds Monica, "she could even be pro-choice, too."

She has already told me she is a liberal Republican, a devout Catholic, *and* pro-choice. She and I might think differently about military expenditure and about Sunday Mass. She grew up working-class in Elmhurst and I grew up pampered in Barranquilla, but I am realizing Monica and I share a good deal of common ground. I know that it is going to be difficult to have the conversation I want to have, sitting in this wood-paneled room with pictures of American presidents and the president of the Hispanic Federation hanging on the wall. What if her mother walks in and I am asking if she would have an abortion?

I offer to take her to lunch.

The more I talk to Monica the more I admire her. She is straightforward and assertive. It amuses me that, at the Argentine restaurant, she asks for *una empanada y una Coca* without the slightest trace of accent. But Monica cannot complete an argument in Spanish. She obviously thinks in English, a language of which she is fully in command. Spanish is more of a low hum in her life, a gentle coo, like the *arrurrú mi niña* her mother probably sang to her in Queens. She has enough Spanish to talk to *mami*, she can sing along with all of Luis Miguel's ballads, but the rest of her life is in English. She spoke Spanish at home, but she read and studied and took the subway in English. She went to Catholic schools and even learned to pray in English.

She is married to a Puerto Rican, but she is quick to point out that he is a Puerto Rican who speaks even less Spanish than she does, a third-generation Puerto Rican. "When we went to Puerto Rico, I was the one who had to ask for directions. That's why I like to tell him, 'Hey, you're a fake, you don't even speak your own language.' Colombians and Ecuadoreans keep a stronger hold on their culture. I can name every last name of my great-great-grandparents. My husband cannot name his own grandmother's maiden name." But even if she is proud of knowing her lineage, I have a feeling she prefers it that her husband speaks bad Spanish and that he is "very Americanized—although I hate using that term," she immediately adds, "because the term reminds me of my uncles' posturing."

"Is your brother like your husband?" I ask. I know she has an older brother. She has told me that the reason she voted Republican was because her brother was in the army.

"Huge," she says, lifting her eyes to the Sheetrock ceiling. "My husband is much more easygoing. For example, he is the one who cooks and cleans at home. My brother, he'll cook but it is not *his* responsibility. He'll cook on a weekend or if he wants to make something different, but it's his wife's responsibility to cook. He

is the typical Latin lover. In high school he would tell me, if so-
and-so calls, don't tell her I'm out with so-and-so. My friends and
I would have to cover up for him."

"Is that different from an American guy?"

"Definitely. My husband was brought up differently. He lived
on his own for a long time before we got married. He knows how
to do for himself. On Saturdays after my class at the Center and
visiting with my mom, I'll walk in and I go, "Oh, that's nice." He's
done the laundry, he cooks. You know, that's nothing for him as
opposed to a more macho who thinks all that stuff is the woman's
responsibility. My brother would *love* for his wife to stay home
and take care of the kids. You know, you can tell, it was a very big
issue for him to marry a virgin the first time he got married, even
though he was such a womanizer."

Monica is contemptuous of this attitude, and I start understanding more as she tells me about her old *novio* Fernando. She
was swept off her feet. "Imagine being sixteen, opening the door
and finding a huge bouquet of flowers from an eighteen-year-old.
I mean, that just never happened in Queens. All those *atenciones*,
the dinners, the gifts. I mean, here, what's the most you did? Someone took you out to the movies."

When she returned to Elmhurst that fall, she was practically
engaged. They wrote letters and he would call all the way from
Colombia. Her friends at school would listen to her stories about
Fernando and, boy, were they impressed. But not as impressed as
when they actually met him. Fernando decided he could not be
apart from Monica and moved to Queens where he too had a
cousin. "My friends were, like, wow, when they saw him. All those
good manners. He would come and pick me up at high school,
take us all in the car, take all the girls home because it was the
proper thing to do. If we wanted to go ice skating or something,
he would pay for all of us. My friends would look at me and say,
'Hey, girl, you've got it made.'"

It seemed so. For a while. When he started demanding that
she not go out unless he was with her, when she could go to a
party only if he was there, when he would not understand why
she was so determined to go to a good college, she started feeling

"stagnant." She remembers thinking, This is the same person that I've been with for five years, but I'm changing and he isn't.

Still, when she decided to break it off, it was not easy.

"Well, maybe the sex was too good," I joke.

As I had supposed, there was none. "The subject of sex really never came up," she says, "which was fine with me. It was as it was supposed to be. I mean, we kissed. We made out to a certain point. When he would say, 'Let's get married,' it was not that he wanted to start a family, it was that he could not come straight out and say, 'Let's have a more intimate relationship.' "

"So why was it so hard to break up?"

"His family knew my family and it was all very proper and what-not."

One day she just said: "You know, Fernando, this is not working."

"And he?"

"He went nuts. 'Whaddaya mean, this is not working? Whadd'about all the time and all this money I've spent on you and whadd'about our families?' " Her Queens accent gets heavier and I am enjoying such a typical Latin tale in it. "Well, after all this," she says, keeping me in suspense, "I find out that all along he had been living with someone else."

Monica never heard from him again. "Kinda strange from a guy who wanted to marry me, no?"

But she heard from his mother, who called her from Colombia. " 'Ay, Monica, I don't want you to hate him,' she said on the phone. 'But you know guys are guys, right? Now, he has a need for an x, y, or z type of woman. So when he is ready for a bigger commitment, I hope you can forgive him. I hope it won't be too late.' That was, as you understand, the last Latin boyfriend I ever had. After that I was ready to forget the gifts and forgo the attention. What did she mean, his mother, that he had to get what he couldn't get from me someplace else? I had the biggest macho experience and that's probably why I married someone totally from the other side of the spectrum."

She has not been back in Colombia since she was eighteen and has no interest in returning. I stop to think if this is true for me too but find that I am not as sure as Monica. As I get up, she tells me she has enjoyed our conversation and I tell her that I have too. If I want to, I can call her anytime, she says, as we say good-bye on the corner and she directs me to the subway.

The elevated train curves and an orange and blue light reflects on the skyscrapers across the river in Manhattan. I feel a sense of calm after this interview that I have not felt before. Talking to Monica has not saddened me or made me angry the way I have been after so many of the interviews I have conducted trying to get a true sense of the lives of women in Latin America and of women of Latin descent in this country. Monica goes off to her husband, who she is happy with, who she can postpone having children with until she feels ready to be a mother. Worrying about her husband's philandering, or men who have sex with men, or clandestine abortions, or men who will order her to shut up, is simply not a part of her life.

Monica could easily have had a life like Luz's, even in Queens. But she refused to be seduced by romantic illusions, or to be enchained by cultural expectations. Her freedom seems exhilarating to me after being surrounded by so many stories of injustice, suffering, and abuse. Monica's life is so splendidly ordinary—the kind of life that should not seem so uncommon, that should have been available to Luz and to every woman.

Epilogue

In Mexico City, the mariachis of the Plaza Garibaldi sing on request about revenge and unrequited love—mostly to men, men who at dawn, and after much tequila, can cry. I've seen them wailing, singing along: "Only once in my garden did hope enter my life." But if you ask the mariachis which is the *ranchera* men requested the most, they all say it is *El Rey* (The King): *"Con dinero y sin dinero hago siempre lo que quiero y mi palabra es la ley. No tengo trono ni reino ni nadie que me comprenda pero sigo siendo el rey."* To paraphrase: I am penniless. I am throneless, but my word is the law, and I continue to be king. In short, I am a man; I do as I please.

In Mexico City, this is often the way it is, at home and on the street. Men get drunk daily and women are not permitted to sit at the bar of cantinas. Men strut freely in the street while women are fearful to leave their homes. An average of eighty-two rapes are committed every day in Mexico City. Women's fears are even more justified, given that police officers have themselves been participants in sexual crimes. In 1990, five policemen rampaged the city raping at least nineteen young women.

Even at the very highest levels of Mexican society, the sodden sentiments of the *rancheras* rule. One cannot attend an official government event in Mexico without seeing squads of young, attractive women—known as *las niñas del PRI*, the initials of the premier political party—hovering like solicitous handmaidens around the assembled male officials. *Las niñas* are ready at a glance to fetch a drink, fill an empty glass, take a message, smiling and silent all the while.

Far south and west of Mexico City, on the Pacific coast off the isthmus of Tehuantepec, next to Chiapas, where the descendants of the Aztecs are currently engaged in a struggle for basic human rights, there is a town called Juchitán, where 150,000 inhabitants live in a society where the roles are reversed. In Juchitán, women are the machos of the Plaza Garibaldi. It is the women who dance and get drunk. One sees them on the street on their way to the bars and balancing boxes of beer on their heads. Here, women are not afraid of rape or the police. It is they who beat up the police, and it is the men whose job is to be sweet, silent, and at their women's beck and call.

I have never been to Juchitán, but word of this extraordinary place has come down to me, mostly from Latin American women. Indeed, some of these same women cite Juchitán as evidence that Latin America is, after all, a *matriarcado*, a matriarchy. These women profess that too much is made of machismo, that it plays little or no role in their lives.

The women of Juchitán are celebrated in a uniquely beautiful book which represents the collaboration of two Mexican women, photographer Graciela Iturbide and writer Elena Poniatowska. Their images and words, alternately tender and bold, capture such things as the exuberance and defiance of market women, like the iguana sellers who, to display their wares, crown their head with these ancient animals. The women, sturdy, round, with long braids and long skirts, dance and joke with each other. Here, women not only talk about sex, they flaunt it. "You should see them arrive, like walking towers, their windows open, their heart like a window, their nocturnal girth visited by the moon. You should see them arrive; they are already the government, they, the people, guardians of men, distributors of food, their children riding astride their hips or lying in the hammocks of their breasts, the wind in their skirts, flowered vessels, the honeycomb of their sex overflowing with men," writes Poniatowska. "Here they come shaking their wombs, pulling the *machos* toward them, the *machos* who, in contrast with them, wear light-colored pants, shirts, leather sandals, and palm hats, which they lift high in the air as they shout: 'Long live Juchitec women!' "

For, as much as I would like to go to Juchitán and see this *matriarcado*, I can't agree with the women who dismiss machismo as harmless and irrelevant because after all our society is like Juchitán, where the real power lies with women, with the mothers and the wives. These women will say conspiratorily that we just let men think they have the power, but ours is the real power. "It is just a silent power," an Argentine woman told me over dinner. She is an artist who came of age in the darkest years of her country's military dictatorship and saw the power of a group of women who took their mourning as the mothers of the disappeared to the streets, namely to the plaza facing the halls of power, where they confronted that power and demanded answers. I agreed with her, Las Madres are heroes; they made the world aware of the atrocities being committed by a group of uniformed men. But they were far from silent.

There is some truth in her comment about mothers and wives being able to influence men. Our societies and our religion are deeply respectful of the maternal. Latin American men *are* close to their mothers. But we need to recognize the difference between the influence that a mother can have on an adult son and the real power needed to change our societies and our lives for the better. Men in Latin America will go visit their mothers every day, and they might make mothers out of their wives, but this does not necessarily translate into power for women.

If power is to be real, it can't stay silent. Silent power has the same connotations as our secret revirginizations, our secret abortions, and our secret orgasms—something manipulative, clandestine, forbidden. We might briefly rattle or subvert institutions by these means, but such measures can never satisfy, and they are not true expressions of our desires, our strengths, our goals. If we accept silent power as our only agent of influence, women will forever be marginalized in both public life and in their most intimate relationships.

The answer to patriarchy is not matriarchy. The answer to having a society where only men are free to be sexual is not having men ignorant of what to do "except put themselves inside women," as Poniatowska writes of the gender roles in Juchitán. The answer to Cato is not the Danaïdes. An equal society is not achieved through a battle of the sexes but through a sharing of power between them. It is about giving girls and boys the same things, be they education, nutrition, knowledge and understanding of their bodies and of their country's laws and institutions.

Even if there are different political systems in Latin America— a one-party state awash in corruption in Mexico; a liberal democracy in Costa Rica; a socialist revolution on crutches in Cuba; a so-called democracy riddled with violence in Colombia—there is a similarity in how men and women see men and how they see each other. A formal *cachaco*, with the airs of a British lord will be appalled by the informality of a *cubano*'s dress and speech, but they are tied together by the culture of machismo. In Bogotá, the highest compliment that can be paid to a dress, a piece of music, a party, even a woman, is to praise that thing or person as "really macho"—*"Eso es una machera,"* an impressed Colombian will say. And in Cuba, if a group of women are talking excitedly and one wants the attention of the others, "Hey girls!" will not do. She calls out *"Cabelleros!"* knowing that if she acts as man among men she has a better chance of being heard.

I can understand how a desolate and distant hamlet in the south of Mexico, where women boss their men around, where women raise their skirts to show off their power, is a fascinating place for an anthropologist, a photographer, or a writer to explore. But I am sure Juchitán is only known to a select group of women, women with a certain level of education and a particular set of interests. That the women of Juchitán control the money *and* do the mothering, that they do the dancing and the drinking, that they not only protest the government but that they *are* the government is unknown to most women in Latin America. "They are very proud of being female," writes Poniatowska, "because they carry their redemption between their legs." Unfortunately, for a large majority of women outside of Juchitán—from the north of Mexico to the tip of Argentina—the opposite holds true.

In this book I wanted to tell the stories of some of these women—the women who have not yet experienced the freedoms of the women of Juchitán, but who, in their individual ways, have either worked toward or simply dreamed of a life in which they would speak and be heard, act on their own initiative, and be accepted and respected.

I am grateful to Iturbide and Poniatowska for expanding the borders of Juchitán with their book, extending visas to all who turns its pages. Their project gives me fresh encouragement about the power of books. In books we can tell truths previously hidden or forcibly suppressed, we can claim greater freedoms and freely celebrate what some would deem shameful. As my own book draws to a close, I wish to thank all the women, children, and men who did not stay silent, who trusted me with the intimate details of their lives. I have learned so much from each of them—and I hope so much for all of them.

Acknowledgments

One of the greatest difficulties I encountered while writing this book was explaining what it would be about—especially to my parents. They accepted my dodges and never stopped sending books, magazines, newspaper clippings, which came with a note attached: *Para tu libro,* for your book. It was always surprising how on target and how useful they all were. For their love, their infinite patience, and unacknowledged understanding, *gracias.*

I owe thanks to many colleagues and friends: to Mark Uhlig, who always told me I could; to James Chace for all the chicken, broccoli, and wamth of Saturday family dinners; to the Saturday dinners gang; to Sherle Schwenninger, who invited me to join the World Policy Institute, providing me with a physical home and a family of colleagues and friends; to everyone at the Institute, especially to "fellow fellow" Bill Berkeley, who diligently read early drafts, giving me useful comments while taking me to lunch. To my editor, Rosemary Ahern, who believed in the book before it was prudent and kept her faith and her patience throughout. She was instrumental in deciphering my unfinished thoughts and turning my Spanglish into proper English. Heather Schroder stood by as agent, friend, and purveyor of the best chocolate birthday cake in New York City

To those who helped me with the research and prevented me from making embarrassing mistakes and generalizations: Jessica Grossman, the super-interviewer, always able to bring back, through her keen eye and her sense of humor, the Barranquilla I left behind more than twenty years ago. To Francis Rivera and Margot Olavarría, who went beyond the call of duty and, as Latin American women, shared their personal stories, thoughts, and insightful criticism—I will miss our talks.

My involvement with the Association Francois-Xavier Bagnoud allowed me to travel to Brazil, Uruguay, and Colombia and meet the most courageous AIDS activists in the region. The energy and commitment of Albina du Boisrouvray, the association's founder, to erase pain and inequality in the world in memory of her son, Francois, served as an inspiration and a guide.

The Fund for Investigative Journalism provided a grant at a crucial time.

My deepest gratitude goes to those who allowed me into their homes, opening their lives—their deepest thoughts, their joys and their hurts, their tears, fears, secrets, and frustrations—to a stranger with a note pad. I hope that this book proves worthy of their trust.

Bibliography

Alan Guttmacher Institute. *Clandestine Abortion: A Latin American Reality.* New York and Washington: 1994.

Almeida Teles, Maria Amélia. *Breve Història do Feminismo No Brasil.* São Paulo: Brasiliense, 1993.

Afshar, Haleh, ed. *Women and Politics in the Third World.* London: Routledge, 1996.

Americas Watch Report. *Criminal Injustice: Violence Against Women in Brazil.* United States of America: Human Rights Watch, 1991.

Arenas, Reinaldo, and Dolores M. Koch, trans. *Before Night Falls.* New York: Penguin, 1993.

Asociación Guatemalteca de Prevención y Control del SIDA. *El Peligro Oculto: La Mujer y el SIDA.* Guatemala: Instituto Panos, 1996

Association for Women in Development. *Women at the Center: Development Issues and Practices for the 1990's.* West Hartford: Kumarian, 1993.

Bermúdez Q, Suzy. *El Sexo Bello: La mujer y la familia durante el Olimpo Radical.* Bogotá: Ediciones Uniandes, 1993.

Buvinic, Mayra. "Women in Poverty: A New Global Underclass." *Foreign Policy* (Fall 1997): 38–53.

Carballo-Diéguez, Alex, PhD., and Curtis Dolezal, PhD. "Contrasting Types of Puerto Rican Men Who Have Sex with Men (MSM)." *Journal of Psychology & Human Sexuality,* Vol. 6(4) (1994): 41–67.

Carrier, Joseph. *De Los Otros: Intimacy and Homosexuality Among Mexican Men*. New York: Columbia University Press, 1995.

Castillo, Ana. *Massacre of the Dreamers: Essays on Xicanisma*. Albuquerque, University of New Mexico Press, 1994.

The Catholic Institute for International Relations. *São Paulo: Growth and Poverty*. London: Bowerdean, 1978.

Chauncey, George. *Gay New York: Gender, Urban Culture, and the Making of the Gay Male World, 1890–1940*. Basic Books, 1994.

Conferencia Mundial Sobre la Mujer, IV. *Informe Nacional de Colombia*. Beijing: September 1995.

Daniel, Herbert, and Richard Parker. *Sexuality, Politics and AIDS in Brazil: In Another World?* London: Falmer, 1993.

De Jesus, Carolina Maria, and David St. Clair, trans. *Child of the Dark: The Diary of Carolina Maria De Jesus*. New York: Dutton, 1962.

De los Ríos, Isabel. *Guía de los Derechos de la Mujer*. Caracas: Isabel De los Ríos, 1994

Departamento de Investigaciones Universidad Central. *NÓMADAS*. Bogotà, vol. 6 (March–September 1997).

Enloe, Cynthia. *Bananas, Beaches and Bases: Making Feminist Sense of International Politics*. Berkeley and Los Angeles: University of California Press, 1990.

Fox, Thomas C. *Sexuality and Catholicism*. New York: George Braziller, 1995.

Franco, Jean. "The Long March of Feminism." *NACLA Report on the Americas* XXXI, no. 4 (Jan/Feb 1998): 10–15.

Freyre, Gilberto. *The Mansions and the Shanties [Sobrados e Mucambos]: The Making of Modern Brazil*. New York: Alfred A. Knopf, 1963.

García Márquez, Gabriel. *Chronicle of a Death Foretold*. New York: Ballantine, 1982.

Gil, Rosa Maria, D.S.W., and Carmen Inoa Vazquez, PhD. *The Maria Paradox: How Latinas Can Merge Old World Traditions with New World Self-Esteem*. New York: Berkeley, 1996.

Grupo Editorial Norma. *Las mujeres en la historia de Colombia: Tomo 1, Mujeres, Historia y Política*. Bogotá, Consejería Presidential para la Politica Social, 1995.

Gruskin, Sofia, ed. *Health and Human Rights* 1, no. 4 (1995): 454–61.

Herek, G. M. and B. Greene, eds. *AIDS, Identity, and Community: The HIV Epidemic and Lesbians and Gay Men, Psychological Perspectives on Lesbian and Gay Issues, 2*. Thousand Oaks: Sage, 1995.

House of Representatives, 102d Congress, 2nd Session, Report 102–1074. *A Decade of Denial: Teens and AIDS in America*. Washington, D.C.: U.S. Government Printing Office, 1992.

Human Rights Watch/Americas. *Chile. Unsettled Business: Human Rights in Chile at the Start of the Frei Presidency*. Vol. VI, 6 (May 1994).

Human Rights Watch/Americas: Human Rights Watch Children's Rights Project. *Generation Under Fire: Children and Violence in Colombia*. United States of America: Human Rights Watch, 1994.

Humans Rights Watch/Americas: Human Rights Watch Women's Rights Project. *Untold Terror: Violence Against Women in Peru's Armed Conflict*. United States of America: Human Rights Watch, 1992.

Instituto de la Mujer. *Mujeres. Latinoamericanas. En Cifras*. Madrid: Instituto de la Mujer, 1993.

Instituto Panos. *Nuestra Voz: Población y desarrollo*. Panos Institute: 1994.

International Conference on AIDS Society, XI. *XI Conference on AIDS, Vol II*. Vancouver: July 7–12, 1996.

Jaquette, Jane S., ed. *The Women's Movement in Latin America: Participation and Democracy*. Boulder and Oxford: Westview, 1994.

Kepner, Charles David, Jr., and Jay Henry Soothill. *The Banana Empire: A Case Study of Economic Imperialism*. New York: Russell & Russell, 1935.

Lancaster, Roger N. *Life Is Hard: Machismo, Danger, and the Intimacy of Power in Nicaragua*. Berkeley and Los Angeles: University of California Press, 1992.

León, Guadalupe. *Del Encubrimiento a la Impunidad: Diagnóstico sobre Violencia de Género.* Ecuador: Ceime, 1995.

León, Magdalena. *Mujeres y Participación Policta: Avances y Desafíos en América Latina.* Bogotá: Transversal, 1994.

Lumsden, Ian. *Machos, Maricones, and Gays: Cuba and Homosexuality.* Philadelphia: Temple University Press, 1996.

Maclaren, Laurel. 1993. *Meeting the Sexual Health Needs of Women: Exploring the Integration of AIDS Prevention and Family Planning Programs.* Prepared for the Pan American AIDS Foundation.

Mann, Jonathan, and Daniel Tarantola, eds. *Aids in the World II.* New York: Oxford University Press, 1996.

Marthe Zapata, Leonello. *El Aborto en Colombia.* Bogotá: Editorial Grijalbo, 1994.

McClausand Sojo, Ernesto. *Las Crónicas de McClausland.* Bogotá: Editorial Espasa, 1996.

NACLA Report on the Americas. "Report on Sexual Politics: Sexual Politics in Latin America." New York, Vol. XXXI, no. 4 (Jan/Feb 1998): 16–43.

Olavarria, Margot. *From Protest to Praxis: The Chilean Women's Movement in Transition.* Master's Thesis, 1995.

Ordoñez, Juan Pablo. *No Human Being Is Disposable: Social Cleansing and Human Rights, and Sexual Orientation in Colombia.* San Francisco: International Gay and Lesbian Human Rights Commission, 1995.

Parker, Richard G. *Bodies, Pleasures, and Passions: Sexual Culture in Contemporary Brazil.* Boston: Beacon, 1991.

Patai, Daphne. *Brazilian Women Speak: Comtemporary Life Stories.* New Brunswick and London: Rutgers University Press, 1988.

Paz, Octavio, and Lysander Kemp, trans. *The Labyrinth of Solitude.* New York: Grove, 1985.

Poniatowska, Elena, and Graciela Iturbide, photographer. *Juchitàn de las mujeres.* Mexico: Ediciones Toledos, 1991.

Posada Carbó, Eduardo. *Una Invitación a la Historia de Barranquilla.* Bogotá: Fondo Editorial CEREC, 1987.

Programa Nacional—DST/AIDS do Ministerio de Saude. *I Encontro Brasileiro de Gays e Lesbicas que trabalham com AIDS. VIII Encontro Brasileiro de Gays e Lesbicas.* Vermelho & Cordiolli, 1995.

Programa Nueva Vida, SOS. *Jovenes de la Calle de Bogota Derecho a la Salud y Prevencion del VIH/SIHA.* Bogotá: 1992.

Rotello, Gabriel. *Sexual Ecology: AIDS and the Destiny of Gay Men.* New York: Dutton, 1997.

Rojas de González, Nelly. *La Pareja: Cómo Vivir Juntos.* Bogotá: Planeta Colombiana, 1994.

Salcedo Castañeda, Lola. *Una Pasión Impresentable: Recuerdos que sobreviven a la brutalidad y violencia de la vida cotidiana.* Bogotá: Planeta, 1994.

Salessi, Jorge, and Beatriz Viterbo, eds. *Médicos maleantes y maricas.* Argentina: Estudios Culturales, 1995.

Schlesinger, Stephen, and Steven Kinzer. *Bitter Fruit: The Untold Story of the American Coup in Guatemala.* New York: Doubleday, 1982.

Sen, Gita, and Rachel C. Snow. *Power and Decision: The Social Control of Reproduction.* Boston: Harvard School of Public Health, 1994.

STD World Congress, IVth. *IXth International Conference on AIDS, Vol. I.* Berlin: June 6–11, 1993.

"Third World, Second Class." Five-Part Series. *Washington Post.* February 14–18, 1993.

Thomas, Florence. *Los estragos del amor: El discurso amoroso en los medios de communicacion.* Bogotá, Editorial Universidad Nacional, 1994.

Transparency International. *1996 International Corruption Perception Index.* www.transparency.de/press/1996.6.2.index.html.

World Bank Conference on Urban Crime and Violence. *Crime and Violence as Development Issues in Latin America and the Caribbean.* Rio de Janeiro: March 2–4, 1997.

Index

Abortions, 32, 57–70, 92, 100, 102–105, 303
  Catholic Church and, 37, 61, 78, 102
  laws prohibiting, 26, 55, 62
  legalizing of, 46, 62, 81, 82, 90
  multiple, 54, 68–69, 78, 103
  self-induced, 31, 33, 49, 60–62, 91, 102, 211
    complications of, 61–62
    methods for, 55–57, 65–67, 69–95, 103–104
    statistics, 54–55
    in United States, 69
    upper classes and, 60, 62
Academy of the Sacred Heart, 8, 11, 58–59, 296
Acorda, Adelaide!, 33–34
Adum, Alfredo, 237–38
AIDS transmission, Latin culture and, 26–36, 46, 213, 218–19, 296
  available information, 92, 96–98
  Catholic Church and, 82
  condom use, *see* Condoms
  men having sex with other men and, *see* Men having sex with other men (MSM), AIDS transmission and
  misconceptions about, 28, 198, 260–61, 262, 263, 269
  prevention campaigns, 50, 92, 96–98, 106–107, 135, 151–52
  statistics, 262–63
  story of upper-class Guatemalan couple, 196–269
  street children and, *see* Street children, AIDS transmission and
  testing for AIDS, 259–62

  transvestites, HIV-positive, *see* Transvestites, HIV-positive
  women infected by their husbands, 28, 31, 33, 37, 42, 46, 138–45, 196–97, 262, 263
Allende, Salvador, 73, 74
Almeida Teles, Maria Amelia (Amelinha), 79–83, 89, 92, 101
Alonso, Maria Conchita, 294
Anal intercourse, 85–87, 213, 240, 294, 296
Arbenz, Jacobo, 229
Arenas, Reinaldo, 146, 149
Argentina, 232, 234
  women's rights in, 18, 74
Arteaga, Rosalía, 7
Aylwin, Mariana, 254

Baker, Lorenzo Dow, 228
Barranquilla, Colombia, 11–12, 16–26, 31–32, 38, 40–43, 53–54, 59–60, 160, 263
  religion in, 13–14
  teenage sexual relationships in, 1–2, 3, 12, 27–28, 38–40
  transvestites in, 4, 27, 40, 108–20
Beauty queens, 19, 20, 45, 64, 271
Before Night Falls (Arenas), 146, 149
BEMFAM, 95–98, 100, 101, 102, 103
Birth control, 12, 46, 58, 81, 100, 142
  Catholic Church and, 33, 37, 82
  lack of communication between partners about, 100
  lack of information about, 58, 90, 211–12
  men's attitudes toward women's use of, 99

in United States, 59
see also specific methods of birth
    control
Bisexuality of Latin men, see Men
    having sex with other men
    (MSM)
Bodies, Pleasure and Passion (Parker),
    146
Bolivia, 10, 232
Bond, Lydia, 178, 179
Brazil, 35, 48–107, 155, 174, 234, 237
    abortion in, 55, 90, 92, 103
    AIDS cases in, 262
    economy of, 70–72
    openness about sex in, 52, 87–88,
        92, 98, 99
    street children in, 179–84
    women's rights in, 18, 44, 74–83,
        87–92
Breve história do feminismo no
    Brasil, 82
Bucaram, Abdala, 237, 238
Buenhogar, 218

Camacho, Dr. Bernardo, 86, 138–39,
    145
Cambio 16, 199, 200
Carballo-Diéguez, Dr. Alex, 110,
    149, 152–53
Cardoso, Fernando Henrique, 92
Carrier, Joseph, 146, 148, 154
Casa Eudes, 184–85
Casa Vida, 136
Catholic Church, 28, 86, 232, 253,
    268
    abortion and, 37, 61, 78, 80, 90,
        102
    birth control and, 33, 37, 82
    divorce law and, 254
    Mass, 13–14, 45
    power of, 83
    reinforcement of gender roles, 27,
        310
    transvestites and, 164, 171–72
    women's devotion to, 44–45, 73, 77
    women's reproductive rights and,
        31, 33, 37, 90, 105, 178

women's rights and, 76, 80, 81,
    198–99
Centers for Disease Control and
    Prevention, U.S., 145
Centro de Estudios e Investigaciones
    de la Mujer Ecuatoriana
    (CEIME), 32, 53
CEPIA (Citizenship, Study, Re-
    search, Information, and Ac-
    tion), 32, 53, 90
Chauncey, George, 148, 149
Children:
    custody of, 10
    HIV-positive, 197, 203, 262, 264
    illegitimate, 252–53
    sexual abuse of, 77–78
    street, see Street children
Chile, 19, 45–46, 73, 92, 155
    divorce law in, 253–54
    women's rights in, 11, 18, 73–74
Chilean Association of the Relatives
    of the Disappeared, 74
Chinchilla, Fabiola, 139–40
Chronicle of a Death Foretold (Gar-
    cía Márquez), 275
Ciudad y los perros, La (Llosa), 29
CLADEM, 53
CNDM (National Council for
    Women's Rights), 88–89, 90, 91
Colombia, 92, 142, 155, 300, 304
    abortion in, 55–57, 60–61
    AIDS statistics, 262–63
    concentration of land ownership,
        229
    corruption in, 232, 234, 235–36
    politics in, 15, 17, 19, 20, 24, 26,
        44, 231, 234, 235–36, 311
    the poor of, upper class and,
        108–109, 115, 116–17, 126,
        158–59
    street children in, 173–74, 175–77,
        184–95
    United Fruit Company and,
        225–27
    violence against homosexuals in,
        156–61
    women's rights in, 6, 10, 18, 19, 44

CONASIDA, 151
Condoms, 27, 35, 52, 58, 92, 136, 137, 150–52, 181–84, 187, 188, 195, 204, 213, 262
  Catholic Church and birth control, 37, 82
  distribution programs in U.S., 296
  men's attitudes toward, 49, 50, 68, 98, 103, 142
  transvestite prostitutes and, 133
  women asking partner to use, 33–34, 49, 97–99, 100–101, 103
Constitutions of Latin American countries, 10, 36, 89, 155, 234
Contraception, see Birth control; see also specific methods
Correa, Gustavo y Alma, 196–97, 199–209, 210, 214–16, 219, 249, 258, 266–67, 268
Correa, Marta, 267–68
Corruption in Latin America, 232–34
Cosmopolitan, 53, 152
Costa Rica, 311
  women in politics in, 6
  women's rights in, 18
Cuba, 146, 149, 311
Curfews, 5, 27–28, 40
Custody of children, 10
Cytotec, 66, 67, 93–95

Day-care centers, 76–77, 79, 89, 106, 180, 247
de Flores Correa, Magdalena, 196–269 passim
  courtship by Manuel, 244–57
  illness and death, 196, 259–67
  marriage of, 196, 257–67
De Los Ostros: Intimacy and Homosexuality among Mexican Men (Carrier), 154
Divorce law, 10, 11, 73, 253–54
Domestic violence, 35, 45, 46, 53, 81, 88, 89, 91, 100
Dominican Republic, 228
  abortion in, 55
  women's rights in, 18
dos Santos, Benedetto, 176

dos Santos, Renildo José, 155
Drag queens, see Transvestites
Duarte, Macarena, 176
Duarte, Patricia, 291–93

Economic dependency of women, 47, 51, 71, 84, 246
Ecuador, 155, 237–38, 299, 304
  women in politics in, 6, 7
  women's rights in, 11, 18
Education of women, 21, 201–202, 219–20, 245
  about sex, see Sex education
Egyptian women, 276–77, 278
Employment of women, 6–7, 9, 10–11, 25, 31, 46, 53–54, 72, 202, 247, 250, 292–93, 302
  as cheap labor force, 36, 231
  in decision-making positions, 247
  forced resignation upon becoming pregnant, 72, 90–91, 231
Endara, Guillermo, 121
Estrada, Dr. Francisco, 156

Family-planning clinics, 34, 64, 95–98, 100–105, 142, 212
First International Conference on Women, 32
Flores, Pedro, 227, 230, 242, 264, 266
Flores, César, 225, 226, 242, 253
Flores, Manuel Flores, 196–269
Flores, Dolores de, 227–28
Folha de São Paulo, 104–105
Ford Foundation, 34
Forjar, 202, 267
Frei, Eduardo, 254
Friedan, Betty, 79

Gabeira, Fernando, 163
Galán, Nely, 289–90, 291, 293–94
Gallegos, Walter, 148
García, Dr. Ricardo, 263
García Márquez, Gabriel, 118, 225–26, 275
Gay New York (Chauncey), 148

General Motors, 231
Guatemala, 92, 174, 237
  United Fruit Company and politics of, 228, 229
  women's rights in, 18
Guevara, Ernesto Che, 149
Guttmacher Institute, Allan, 55, 61

Haag, Dr. Alejandro, 53
Haiti, 35, 262
Health and Human Services, U.S. Department of, 271
Heterosexual men:
  having sex with other men, see Men having sex with other men (MSM)
  marriage and, see Marriage
Homophobia, 27, 113, 136, 150, 152
Homosexuals, 146, 147–49, 152, 154
  AIDS among, 26
  derogatory names for, 27, 113
  differences between gays and transvestites, 164, 165
  gay movement, 148–49
  prostitution, see Prostitution, male
  transvestites, see Transvestites
  violence against, 154–61
  see also Men having sex with other men (MSM)
Honduras, 6, 18, 228
Human Rights Watch, 91–92
Hurtado, Álvaro Gómez, 15
Hymen reconstruction, 271–89

Illegitimate children, 252–53
Immigration and Naturalization Service, U.S., 300
Inheritance law, 10
International Development Bank, 35
International Lesbian and Gay Association, 156
Isto É, 99
Iturbide, Graciela, 309, 312

Javier de Nicolo, Father, 176–77
Jovana Baby, 163, 164–65, 166, 169, 170, 172–73

Juchitán, Mexico, women of, 309–12

Keith, Minor, 226
Korean women, 276

Labyrinth of Solitude (Paz), 287
Lancaster, Roger, 148, 149
Lancet, The, 276, 278
Latina, 291–93, 294
Latin American Integration Center, 298–301
León, Guadalupe, 7
Life Is Hard: Machismo, Danger and the Intimacy of Power in Nicaragua (Lancaster), 149
Linero, Oswaldo Henríquez, 160
Little Bit of This and a Little Bit of That, A, 151
Los Estagos del Amor (Thomas), 218
Lucero, Beatriz Merino, 31
Lumsden, Ian, 149
Lusinchi, Jaime, 237

McCausland, Ernesto, 116
Machismo, 29, 31–32, 142, 177, 247, 311
  banana republics and, 228, 231
  cultural enforcement of, 6
  Hispanics in the U.S. and, 16, 274, 300
  men having sex with other men and, see Men having sex with other men (MSM), the active partner considered macho
Making Feminist Sense of International Politics: Bananas, Beaches & Bases (Enloe), 228
Maldonado, Miguelina, 26, 33
Mann, Dr. Jonathan, 35, 214
Mano Negra (Black Hand), 158, 159
Maria Paradox: How Latinas Can Merge Old World Traditions and New World Self-Esteem, The, 292, 293
Marriage, 105–106
  among upper-class families, 15, 248–51

Marriage (*cont.*)
  infidelity of men, 49, 50, 51, 52, 70,
    138–39, 143, 144, 167, 236–37
  with other men, *see* Men having
    sex with other men (MSM);
    Street children; Transvestites,
    as prostitutes
  pregnancy and, *see* Pregnancy,
    marriage and
  surname, taking of husband's, 8,
    10, 46, 220, 236, 247–48
  virginity and, *see* Virginity
  woman's success linked to her,
    220, 246, 290
Mass, 13–14, 45
Maternity leave, 89, 91
Matriarchy, 309–10, 311
Mejía, María Emma, 20, 36
Men:
  age at first intercourse, 98, 136,
    240
  control over women's lives, 7, 17,
    46
  having sex with other men, *see*
    Men having sex with other men
    (MSM)
  machismo, *see* Machismo
  married, *see* Marriage
  patriarchal authority, *see* Patriar-
    chal authority
  sexuality of, beliefs about, 212–13,
    230
  sex with prostitutes, *see* Pros-
    titution; Transvestites, as
    prostitutes
  sex with servants, 239–40
  see also Women
Men having sex with other men
  (MSM), 44, 51, 134–95
  the active partner considered
    macho, 27, 110–11, 131, 134,
    136, 144–50, 152, 153, 154–55
  AIDS transmission and, 26–27,
    28–29, 37, 128, 135–36, 137,
    138–45, 150, 167
  street children and, *see* Street
    children, prostitution by

  see also Transvestites, as prostitutes
Menstruation:
  girl's understanding of, 58, 86, 201
  hymen reconstruction and, 282
Mexico, 146, 156, 175, 237, 308–10
  corruption in, 232, 311
  politics in, 15
  women's rights in, 15
Miami, Florida, 221–22, 227
Miami Herald, 28–29
Moreira Neves, Dom Lucas, 82
Mother Jones, 296
Mothers of the Plaza de Mayo, 74
Movimento de Meninos e Minenas
  da Rua, 176
Mujer, 46
Mulher Accion, 79

National Conference of Bishops of
  Brazil (CNBB), 82
National Council for Women's Rights
  (CNDM), 88–89, 90, 91
National Health and Social Life Sur-
  vey, U.S., 162
New York Board of Education, 296
New York Times, 20, 127, 232, 233,
  271
New York Times Magazine, 289, 293
Nicaragua, 46, 155, 174
  women's rights in, 18
Nieves, Luis, 33, 151
Nos Mulher, 79, 80

O Movimento do Custo de Vida, 76
One Hundred Years of Solitude (Gar-
  cía Márquez), 226, 245
Oral sex, 154, 294
Ordóñez, Juan Pablo, 160
Ortega, Daniel, 45

Panama, 120–21, 175, 234
  corruption in, 232–33
  women's rights in, 11, 17–18
Panama Canal Commission, 233
Pan-American Health Organization
  (PAHO), 178, 184
Panos Institute, 35

Pantoja, John, 118–19, 120, 126
Paraguay:
    women's rights in, 18
Parker, Richard, 146, 149
Parrish, Karl C., 40, 41
Pasión Impresentable (Salcedo), 220
Patriarchal authority, 10, 231
    AIDS transmission and, 35, 219
Paz, Octavio, 287
Pérez, Augusto, 135–36, 246
Pérez Balladardes, Ernesto, 232
Peru, 155, 234
    abortion in, 55
    women's rights in, 11, 18, 31, 35
Pinochet, General Augusto, 45–46, 73
Pitanguy, Jacqueline, 62, 88, 89–90, 91, 92, 101
Plastic surgery, 270–89
    hymen reconstruction, 271–89
Poder Femenino, 73–74
Politics and power, 24
    banana plantations and, 224–29
    corruption, 232–34
    as male domain, 6, 14–15, 17, 19–20, 21, 26, 230, 233–34
    sharing of, 310–12
    women in, 6–7, 19–20, 26, 31, 36, 46, 73–74
    women's issues and, 44
    see also under individual countries
Poniatowska, Elena, 309–12
Population Council, 35
Poverty, 45
    among women, 36–37
    in Colombia, *see* Colombia, the poor of, upper class and
    street children and, *see* Street children
Power, *see* Politics and power
Pregnancy, 64, 211, 212
    abortion of, *see* Abortions
    job loss and, 72, 90–91, 231
    knowledge about sex and, 12
    marriage and, 1, 8, 20, 42, 54, 211
Pro-familia, 142
Property rights, 10

Prostitution, 4, 58, 85, 241
    adolescent male sex with prostitutes, 121–25, 215–16, 236, 241
    male, 136–37, 155
        by street children, *see* Street children, prostitution by
        by transvestites, *see* Transvestites, as prostitutes

Rape, 32, 36, 100, 183, 308
    judicial systems and, 91
    laws concerning, 17–18, 26, 31, 35
Reiss, Toni, 164, 169, 172
RENATA, 172–73
Restrepo, Jamie, 176–77, 178
Rhythm method, 63, 64, 67, 102
Rockefeller Foundation, 34
Rodríguez, Orlando, 118

Saez, Irene, 20, 36
Sales, Dom Eugênio, 171–72
Salinas, Carlos, 237
Samper, Ernesto, 222
Samper, Soledad de, 83, 84
Sanín, Noemí, 20, 36, 46
Sarney, Jose, 88
Schroder, Tom, 28–29
Semana, 50–51
Serrano, Jaime, 237
Sex education, 44, 101–102, 206, 234, 296
    absence of, 12, 54, 58, 86, 141–42, 201, 208, 211–12, 213, 303
Sexual abuse, 77–78
Sexually transmitted diseases (STDs), 84–85, 213
    AIDS, *see* AIDS transmission, Latin culture and
Shakira, 217–18
Shalala, Donna, 271
Silva, Luis Ignacio da (Lula), 92
Street children, 30, 78, 135, 173–95
    AIDS transmission and, 135, 178, 179, 184–90
    prostitution by, 135–36, 178, 180–83, 185–94
        clients, 135–36, 182–83, 187, 192

Street children (*cont.*)
  violence against, 173–74, 178, 186, 190–93
Suplicy, Marta, 52, 88, 163
Szterenfeld, Dr. Celia, 163

Tabelinha, see Rhythm method
Thomas, Florence, 218
Toro, Monica, 300–307
Torres, Archbishop Félix María, 117
Transvestites, 27, 30–31, 40, 108–38, 153, 161–73, 187–88
  backgrounds of, 132, 133, 135
  conference in Brazil, 161–73
  differences between gays and, 164, 165
  discrimination against, 164, 167, 170–71
  femininity and, 111–14
  HIV-positive, 30, 135–36, 137, 188
  male sexual initiation and, 121–26
  as prostitutes, 4, 30, 111, 121–29, 159–60, 167, 170
    clients of, 130–31, 134, 159–60
    condom use, 133
    reasons for going to, 131, 134
  violence against, 137–38, 154–56, 159–60, 166, 167, 172
Turizo, Gustavo, 114, 119–20, 126, 159

Uganda, 35
União de Mulheres de São Paulo, 81
United Fruit Company, 225–29, 231
United Nations:
  AIDS Report, 263
  women's rights and, 32, 34, 76, 79
United States:
  Latin American politics and, 228–29, 231
  Latin community in, 15–16, 270–307
U.S. Department of Health and Human Services, 271
Urban: The Latino Magazine, 297
Uribe Escobar, Ricardo, 105–106
Uruguay, 176, 233
  women's rights in, 74

Vagina, surgery to tighten walls of, 286
Vanidades, 218
Vargas Llosa, Mario, 29
Veja, 82
Velandia, Manuel, 148
Venezuela, 237
  patriarchal society, laws enforcing, 10
  women in politics in, 6, 20
Villada, Javier, 184–86
Virginity, 27, 28, 142, 207, 208, 212, 219, 221, 249
  hymen reconstruction, 271–89
  teenage sexual practices to preserve, 210–11, 213, 240, 296
Vogue, 293

Washington Post, 254
Women:
  abortion and, *see* Abortions
  adulterous, 17–18
  AIDS transmission to married, *see* AIDS transmission, Latin culture and, women infected by their husbands
  birth control, *see* Birth control
  Catholic Church and, *see* Catholic Church
  circumcision, female, 271
  conservative values and, 73–74
  domestic violence, *see* Domestic violence
  education of, 21, 201–202, 219–20, 245
  employment of, *see* Employment of women
  empowerment of, 34, 43, 292–93
  hymen reconstruction, 271–89
  international conferences, 32, 247
  legal system perpetuating inequality of, 10–11, 17–18, 35–47
  media's reflection on roles of, 217–18